SwiftUI Animations by Tutorials

First Edition

by Irina Galata & Bill Morefield

SwiftUI Animations by Tutorials

Irina Galata & Bill Morefield

Notice of Rights

Notice of Liability

Trademarks

ISBN: 978-1-950325-79-5

Table of Contents

Book License

By purchasing *SwiftUI Animations by Tutorials*, you have the following license:

- You are allowed to use and/or modify the source code in *SwiftUI Animations by Tutorials* in as many apps as you want, with no attribution required.
- You are allowed to use and/or modify all art, images and designs that are included in *SwiftUI Animations by Tutorials* in as many apps as you want, but must include this attribution line somewhere inside your app: "Artwork/images/designs: from *SwiftUI Animations by Tutorials*, available at www.kodeco.com".
- The source code included in *SwiftUI Animations by Tutorials* is for your personal use only. You are NOT allowed to distribute or sell the source code in *SwiftUI Animations by Tutorials* without prior authorization.
- This book is for your personal use only. You are NOT allowed to reproduce or transmit any part of this book by any means, electronic or mechanical, including photocopying, recording, etc. without previous authorization. You may not sell digital versions of this book or distribute them to friends, coworkers or students without prior authorization. They need to purchase their own copies.

All materials provided with this book are provided on an "as is" basis, without warranty of any kind, express or implied, including but not limited to the warranties of merchantability, fitness for a particular purpose and noninfringement. In no event shall the authors or copyright holders be liable for any claim, damages or other liability, whether in an action of contract, tort or otherwise, arising from, out of or in connection with the software or the use or other dealings in the software.

All trademarks and registered trademarks appearing in this guide are the properties of their respective owners.

Before You Begin

This section tells you a few things you need to know before you get started, such as what you'll need for hardware and software, where to find the project files for this book, and more.

What You Need

To follow along with this book, you'll need the following:

- **Xcode 14 or later**. Xcode is the main development tool for iOS. You'll need Xcode 14 or later for the tasks in this book. SwiftUI evolves rapidly so having the latest version of Xcode can be crucial to having a smooth reading experience. You can download the latest version of Xcode from Apple's developer site here: apple.co/2asi58y
- **An intermediate level knowledge of Swift and SwiftUI**. This book teaches you how to leverage basic and advanced animations in SwiftUI. Even though you'll use Swift and SwiftUI throughout this book, its focus isn't about these topics, so you should have at least an intermediate-level knowledge of Swift.

If you want to try things out on a physical iOS device, you'll need a developer account with Apple, which you can obtain for free. However, all the sample projects in this book will work just fine in the iOS Simulator bundled with Xcode, so a paid developer account is completely optional.

Book Source Code & Forums

Where to Download the Materials for This Book

The materials for this book can be cloned or downloaded from the GitHub book materials repository:

- https://github.com/kodecocodes/sat-materials/tree/editions/1.0

Forums

We've also set up an official forum for the book at https://forums.kodeco.com/c/books/swiftui-animations-by-tutorials. This is a great place to ask questions about the book or to submit any errors you may find.

"To my family"

— *Irina Galata*

"To my parents for buying me that first computer when it was a lot weirder idea than it is now. To all my family for putting up with all the time I spend at a keyboard."

— *Bill Morefield*

About the Authors

Irina Galata is an author of this book. She is a software engineer living in Linz, Austria originally from Ukraine. She's passionate about mobile software development and especially animations. In her free time she's often busy with learning languages, gaming, sewing jackets, or making homemade pasta. Irina‘s GitHub account is @igalata.

Bill Morefield is an author of this book. He's spent most of his professional life writing code. He bought his first Apple computer to learn to program for the iPhone and got hooked on the platform. He manages the development and cloud team for a college in Tennessee, where he still gets to write code on occasion. When not attached to a keyboard he enjoys hiking and photography.

About the Editors

Renan Dias is a tech editor of this book. He is an iOS software engineer in love with Swift. Renan is always trying to learn more about new technologies. When not studying, you can find him playing video games, watching Disney/Pixar movies or reading manga.

Eli Ganim is a tech editor of this book. He is a Software Engineer who's passionate about teaching, writing and sharing knowledge with others. He lives in Israel with his wife and kids.

April Rames is the English language editor of this book. She's a former high school English and theatre teacher and director. When not volunteering at her daughters' school, she usually spends her time being asked to pretend to be a unicorn, zombie princess or superhero. In her spare time, she enjoys reading, making pasta and exploring the Gulf Coast with her family.

Shai Mishali is the final pass editor on this book. He's an experienced, award-winning iOS specialist; as well as an international speaker, and a highly active open-source contributor and maintainer on several high-profile projects - namely, the RxSwift Community and RxSwift projects, but also releases many open-source endeavors around Combine such as CombineCocoa, RxCombine and more. As an avid enthusiast of hackathons, Shai took 1st place at BattleHack Tel-Aviv 2014, BattleHack World Finals San Jose 2014, and Ford's Developer Challenge Tel-Aviv 2015. You can find him on GitHub and Twitter as @freak4pc.

Introduction

SwiftUI has absolutely changed our lives when it comes to developer experience and developer productivity. We can make beautiful apps extremely quickly, get instant feedback from SwiftUI previews, and iterate. SwiftUI also enables developers to easily leverage most common animations using simple SwiftUI modifiers, which makes it a pleasure to use. But it also begs the question: "How do I make my app stand out if everyone is using the same standard animations?"

It cannot be overstated how much animations matter in an app. It's not just about usability, it's about your app's "signature", a feel of quality and craftsmanship, the comforting feeling your users get that you're going above and beyond to take care of them. Animations are what separate good apps from the best.

This book aims to push the envelope for seasoned developers who might know how to leverage SwiftUI's basic animation system but aren't aware of the many advanced concepts they can leverage to bring their animations to that next level of craftsmanship and interactivity, broadening the reader's horizons and creative thinking.

Throughout your journey, you'll learn everything you need to create outstanding and memorable animations. You'll learn about the engine that drives SwiftUI animations, explore animations, transitions, matched geometry, gestures and everything in between!

How to Read This Book

While this book was built to read linearly, each chapter should stand on its own. If a specific topic in one of the chapters piques your interest, feel free to browse around and explore.

Section I: SwiftUI Animations by Tutorials

Chapter 1: Introducing SwiftUI Animations

By Bill Morefield

Small touches can help your app stand out from the competition in the crowded App Store. Animations provide one of these small delightful details.

Used correctly, animations show an attention to detail that your users will appreciate and a unique style they'll remember. Using animations purposefully provides your users subtle and practical feedback as your app's state changes.

Up until the release of SwiftUI, creating animations was quite a tedious task, even for the simplest of animations. Luckily, SwiftUI is often clever enough to automatically animate your state changes, or provide you with more granular control when the default animations don't cut it.

First, you'll explore the basic native animations included in SwiftUI resulting from **state changes**, the transformation of a value that a view depends on. You'll then explore **view transitions**, a type of animation that SwiftUI applies to views when inserted or removed from the screen. These animations provide a base of knowledge you'll use throughout this book.

Creating Animations

To begin, download and extract the materials for this chapter. Open the **starter** folder, which contains the starter project for this chapter. Then, open **AnimationCompare.xcodeproj** to start working on this chapter.

Run the project by selecting **Product ▸ Run** or press **Cmd-R**. When the project starts in the simulator, you'll see two tabs:

The first tab contains the user interface for an app that helps a developer explore different types of animations and manipulate various animation parameters to see their effects. The user can add multiple animations and run them in tandem.

The second tab contains a red square you can show or hide using a button. You'll use this tab to explore view transitions later in this chapter.

Exploring the Starter App

Inside the **Models** folder, open **AnimationData.swift**. You'll find the `AnimationData` struct, which holds the properties used by the different types of built-in animations.

Open **AnimationCompareView.swift** and look for the **Add Animation** button. When the user taps it, the app creates a new struct with a set of default values and adds it to the `animations` array. The user can change these values, but none of the animations work yet. You'll fix that now.

First, look for the `location` state property:

```
@State var location = 0.0
```

As the state changes, you'll use this property to animate views in your app. First, you need to provide a way for the user to change this state. Immediately inside the `VStack`, add the following code:

```
// 1
Button("Animate!") {
  // 2
  location = location == 0 ? 1 : 0
}
.font(.title)
.disabled(animations.isEmpty)
```

The code above:

1. Creates a button that changes the state property `location` to animate views when tapped.
2. Toggles the value of `location` between 0.0 and 1.0. You'll use this later to animate the views on screen.

Notice that you disable the button when the `animations` array is empty. This prevents users from tapping the button before creating any animations.

Adding Your First Animation

Open **AnimationView.swift**. Near the top of the view, look for this line:

```
@Binding var location: Double
```

This property contains the `location` passed in from the parent view. When the value changes in `AnimationCompareView`, it also changes inside this view, since it's a `Binding`. Inside each `AnimationView`, SwiftUI will notice the state change and trigger two animations that you specify.

Currently, `AnimationView` contains a `Text` view wrapped inside a `GeometryReader`. Replace this `Text` view with:

```
HStack {
  // 1
  Image(systemName: "gear.circle")
    .rotationEffect(.degrees(360 * location))
  Image(systemName: "star.fill")
    // 2
    .offset(x: proxy.size.width * location * 0.8)
}
.font(.title)
// 3
.animation(
  // 4
  .linear(duration: animation.length),
  // 5
  value: location
)
```

Here's what each part of the new view does:

1. You place two images in an `HStack`. You apply a rotation effect to the first image that multiplies the `location` property by 360 degrees. Since `location` will vary between zero and one, the result will toggle between zero and 360 degrees. The key is that a change in `location` changes the view's state.

2. The second image has an offset applied that multiples the width of the view, taken from the `GeometryProxy`, by the `location` property and multiples that by `0.8`. As a result, when `location` is zero, the offset is zero, and when `location` is one, the offset is 80% of the width of the view. Since SwiftUI applies the offset to the view's leading edge, multiplying by 0.8 keeps the view from floating off the screen.

3. There are several ways to tell SwiftUI you want to animate a state change. Here you use `animation(_:value:)` on the `HStack`. This method creates the most straightforward SwiftUI animation, an **implicit animation**. You apply it to the `HStack` so that both views included within have the animation applied to them. Sounds simple? That's the beauty of animations in SwiftUI!

4. The first parameter to `animation(_:value:)` defines the type of animation, which is a linear animation in this case. You then pass the `duration` parameter, telling SwiftUI the animation should take the amount of time specified in `animation.length` to complete. Most animations should last between 0.25 and 1.0 seconds as these values allow the user time to notice the animation without feeling too long and intrusive.

5. When you apply an implicit animation, you specify the value whose change will trigger the animation. Explicitly setting the state change lets you use different animations with different state changes.

Run the app and add an animation. Next, tap **Animate!**. The gear icon makes one revolution, and the star slides to the right side of the view.

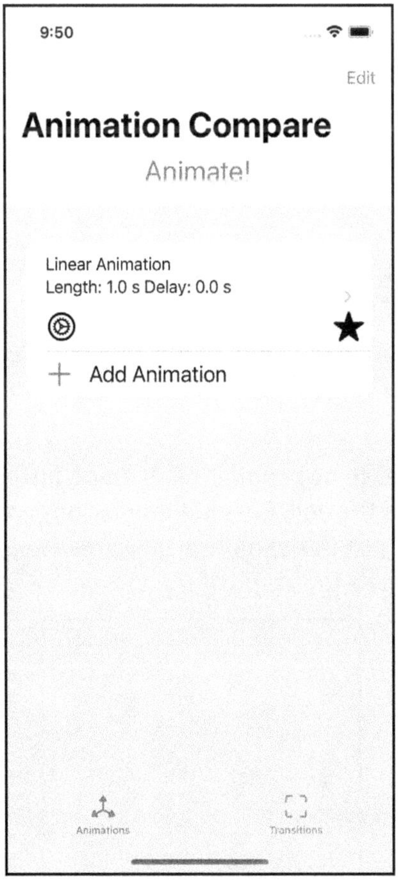

Linear Animation

If you tap **Animate!** again, you'll see the gear spin in the opposite direction while the star slides back to the left. Think for a moment about why the opposite movement takes place. Here's a hint: remember what the **Animate!** button does.

Since the **Animate!** button returns the property to its original value of zero, the animation reverses. The `rotationEffect(_:anchor:)` method interprets greater values as clockwise rotation. Therefore, the initial change from zero to one turns into a degree change from zero to 360. This change animates as a set of increasing clockwise rotations. The change back to zero causes counterclockwise animation as the value decreases.

Linear animations work best for views that pass through but do not start or end within the scene. In the real world, a car passing by a window would look routine while moving at a constant speed, but a vehicle instantly achieving full speed from a stop would seem odd. Our minds expect something that starts or stops within our view to accelerate or decelerate.

In the next section, you'll explore **eased animations**, another type of animation that matches this behavior.

Creating Eased Animations

Instead of linear movement, eased animations provide acceleration or deceleration at one or both endpoints. The types of eased animations differ by where the change in speed applies.

The most common is the **ease out** animation. It starts faster than a linear animation before decelerating toward the end. Ease out animations are often the best choice in a user interface since that fast initial motion gives the feeling your app is quickly responding to the user. Here's the graph of the movement against time:

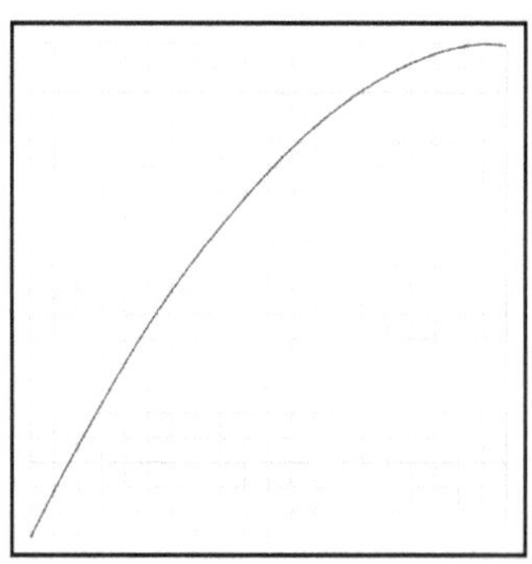

Ease Out

An **ease in** animation reverses these steps. It starts more slowly than a linear animation before accelerating. If you were to graph the movement against time, it would look like this:

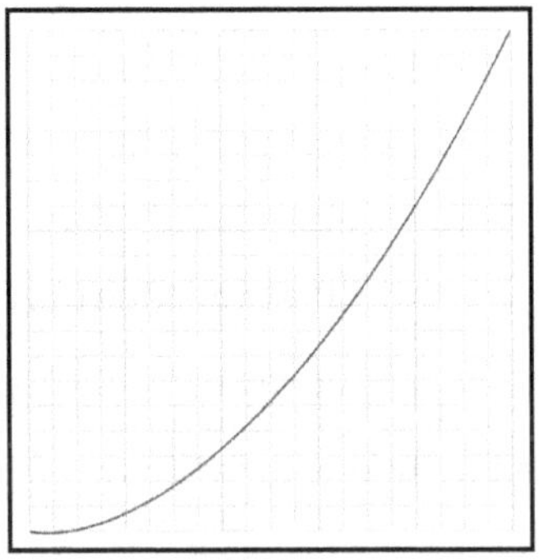

Ease In

The next eased animation combines the previous two. **Ease in-out** animations accelerate, as in the ease in animation, before decelerating, as in the ease out animation. For ease in and ease in-out animations, you usually want to keep the duration less than 0.5 seconds so it feels more responsive to your user.

The movement graphed against time looks like a combination of the other two graphs:

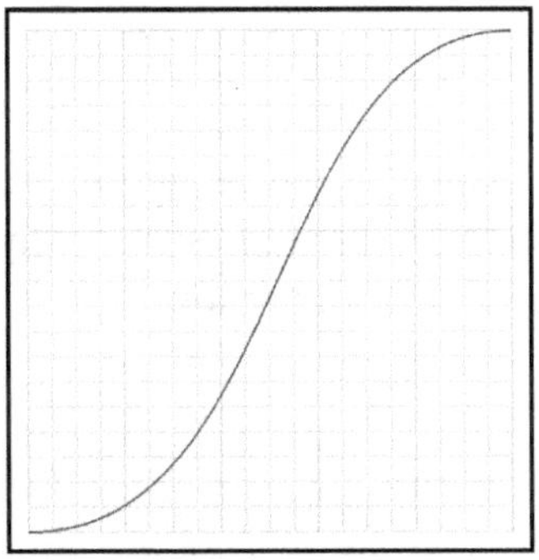

Ease In Out

Applying Eased Animations

The app already lets the user select eased animations, so next, you'll add support for those. Open **AnimationView.swift** and add the following new computed property after the `location` property:

```
var currentAnimation: Animation {
  switch animation.type {
  case .easeIn:
    return Animation.easeIn(duration: animation.length)
  case .easeOut:
    return Animation.easeOut(duration: animation.length)
  case .easeInOut:
    return Animation.easeInOut(duration: animation.length)
  default:
    return Animation.linear(duration: animation.length)
  }
}
```

This computed property converts the `AnimationType` enum of `animation` to the matching SwiftUI animation using a duration from the `length` property.

Next, change the `animation(_:value:)` modifier to:

```
.animation(
  currentAnimation,
  value: location
)
```

This code sets the animation using the new computed property you just added, so it has the animation specified in the `animation` struct. Any animation you haven't implemented will fall back to a linear animation.

Run the app and create two animations. Tap the second and change the type to **Ease In-Out**.

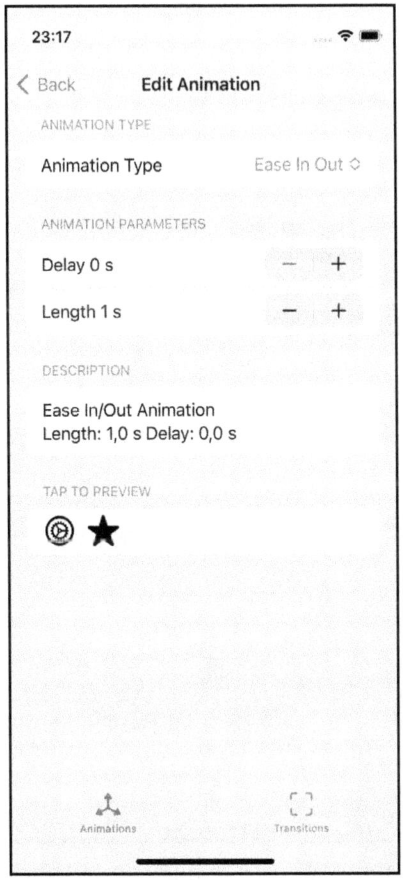

Changing animation to ease in out.

Tap **Back** and then **Animate!** to see the difference between the two animations.

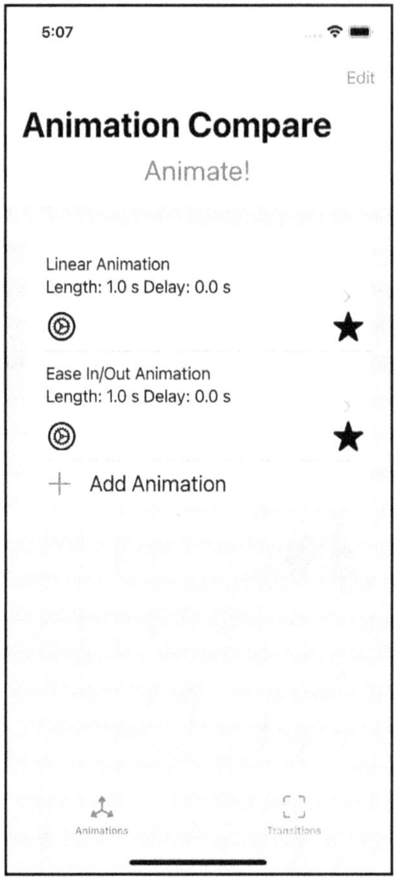

Comparing eased and linear animations

You can slow down animations inside the Simulator using the **Debug ▸ Slow Animations** toggle to better view the sometimes subtle differences between animations.

Notice the ease in out animation moves slower at first before passing the linear animation and then slowing down at the end. Since you specified the same `duration` for both animations, they take the same time to complete.

Add two more animations and set one to Ease In and the other to Ease Out. Change the length of one animation and rerun it to see how they compare. Notice the shape of the animation doesn't change. Only the time it takes the animation to complete changes.

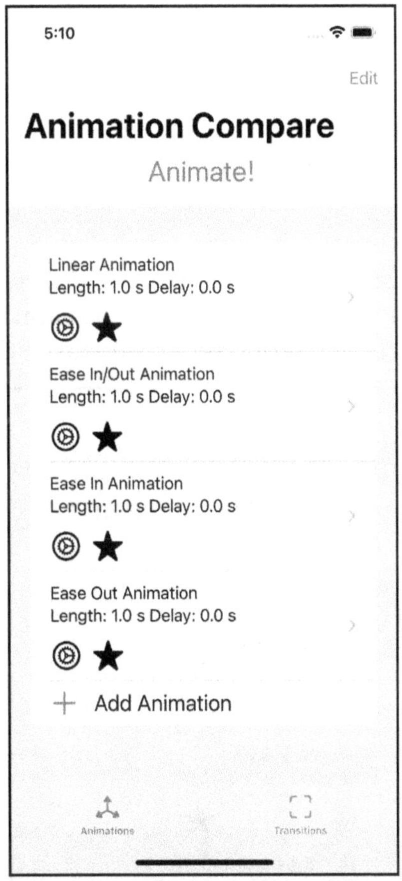

Comparing multiple animations

While the linear and eased animations let you set the animation's duration, SwiftUI also provides general modifiers you can apply to *any* animation.

In the next section, you'll learn two common modifiers that help you customize the duration of your animation.

Modifying Animations

By default, an animation starts immediately when the state changes, but since your app lets the user specify a delay for each animation, you'll add support for it. Open **AnimationView.swift** and replace the current `animation(_:value:)` modifier with:

```
.animation(
  currentAnimation
    .delay(animation.delay),
  value: location
)
```

You add the `delay(_:)` modifier to the animation and specify the delay in seconds. Run the app and add two animations. Edit the second animation and set the delay to 0.5 seconds. Tap **Back** and tap the **Animate!** button to see the effect.

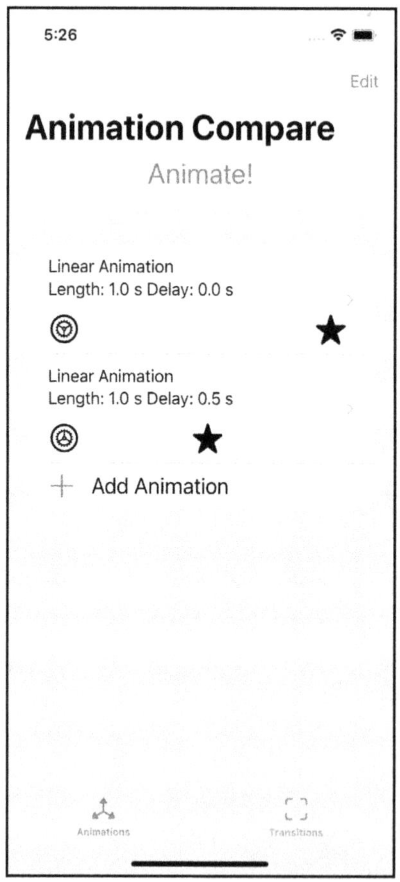

While the first animation begins when you tap the button, the second animation doesn't start until 0.5 seconds later. A delay doesn't affect the duration or movement of the animation. However, it can provide a sense of flow or order between multiple animations tied to a single state change.

Changing Animation Speed

Another useful modifier lets you change the animation's speed independent of type and parameters. You add the `speed(_:)` modifier and pass a ratio of the base speed to the desired speed.

A value lower than one will result in a slower animation, while a value greater than one will speed up the animation.

You'll use this to implement a slowdown effect that will make it easier for the user to notice the differences between animations, similar to the Simulator menu option.

Open **AnimationCompareView.swift**. Add the following new property after the existing ones:

```
@State var slowMotion = false
```

You'll use this boolean property to indicate when the user wants to slow the animations. Next, add the following toggle control to the view as the first item inside the `List`, before the `ForEach`:

```
Toggle("Slow Animations (¼ speed)", isOn: $slowMotion)
```

Now the user can use this toggle to specify when they want to slow down the animations. Next, open **AnimationView.swift** and add the following property.

```
var slowMotion = false
```

The parent view can now indicate when to slow down the animations on this view, defaulting to `false`.

Next, replace the existing animation modifier with:

```
.animation(
  currentAnimation
    .delay(animation.delay)
    .speed(slowMotion ? 0.25 : 1.0),
  value: location
)
```

Recall that values lower than one passed to the `speed(_:)` modifier cause the animation to slow down. Passing 0.25 will cause the animation to take four times as long (`1 / 0.25 = 4`) as it otherwise would have.

Go back to **AnimationCompareView.swift**. To pass the new property to the view, add the new `slowMotion` parameter to your `AnimationView`:

```
AnimationView(
  animation: animation,
  location: $location,
  slowMotion: slowMotion
)
```

Run the app, add an animation and tap the **Animate!** button. You'll see the familiar one-second linear animation. Now toggle on **Slow Animations** and tap **Animate!** again.

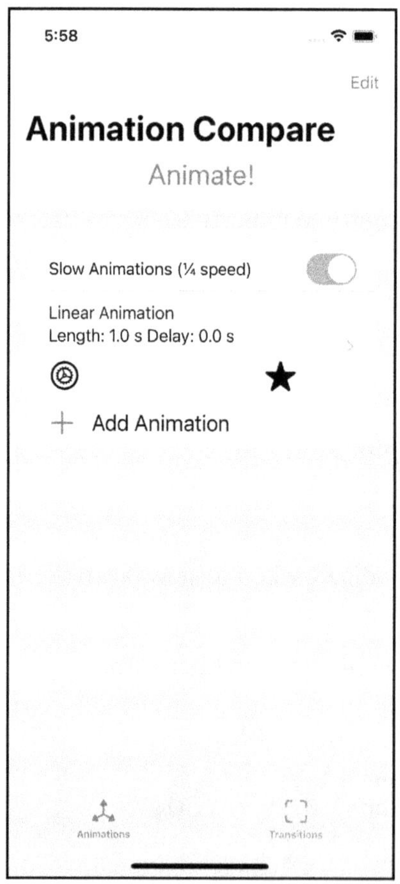

Using speed(_:) to slow animations

Your animation now takes four seconds, or four times longer, to complete. To verify all animations run slower, add another animation and change its length to 0.5 seconds.

When you animate them, you'll see the second animation takes two seconds (4 x 0.5 seconds) or half as long as the first animation.

Now that you've seen some of the modifiers you can apply to animations, you'll look at the last type of animation: **spring animation**.

Springing Into Animations

Spring animations are popular because they seem more natural. They usually end with a slight overshoot and add some "bounce" at their end. The animation values come from the model of a spring attached to a weight.

Imagine a weight attached to one end of a spring. Attach the other end to a fixed point and let the spring drop vertically with the weight at the bottom. The weight will bounce several times before coming to a full stop.

The slowdown and stop come from friction acting on the system. The reduction creates a **damped** system. Graphing the motion over time produces a result like this:

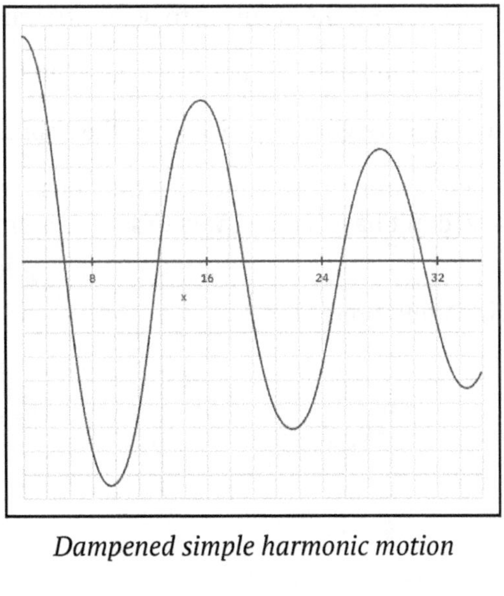

Dampened simple harmonic motion

There are two types of spring animations. The `interpolatingSpring(mass:stiffness:damping:initialVelocity:)` animation uses this damped spring model to produce values. This animation type preserves velocity across overlapping animations by adding the effects of each animation together.

To experiment with this, open **AnimationView.swift** and add the following new case to the `currentAnimation` computed property, before the `default` case:

```
case .interpolatingSpring:
  return Animation.interpolatingSpring(
    // 1
    mass: animation.mass,
    // 2
    stiffness: animation.stiffness,
    // 3
    damping: animation.damping,
    // 4
    initialVelocity: animation.initialVelocity
  )
```

Each of the parameters maps to an element of the physical model. Here's what they do:

1. **mass** reflects the mass of the weight.
2. **stiffness** defines how resistant the spring is to being stretched or compressed.
3. **damping** maps to gravity and friction that slows down and stops the motion.
4. **initalVelocity** reflects the weight's velocity when the animation starts.

Notice that these parameters aren't correlated with the linear and eased animations you used earlier. You also don't have a direct way to set the animation length as you did before.

Run the app and add two animations.

Change the type for the second one to an **Interpolating Spring** and keep the default values, which include the default `mass` and `initialVelocity` if you don't specify them to the method.

Default interpolating spring animation.

Go back to the main screen and tap **Animate!**, and you'll see a much different animation. The star and gear move past the end point before bouncing slightly backward. The movement will repeat with the motion decreasing until it stops.

Even with the extra movement, the spring completes faster than the one-second linear animation.

> **Note**: Before moving on, try to experiment with the different animation parameters and get a grasp for how each of them effects the animation.

Increasing the mass causes the animation to last longer and bounce further on each side of the end point. A smaller mass stops faster and moves less past the end points on each bounce.

Increasing the stiffness causes each bounce to move further past the end points but with a smaller effect on the animation's length.

Increasing the damping slows the animation faster. If you set an initial velocity, it changes the initial movement of the animation.

Another Way to Spring

SwiftUI provides a second spring animation method you can apply using the `spring(response:dampingFraction:blendDuration:)` method. The underlying model doesn't change, but this method abstracts the four different physics-based arguments with two simpler arguments.

Open **AnimationView.swift** and add the following case before the `default` case:

```
case .spring:
  return Animation.spring(
    response: animation.response,
    dampingFraction: animation.dampingFraction
  )
```

The `spring`'s `response` and `dampingFraction` internally map to the appropriate physics-based values of `interpolatingSpring`.

The `response` parameter acts similarly to the mass in the physics-based model. It determines how resistant the animation is to changing speed. A larger value will result in an animation slower to speed up or slow down.

The `dampingFraction` parameter controls how quickly the animation slows down. A value greater than or equal to one will cause the animation to settle without the bounce that most associate with spring animations.

A value between zero and one will create an animation that shoots past the final position and bounces a few times, similarly to the previous section.

A value near one will slow faster than a value near zero. A value of zero won't settle and will oscillate forever, or at least until your user gets frustrated and closes your app.

Note that you aren't using the `blendDuration` parameter of `spring(response:dampingFraction:blendDuration:)` as that only applies when combining multiple animations, which is more advanced than you'll examine in this chapter.

Run the app and add two animations. Change the type of the first to **Interpolating Spring** and the type of the second to **Spring**. Tap **Animate!**, and you'll notice that the animations are similar despite the different parameters.

Change the first animation to **Spring** and experiment by changing the values to see the effect of `mass` and `stiffness` on the animation. Slowing the animation down will help with the often subtle differences between spring animations.

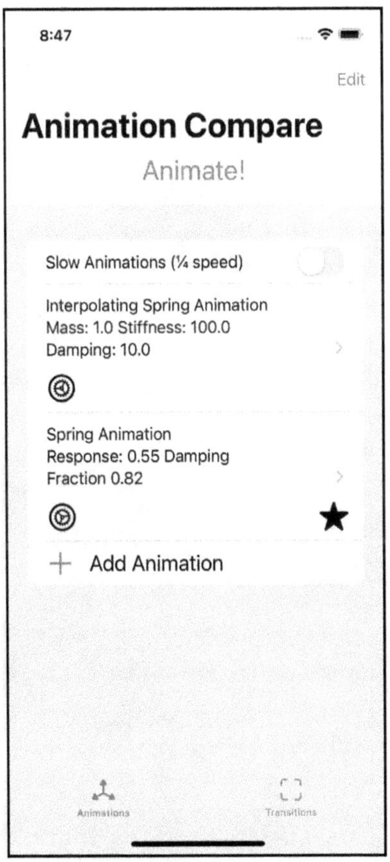

Comparing spring animations.

You now understand the basics of SwiftUI animations and can use the app to explore and fine-tune animations in your apps.

Next, you'll look at one final category of animations: **view transitions.**

Using View Transitions

View transitions are a subset of animations that animate how views appear or vanish. You'll often use them when a view only appears when your app is in specific states. Open **TransitionCompareView.swift**. You'll see a simple view consisting of a button that toggles the boolean `showSquare` property. When `showSquare` is `true`, it shows a red square with rounded corners.

Run the app, go to the **Transitions** tab and tap the button a few times to see it in action.

Note that there's no animation when the square appears and vanishes. That's because transitions only occur when you apply an animation to the state change. Earlier in the chapter, you used implicit animations where the `animation(_:value:)` modifier implied SwiftUI should animate the view. Now, you will explicitly tell SwiftUI to create an animation when `showSquare` changes. To do so, go to the action for the button and change it to:

```
withAnimation {
  showSquare.toggle()
}
```

With the animation applied, you can apply a transition using the `transition(_:)` modifier on a view. Look for the conditional statement to show the rectangle and add the following modifier after `foregroundColor()`:

```
.transition(.scale)
```

Run the app and repeat the steps. You'll see the square shrink to a single point.

You can also use this explicit `withAnimation(_:_:)` function on the animations you used earlier in this chapter. However, it can only specify a single animation and will apply that animation to all changes resulting from the code within the function.

The scale transition you applied here makes the view appear to originate or vanish by scaling to a provided ratio of the view's size. By default, the view scales down to zero at a point in its center. You can change either of these values.

Change the transition for the rounded square to:

```
.transition(.scale(scale: 2.0, anchor: .topLeading))
```

Run the app. When you hide the view, the square will expand to twice its original size, with the scaling centered around the top leading corner of the view before vanishing.

> **Note**: When running in the simulator, the vanishing of the scale animation might end abruptly due to a bug in SwiftUI. If this happens to you, try running the code on a device, or a different Simulator.

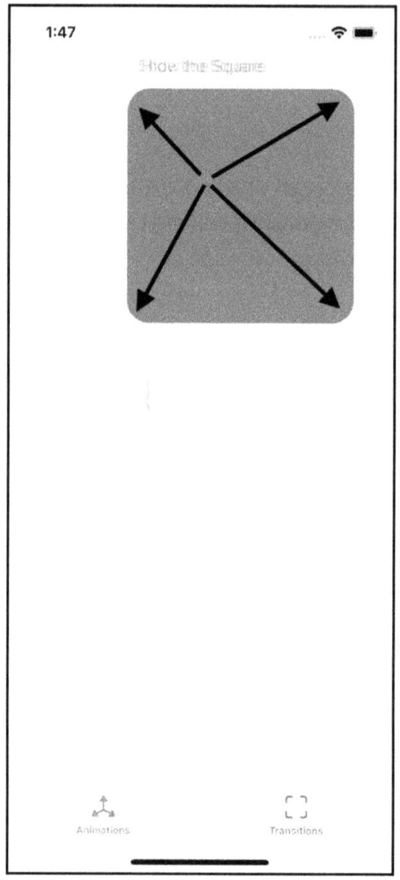

Additional Transitions

You can specify the default fade transition using the `opacity` transition. Change the transition to read:

```
.transition(.opacity)
```

Run the app. You'll see the view now vanishes and appears with a fade-in/out animation.

Another transition is `offset(x:y:)`, which lets you specify that the view should offset from its current position. Change the transition to read:

```
.transition(.offset(x: 10, y: 40))
```

Run the app. The view slides slightly to the right and down before being removed. When it returns, it appears at the same position it vanished from before returning to the original location.

You can also specify the view should move towards a specified edge using the `move(edge:)` transition. Change the current transition to:

```
.transition(.move(edge: .trailing))
```

Run the app. Now the view slides off toward the trailing edge when you tap the button to hide it. When you show the square, the view will appear from the same edge it moved toward before vanishing.

Having a view transition by appearing on the leading edge and vanishing toward the trailing edge is common enough that SwiftUI includes a predefined specifier: the `slide` transition. Change the transition to:

```
.transition(.slide)
```

Run the app, and you'll see the view acts similar to the `move(edge:)` transition it replaced, except the view now appears from the leading edge and vanishes toward the trailing edge. This transition provides different animations for inserting and removing the view.

Head over to the next section to learn how you too can create these custom asynchronous transitions!

Using Asynchronous Transitions

You can specify different transitions when the view appears and vanishes using the `asymmetric(insertion:removal:)` method on `AnyTransition`.

Add the following code after the `showSquare` state property:

```
// 1
var squareTransition: AnyTransition {
  // 2
  let insertTransition = AnyTransition.move(edge: .leading)
  let removeTransition = AnyTransition.scale
  // 3
  return AnyTransition.asymmetric(
    insertion: insertTransition,
    removal: removeTransition
  )
}
```

Here's how your new transition works:

1. You specify the transition as a computed property on the view. Doing so helps keep the view code less cluttered and makes it easier to change in the future.

2. Next, you create two transitions. The first is a `move(edge:)` transition and the second is a `scale` transition.

3. You use the `.asymmetric(insertion:removal:)` transition and specify the insertion and removal transition for your view.

Finally, change the transition to read:

```
.transition(squareTransition)
```

This method tells SwiftUI to apply the transition from the `squareTransition` property to the view.

Run the app. When you tap the button, you'll see the view does as you'd expect. The view appears from the leading edge and scales down when removed.

You've now explored the basics of animations and view transitions in SwiftUI. In the remainder of this book, you'll delve deeper into more complex animations.

Challenge

Modify the transitions view for this chapter's app to let the user specify a single transition or separate insert and removal transitions. For each type of transition, let the user select the additional values supported by the transition. Apply these transitions to the square when the user taps the button.

To help you get started, you'll find data structures that can hold the properties for transitions in **TransitionData.swift**. You'll also find a view letting the user specify these properties in **TransitionTypeView.swift**. Check the challenge project in the materials for this chapter for a possible solution.

Key Points

- SwiftUI animations are driven by state changes. The change of a value that affects a view.
- **View transitions** are animations applied to views when SwiftUI inserts or removes them.
- **Linear animations** represent a constant-paced animation between two values.
- **Eased animations** apply acceleration, deceleration or both to the animation.
- **Spring animations** use a physics-based model of a spring.
- You can delay or change the speed of animations.
- Most animations should last between 0.25 and 1.0 seconds in length. Shorter animations often aren't noticeable, while longer animations risk annoying your user who just wants to get something done.
- View transitions can animate by opacity, scale or movement. You can use different transitions for the insertion and removal of views.

Where to Go From Here?

- Chapter 19: Animations & View Transitions in SwiftUI by Tutorials (https://www.kodeco.com/books/swiftui-by-tutorials/v4.0/chapters/19-animations-view-transitions) contains an examination of the basics of animation within an app, including some you won't see until later in this book.
- The WWDC 2018 session, Designing Fluid Interfaces (https://developer.apple.com/videos/play/wwdc2018/803), also details gestures and motion in apps.
- For more on how to use animations and transitions in your apps, see the Human Interface Guidelines (https://developer.apple.com/design/human-interface-guidelines/).

Chapter 2: Getting to Know SwiftUI Animations

By Irina Galata

In this chapter, and the three following it, you'll work on an app designed to sell tickets for sports events. You'll use the concepts you learned in the previous chapter to make it stand out. Your first objective is to replace the plain activity indicator when refreshing the events screen with an interactive pull-to-refresh animation.

Getting Started

First, download the materials for this chapter and open **starter/SportFan.xcodeproj**. You'll see a few Swift files waiting for you in advance, so you can start working immediately.

Open **ContentView.swift** and ensure the preview is visible. If it isn't, enable it by pressing **Opt-Cmd-Return*** Xcode menu option. If you prefer using a simulator, run the app.

Your app currently has only one screen — the events list that previews all upcoming games. If you're eagerly waiting for a specific game that wasn't announced yet, you can pull the list down to fetch the latest data.

In a real-world app, it might take a while to send a request to a server, wait for a response, process it and display it appropriately. So, you must let the user know the request is still ongoing. The built-in activity indicator the app currently uses is a great way to do so, but it's a missed opportunity to make your app unique and memorable.

Using GeometryReader for a Custom Pull-to-Refresh

What would be a fitting animation for a sports-related mobile app? A jumping basketball would do the trick. Its bright color and physically plausible movement make the animation more engaging and fit the app's topic.

Currently, although convenient, the `.refreshable` modifier, found in line 43 in **ContentView.swift**, doesn't offer the flexibility you need to implement a custom animation. It may do so in future releases of SwiftUI, but today you'll use a different approach.

You'll make manual calculations to detect when a user swipes the container to a specific distance to trigger the data update. To achieve this, you'll use SwiftUI's `GeometryReader`. It's a view that provides vital information suggested by its parent - in this case, a `ScrollView`, such as its size, frame and safe area insets.

Drafting the Animation

In iOS, a `ScrollView` has a *bounce effect* by default. Once you reach a boundary of its content, such as the top or bottom of a vertical container or the leading or trailing edge of a horizontal one, you can scroll a bit past the initial or final position. When you lift your finger, it bounces back.

This feature is the foundation of your animation. You'll put `GeometryReader` inside `ScrollView` alongside its content. When you pull the content on top, the geometry reader view will be pulled as well, which allows you to catch the exact value of the scroll offset and use it as needed.

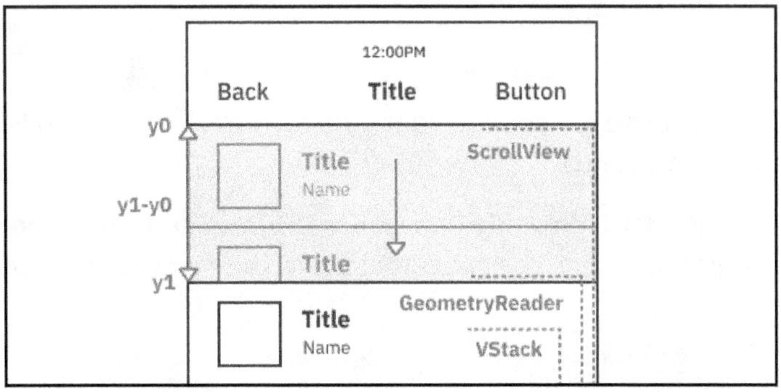

The initial value of the geometry reader's y-axis offset is marked **y0** in the diagram above.

Once a user starts pulling the content down, GeometryReader's and VStack's frames follow the movement with the same velocity. Through GeometryReader, you'll access the current **y1** value at every moment of the gesture, calculate the distance traveled and decide whether the app should trigger a refresh.

Outlining the Geometry Reader

First, create a new Swift file named **PullToRefresh.swift** and add the following enum to it:

```
enum AnimationState: Int {
  case idle = 0,
       pulling,
       ongoing
}
```

Since your animation will consist of multiple phases, you need an enum representing its current state. It's .idle before a user starts interacting with the scroll view, .pulling while the gesture is in progress and then transitions to .ongoing to indicate the ongoing refresh.

> **Note**: An enum is an optimal way to handle state changes since, by its nature, it prevents you from ending up in an invalid state: a variable of the AnimationState type can have only one value out of three.

Add a new PullToRefresh struct below the enum:

```
struct PullToRefresh: Equatable {
  var progress: Double
  var state: AnimationState
}
```

Soon, you'll use it to share the state of your pull-to-refresh animation between its components and ContentView.

Next, create a new **SwiftUI View** file named **ScrollViewGeometryReader.swift**. Add the following properties inside the generated ScrollViewGeometryReader:

```
// 1
@Binding var pullToRefresh: PullToRefresh

// 2
let update: () async -> Void
```

```
// 3
@State private var startOffset: CGFloat = 0
```

Here's what the code above does:

1. You use the `@Binding` property wrapper for the `pullToRefresh` property to establish a two-way connection between `ContentView` and `ScrollViewGeometryReader`. The main container passes a `PullToRefresh` instance to the geometry reader. The geometry reader updates its properties when a user interacts with a scroll view to tell `ContentView` when the animation should start or finish.

2. You call the closure every time your `ScrollViewGeometryReader` determines that a refresh is needed. You mark it as `async` to tell the compiler that this closure's execution might suspend to wait for a response since you'd typically request the data from a server.

3. You need to keep the initial value of the y-axis offset, **y0**, to compare it to the current offset of the geometry reader and calculate the length of a user's swipe.

Xcode may have generated a `struct` called `ScrollViewGeometryReader_Previews`, which comes in handy when you want to immediately see the preview of your SwiftUI view without building the app. You can safely remove it now since `ScrollViewGeometryReader` won't be visible to users, so there's nothing to see in the preview.

Next, replace the content of `body` with:

```
GeometryReader<Color> { proxy in // 1
  // TODO: To be implemented
  return Color.clear // 2
}
.task { // 3
  await update()
}
```

Here, you:

1. Add `GeometryReader`, where you pass a closure that receives an instance of `GeometryProxy` and returns some content.

2. If you don't want the content of the reader to be visible to a user, you can simply return a transparent view.

3. Use `task` to trigger data fetching right before the view appears on the screen.

Using GeometryProxy

Now, it's time to do a bit of math. First, create a constant for the maximum offset, which a scroll view needs to reach to trigger the pull-to-refresh.

Create a new **Constants.swift** file and add the following to it:

```
enum Constants {
  static let maxOffset = 100.0
}
```

Here's the exciting part! Make a function inside `ScrollViewGeometryReader`, beneath its `body`, where you'll make all the calculations needed for the animation:

```
private func calculateOffset(from proxy: GeometryProxy) {
  let currentOffset = proxy.frame(in: .global).minY

}
```

`calculateOffset` accepts a `GeometryProxy`, which is the base for all the computations. You retrieve the frame of `GeometryProxy` and assign its `minY` to `currentOffset`. That's the **y1** you saw earlier in the sketch.

Next, add this `switch` below `currentOffset`. It'll control the `pullToRefresh` state:

```
switch pullToRefresh.state {
case .idle:
  startOffset = currentOffset // 1
  pullToRefresh.state = .pulling // 2

case .pulling where pullToRefresh.progress < 1: // 3
  pullToRefresh.progress = min(1, (currentOffset -
startOffset) / Constants.maxOffset)

case .pulling: // 4
  pullToRefresh.state = .ongoing
  pullToRefresh.progress = 0
  Task {
    await update() // 5
    pullToRefresh.state = .idle
  }

default: return
}
```

A few important things happen in the code snippet:

1. If `state` is still `.idle`, you set `startOffset` to `currentOffset`. That means the gesture has just started, and it's the initial value of the offset. Therefore it's **y0**.
2. You change the state to `.pulling` as a user starts interacting with the scroll view.
3. Now, you calculate the progress of the gesture where your **y1** currently is between **y0** and its maximum value **y0** + **maxOffset**. This value will lay between 0 and 1.
4. Once the offset reaches its maximum value, but before the update starts, you change the state property to `.ongoing`.
5. Since `update` is asynchronous, you create a new `Task` to invoke it and use the `await` keyword to suspend the task and wait for the function to return a result. Once you get the value, the execution resumes, and you use `pullToRefresh` to say the update is complete and the animation is back to `.idle`.

Since you've implemented the function, replace the `TODO` comment inside the geometry reader with:

```
Task { calculateOffset(from: proxy) }
```

Because you may modify some state variables inside `calculateOffset(from:)`, the compiler prevents you from executing it synchronously while the view's body renders, preventing you from potentially entering a loop and causing undefined behavior.

Go back to `ContentView` and add an instance of `PullToRefresh` inside the `struct`:

```
@State var pullToRefresh = PullToRefresh(progress: 0,
state: .idle)
```

To verify that your geometry reader can determine when to refresh the data correctly, replace everything inside the `body` of `ContentView` with:

```
ScrollView {
  ScrollViewGeometryReader(pullToRefresh: $pullToRefresh) { // 1
    await update()
    print("Updated!")
  }
  ZStack(alignment: .top) {
    if pullToRefresh.state == .ongoing { // 2
      ProgressView()
    }
    LazyVStack { // 3
```

```
        ForEach(events) {
          EventView(event: $0)
        }
      }
      .offset(y: pullToRefresh.state == .ongoing ?
Constants.maxOffset : 0) // 4
    }
  }
```

Here's what you just did:

1. You put the newly implemented `ScrollViewGeometryReader` inside the scroll view, passing a binding to `pullToRefresh` and a closure to invoke when the update is needed.
2. If the update is ongoing, you show a regular progress view. Later, you'll replace it with a bouncy basketball. But to verify whether the math works, you use a built-in view for now.
3. `LazyVStack` contains the events views instead of a `List`.
4. To give the future animation enough space on the screen, you move the events container down using its `offset` modifier.

The first iteration of your custom pull-to-refresh solution is ready. Hooray! Now, refresh the preview in `ContentView` or run the app.

As you finish pulling the scroll view, a progress wheel appears, spins for a few seconds and disappears. At the same time, the events list refreshes if any earlier events appear. Don't worry about its abrupt, non-animated appearance at the moment — you'll deal with it soon.

It's also worth checking the output in Xcode. You'll see an `Updated!` message print once the app starts and every time you trigger an update during the idle state. In other words, no excessive updates should occur:

```
Updated!
Updated!
Updated!
```

Triggering an Animation Explicitly

Until now, you've built the necessary foundation for your animation using the implementation particularities of the system components and the API offered by SwiftUI.

Now, your goal is to render a ball while the data refreshes and make it jump using **explicit** animations. Then, you'll enhance your animation by adding physical details like rotation, a shadow and even squashing when the ball reaches the bottom.

Before you start, add some new constants to your **Constants.swift** file, inside the `enum`:

```
static let ballSize = 42.0
static let ballSpacing = 8.0
static let jumpDuration = 0.35
```

Then, create a new SwiftUI view file called **BallView.swift** and add the following property to the generated view `struct`:

```
@Binding var pullToRefresh: PullToRefresh
```

`BallView` is the third component of your animation connected via `PullToRefresh`. Now, any time the state changes inside `ScrollViewGeometryReader`, `BallView` also gets notified.

Delete `BallView_Previews`. Then, add:

```
struct Ball: View {
  var body: some View {
```

```
      Image("basketball_ball")
        .resizable()
        .frame(
          width: Constants.ballSize,
          height: Constants.ballSize
        )
    }
}
```

This code makes the ball image easy to reuse without code duplication.

Animating Offset

Next, create a new SwiftUI view file — **JumpingBallView.swift**, which will be responsible for rendering the jumping ball.

Keep the generated preview `struct` to work on and adjust this part of the animation separately from the app.

> **Note**: You can modify a view in its preview without affecting its appearance in the app. If you zoom the ball in by adding `.scale(4)` in `JumpingBallView_Previews`, you can inspect your animation closely and keep its correct size in other components.

Now, add the two following properties inside `JumpingBallView` to keep track of the animation state and offset of the view:

```
@State private var isAnimating = false

var currentYOffset: CGFloat {
  isAnimating
    ? Constants.maxOffset - Constants.ballSize / 2 -
Constants.ballSpacing
    : -Constants.ballSize / 2 - Constants.ballSpacing
}
```

In the computed `currentYOffset` property above, if `isAnimating` is `true`, the animation is ongoing, and you offset the ball to its bottom position, the "surface". Always remember to account for the size of the ball. The view's position corresponds to its **top left** corner. Therefore, you operate with half of its size to coordinate the position of the center. Also, keep spacing in mind to avoid overlapping the ball and the content. You *deduct* both of these values from the final offset to move the ball **up** relatively to it.

> **Note**: In iOS, the center of the coordinate system, the intersection of the x and y-axis, is located in the top left corner. Therefore, the values grow positively on the x-axis when moving towards the right side and downwards along the y-axis.

With these calculations behind you, you can simply add your new `Ball` with the computed `y` offset. Replace `JumpingBallView`'s body with:

```
Ball()
  // 1
  .offset(y: currentYOffset)
```

To make the ball jump the moment it appears, add `.onAppear` to the ball image right after `.offset`:

```
.onAppear {
  withAnimation(
    .linear(duration: Constants.jumpDuration)
    .repeatForever()
  ) { // 1
    isAnimating = true // 2
  }
}
```

It took a while to start animating, but you're there! Here's what you achieved above:

1. Using `withAnimation()`, you **explicitly** tell SwiftUI to animate the view properties changes resulting from the modifications inside the closure for a defined amount of time - `jumpDuration` - and repeat it forever.
2. By modifying `isAnimating`, you trigger the ball's offset change, which now animates according to the animation properties you passed to `withAnimation()`.

Before trying out your changes, add `JumpingBallView` to `BallView`'s `body`, like so:

```
switch pullToRefresh.state {
case .ongoing:
  JumpingBallView() // 1
default:
  EmptyView() // 2
}
```

In the code above, you display a `JumpingBallView` if the animation is ongoing, or a simple `EmptyView` otherwise.

Last but not least, you'll completely replace `ProgressView` with the `BallView` you created. Go to `ContentView` and replace the `if pullToRefresh.state == .ongoing` condition with:

```
BallView(pullToRefresh: $pullToRefresh)
```

Now, refresh the preview and see your animation's first steps, or jumps.

Well, you may not be impressed just yet. The ball moves oddly and unnaturally.

However, in the first chapter, you learned that interpolating functions can significantly affect an animation's feel. It's time to apply one.

Replace the invocation of `withAnimation()` in `JumpingBallView` with:

```
withAnimation(
  .easeInOut(duration: Constants.jumpDuration)
  .repeatForever()
) {
```

Check the preview of `JumpingBallView` to see the difference. The movement is much more realistic now, but there are so many more things you can improve.

Animating Rotation and Scale

First, make the ball rotate and squash while jumping. Add the following two properties to `JumpingBallView`:

```
@State private var rotation = 0.0
@State private var scale = 1.0
```

Now, add `.rotationEffect` and `.scaleEffect` to the ball *above* `.offset`. The order is important! If you reverse the order, the animation will look jarring.

```
.rotationEffect(
  Angle(degrees: rotation),
  anchor: .center
) // 1
.scaleEffect(
  x: 1.0 / scale,
  y: scale,
  anchor: .bottom
) // 2
```

Here, you:

1. Use degrees for the rotation measurement and set the center of the ball as the rotation's anchor.

2. Squash the ball around its bottom side as it hits the surface on the bottom by scaling it along the x-axis inversely to the y-axis.

The final touch is to animate those properties. Make a new function inside `JumpingBallView` right below its `body`:

```
private func animate() {
  withAnimation(
    .easeInOut(duration: Constants.jumpDuration)
    .repeatForever()
  ) { // 1
    isAnimating = true
  }

  withAnimation(
    .linear(duration: Constants.jumpDuration * 2)
    .repeatForever(autoreverses: false)
  ) { // 2
    rotation = 360
  }

  withAnimation(
    .easeOut(duration: Constants.jumpDuration)
```

```
      .repeatForever()
    ) { // 3
      scale = 0.85
    }
  }
```

Here's what you did:

1. Since you need to trigger all these animations the moment the ball appears, you move the previously-created jumping animation alongside new ones to a separate function.
2. To make the ball rotate indefinitely without changing its direction, you disable auto-reverse. By doubling the duration, you force the ball to make a whole rotation before returning to the top position.
3. You use `.easeOut` to squash the ball since you want it to slow down slightly as the ball hits the surface to amplify the effect. Making `scale` less than `1` increases the ball horizontally and makes it smaller vertically, imitating squashing.

Update the `.onAppear` action of `JumpingBallView` to only invoke your new `animate()` method:

```
.onAppear {
  animate()
}
```

Run your app again, and you'll see the ball now rotates nicely and gets squashed at its bottom, just as expected — great progress!

Animation Opacity

The ball is ready, but what about a little touch of shadow? Add a new property to `JumpingBallView` to define the shadow's height:

```
private let shadowHeight = Constants.ballSize / 2
```

Then, in `JumpingBallView`'s `ZStack`, you wrap the ball image in `body` and add some shadow to the ball. Replace the `body` with:

```
ZStack {
  Ellipse()
    .fill(Color.gray.opacity(0.4))
    .frame(
      width: Constants.ballSize,
      height: shadowHeight
```

```
    )
    .scaleEffect(isAnimating ? 1.2 : 0.3, anchor: .center) // 1
    .offset(y: Constants.maxOffset - shadowHeight / 2 -
Constants.ballSpacing) // 2
    .opacity(isAnimating ? 1 : 0.3) // 3

  Ball()
    .rotationEffect(
      Angle(degrees: rotation),
      anchor: .center
    )
    .scaleEffect(
      x: 1.0 / scale,
      y: scale,
      anchor: .bottom
    )
    .offset(y: currentYOffset)
    .onAppear { animate() }
}
```

Here's what you added:

1. You draw a translucent gray ellipse behind the ball and make its size animate with the jumping ball by reusing `isAnimating`. It becomes larger when the ball reaches the surface and shrinks when the ball is in the air.
2. You position the shadow exactly beneath the ball.
3. Like you did for scaling, you make the shadow change its opacity depending on the ball position. When it's closer to the bottom, the shadow is darker.

Take a look at the preview:

Great job! Remember to keep an eye on the whole screen's integrity when working on a single component. Run the app to see the entire picture.

Making a Complete Picture

Your pull-to-refresh animation looks impressive but still feels somewhat out of place. The ball appears out of nowhere and then disappears. The user hardly anticipates this happening, and it can be off-putting.

To make it more natural, you must prepare the user and make it clear how the ball got to the screen. What could be more logical than a ball rolling towards you rather than just appearing in front of your nose?

You'll make the ball roll in from the left corner toward the center before it starts jumping.

First, for quick access to the value of half of the screen width, add a handy extension to the bottom of **BallView.swift**:

```
extension UIScreen {
  static var halfWidth: CGFloat {
    main.bounds.width / 2
  }
}
```

Add a new `struct` in **BallView.swift** to implement the entrance of the animation:

```
struct RollingBallView: View {
  @Binding var pullToRefresh: PullToRefresh
  private let shadowHeight: CGFloat = 5

  private let initialOffset = -UIScreen.halfWidth
    - Constants.ballSize / 2 // 1

  var body: some View {
    let rollInOffset = initialOffset
      + (pullToRefresh.progress * -initialOffset) // 2
    let rollInRotation = pullToRefresh.progress * .pi * 4 // 3

    ZStack {
      Ellipse()
        .fill(Color.gray.opacity(0.4))
        .frame(
          width: Constants.ballSize * 0.8,
          height: shadowHeight
        )
        .offset(y: -Constants.ballSpacing - shadowHeight / 2)

      Ball()
        .rotationEffect(
          Angle(radians: rollInRotation),
          anchor: .center
```

```
        )
        .offset(y: -Constants.ballSize / 2 -
Constants.ballSpacing)
    }
    .offset(x: rollInOffset) // 4
  }
}
```

You're already familiar with this setup. You have a `ZStack` with a shadow and a ball inside. Here's how the movement is different:

1. The ball's starting position in the animation is right behind the left corner of the screen. So, to move it from the center of the screen, where SwiftUI puts it by default, you need to apply a negative offset of half of the screen width and half of the ball size.

2. You use `PullToRefresh`'s `progress` value to move the ball with the same velocity as the user's gesture. It reaches the screen's center when the scroll view reaches its maximum offset. When the progress is `0`, `rollInOffset` equals `initialOffset`. When the progress is `1`, the offset is `0`, bringing the ball back to the center.

3. You apply the value of `progress` to the rotation and offset, too.

4. Since the horizontal offset of the shadow is identical to that of the ball, you can apply the offset to their parent view, the `ZStack`.

To bring this part of the animation to the picture, add a new condition, `case .pulling`, to the body of `BallView`, so the `switch` statement looks like this:

```
switch pullToRefresh.state {
case .ongoing:
  JumpingBallView()
case .pulling:
  RollingBallView(pullToRefresh: $pullToRefresh)
default:
  EmptyView()
}
```

Now, when the pulling gesture is ongoing, but the update hasn't started yet, you display the rolling ball.

Run the app to check it out:

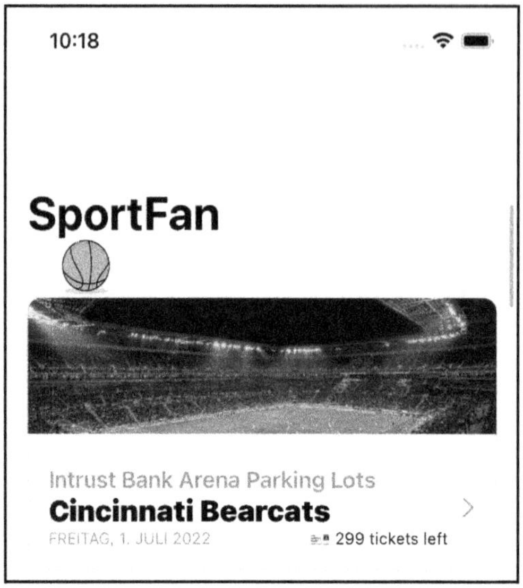

Finishing the Animation Gracefully

A natural way for the ball to disappear from the screen would be rolling away from the user after it stops jumping. All `RollingBallView` needs are a few adaptations to make it possible.

You'll add two new states to your animation:

1. The state transitions to `.preparingToFinish` right after the app completes the update to tell the ball to return to the top from whatever position it's at while jumping.
2. Once the ball is back to the top position, the state transitions to `.finishing` to tell `BallView` to switch back to `RollingBallView` to show the final part of your pull-to-refresh animation.

Go back to `AnimationState` in **PullToRefresh.swift** and add the `preparingToFinish` and `finishing` cases:

```
case idle = 0,
     pulling,
     ongoing,
     preparingToFinish,
     finishing
```

Then, add some new values to your `Constants` enum over at **Constants.swift**:

```
static let timeForTheBallToReturn = 0.3
static let timeForTheBallToRollOut = 1.0
```

You give the ball 300 milliseconds to finish the jumping motion and a full second to roll off the screen.

Add the following handy helper function to **ScrollViewGeometryReader.swift**. You'll use it to delay the execution of a piece of code:

```
func after(
  _ seconds: Double,
  execute: @escaping () -> Void
) {
  Task {
    let delay = UInt64(seconds * Double(NSEC_PER_SEC))
    try await Task<Never, Never>
      .sleep(nanoseconds: delay)
    execute()
  }
}
```

Then, replace the `Task` in `calculateOffset(from:)`'s `.pulling` case with:

```
Task {
  await update()
  pullToRefresh.state = .preparingToFinish // 1
  after(timeForTheBallToReturn) {
    pullToRefresh.state = .finishing // 2
    after(timeForTheBallToRollOut) {
      pullToRefresh.state = .idle // 3
      startOffset = 0
    }
  }
}
```

Here's what you added:

1. Instead of transitioning back to the idle state, your animation moves to a new phase — `.preparingToFinish`. It signals the ball to come back to the top to smooth the transition to the rolling out phase.

2. After that, the state transitions to `.finishing`. At this moment, the rolling ball replaces the jumping one.

3. Finally, once the ball is gone, you reset the animation state, setting its state to `.idle` and the offset to `0`. Now, the pull-to-refresh is in a valid state to execute again if needed.

To make the jumping ball react to the state change, add `PullToRefresh` to `JumpingBallView`:

```
@Binding var pullToRefresh: PullToRefresh
```

Update the shadow's `.fill` modifier to make it transparent when the ball stops jumping. Reminder: it's the `Ellipse` inside the `ZStack`:

```
.fill(
  Color.gray.opacity(
    pullToRefresh.state == .ongoing ? 0.4 : 0
  )
)
```

Then, tell the ball to move to the top by updating the `currentYOffset` property to:

```
var currentYOffset: CGFloat {
  isAnimating && pullToRefresh.state == .ongoing
  ? Constants.maxOffset - Constants.ballSize / 2 -
Constants.ballSpacing
  : -Constants.ballSize / 2 - Constants.ballSpacing
}
```

You'll work with implicit animations later in the chapter. For now, you'll use a little trick to tell SwiftUI to animate a state change to `.preparingToFinish` for `timeForTheBallToReturn` to smooth its move upwards. Add the following modifier to after `Ball`'s `offset` modifier and before its `onAppear`:

```
.animation(
  .easeInOut(duration: Constants.timeForTheBallToReturn),
  value: pullToRefresh.state == .preparingToFinish
)
```

Finally, don't forget to adjust the `JumpingBallView`'s initializer in the preview `struct`. If you don't, you'll get a compilation error:

```
JumpingBallView(
  pullToRefresh: .constant(
    PullToRefresh(
      progress: 0,
      state: .ongoing
    )
  )
)
```

You're done with `JumpingBallView`. Now to the rolling ball.

To animate the ball's rotation, offset and shadow while rolling out, add two new properties to `RollingBallView` in **BallView.swift**:

```
@State private var rollOutOffset: CGFloat = 0
@State private var rollOutRotation: CGFloat = 0
```

Then, update the x offset of the `ZStack` to change depending on the state:

```
.offset(x: pullToRefresh.state == .finishing ? rollOutOffset :
rollInOffset)
```

Do the same for the ball's `.rotationEffect`:

```
.rotationEffect(
  Angle(
    radians: pullToRefresh.state == .finishing
      ? rollOutRotation
      : rollInRotation
  ),
  anchor: .center
)
```

To animate these properties, add a new function to `RollingBallView`:

```
private func animateRollingOut() {
  guard pullToRefresh.state == .finishing else {
    return
  }

  withAnimation(
    .easeIn(duration: Constants.timeForTheBallToRollOut)
  ) {
    rollOutOffset = UIScreen.main.bounds.width
  }

  withAnimation(
    .linear(duration: Constants.timeForTheBallToRollOut)
  ) {
    rollOutRotation = .pi * 4
  }
}
```

And invoke by attaching an `.onAppear` modifier to the `ZStack`:

```
.onAppear {
  animateRollingOut()
}
```

Update the `switch` statement in `BallView` to account for the new states. Adding `.finishing` and `.preparingToFinish` and passing the `pullToRefresh` binding to `JumpingBallView`. The entire `switch` statement should look like this:

```
switch pullToRefresh.state {
case .ongoing, .preparingToFinish:
  JumpingBallView(pullToRefresh: $pullToRefresh)
case .pulling, .finishing:
  RollingBallView(pullToRefresh: $pullToRefresh)
default:
  EmptyView()
}
```

Now, the rolling ball view displays both the animation's entrance, `.pulling`, and its exit, `.finishing`. The jumping ball will take over the `.ongoing` and `.preparingToFinish` phases.

As a final touch, update the `.offset` of the `LazyVStack` in the `ContentView` to wait for the ball to stop jumping before getting back to the initial position:

```
.offset(y: [.ongoing, .preparingToFinish]
  .contains(pullToRefresh.state) ? Constants.maxOffset : 0
)
```

Run the app to see the latest changes.

Now the animation doesn't look out of place and has a logical and seamless flow. Only a few final touches are missing!

Polishing With Implicit Animations and Advanced Interpolation Functions

Explicit animations are great for triggering an animation at a specific point or animating *multiple* view properties by modifying a variable in a single place. Remember how `isAnimating` was solely responsible for the shadow animating its opacity and scaling perfectly to the beat of the ball?

On the other hand, you may need to animate *one single view* depending on a variable value that you modify in *multiple places*. That's where **implicit** animations come to the rescue, using `View`'s modifier — `.animation(:value:)`. SwiftUI animates any change to the `value` parameter using the animation you pass as the first argument.

For instance, `pullToRefresh.state` affects the offset of the events container when pull-to-refresh starts and finishes. If you animate this change explicitly via `withAnimation` to enhance the container's movement, you'll break the behavior of other views dependent on the shared state.

An easy way to achieve this change in an isolated manner is to add the `.animation(:value:)` below the `.offset` of the `LazyVStack` in `ContentView`:

```
.animation(
  .easeInOut(duration: Constants.timeForTheBallToReturn),
  value: pullToRefresh.state
)
```

That smooths the movement slightly, but you can go further using a spring animation for the pull-down movement.

Add these new properties to `ContentView`:

```
private let ease: Animation = .easeInOut(
  duration: Constants.timeForTheBallToReturn
)
private let spring: Animation = .interpolatingSpring(
  stiffness: 80,
  damping: 4
)
```

With the setup above, you instantiate a bouncy spring animation with a relatively low damping and ensure the animation bounces a few more times before settling down.

Now replace the `.animation(:value:)` modifier you added recently with:

```
.animation(
  pullToRefresh.state != .finishing ? spring : ease,
  value: pullToRefresh.state
)
```

The code above lets you alternate between two different timing curves, ease and spring, depending on the state of the pull-to-refresh.

Run the app and check out what you have so far — simply remarkable and delightful!

Creating a Custom Timing Curve

While working with animations or computer graphics in general, you inevitably end up needing a rather specific or unusual timing curve.

Interestingly, engineers faced this problem before animations as we know them came into existence. In the 1960s, the auto industry reluctantly introduced software into the car design process. One of the challenges they faced was programming the complex curves of a car's bodywork.

At the time, Pierre Bézier, a french engineer, came up with a mathematical formula defined by a set of "control points" describing a smooth and continuous curve.

Nowadays, any graphic design tool like Photoshop, Figma or Sketch will offer you Bézier curves to build complex curves. And SwiftUI is no exception. This lets you create a custom interpolation function by defining a quadratic Bézier curve with two control points:

```
static func timingCurve(
  _ c0x: Double,
  _ c0y: Double,
  _ c1x: Double,
  _ c1y: Double,
  duration: Double = 0.35
) -> Animation
```

To build such a curve, you may use one of many online tools for Bézier curves preview, such as cubic-bezier.com. By dragging the control points, you'll receive precise coordinates to achieve the curve.

To enhance the rolling-in animation of the ball, you can use a custom timing curve to make it bounce sideways slightly, as if the ball was affected by inertia, if the user stops pulling the events container for a brief moment halfway through.

Add a new property inside `RollingBallView`:

```
private let bezierCurve: Animation = .timingCurve(
  0.24, 1.4, 1, -1,
  duration: 1
)
```

Immediately apply it on the `ZStack` in the `body` property of `RollingBallView`:

```
.animation(
  bezierCurve,
  value: pullToRefresh.progress
)
```

Run the app one final time and play with your now-complete pull-to-refresh animation. Fantastic progress!

Don't hesitate to experiment with the numbers and the interpolating functions. That's the fun part of crafting animations. :]

Key Points

- `GeometryReader` is a SwiftUI view, which takes up all the space provided by its parent and allows accessing its size, frame and safe area insets through a `GeometryProxy`.
- Avoid performing state changes directly inside a view's body, as it may cause an undesired render loop.
- Use interpolation functions to make animations feel more natural and physically realistic.
- Try not to catch a user off guard with your animations. The behavior should be expected and well placed in the app.
- Use `withAnimation()` to animate multiple views or properties of a view from one place **explicitly**.
- Use `.animation(:value:)` to trigger a single view animation by modifications happening in the shared state of multiple components **implicitly**.
- A Bézier curve is defined by a set of control points and can be helpful in various aspects of computer graphics.

Where to Go From Here?

1. If you want to learn more about different Bézier curves, visit the Wikipedia page (https://en.wikipedia.org/wiki/Bezier_curve). It offers a detailed and demonstrative overview.
2. Disney's animation principles (https://en.wikipedia.org/wiki/Twelve_basic_principles_of_animation) may be handy when developing an animation on a mobile device. A few of them, like "Squash and stretch", "Anticipation" or "Slow in and slow out," may already be familiar to you. :]

Chapter 3: View Transitions

By Irina Galata

In the previous chapter, you started working on a sports-themed app to sell game tickets. You managed to improve its pull-to-refresh animation, turning the system loading wheel into a fun and memorable interaction.

In this chapter, you'll work on a new screen that contains a game's details as the next step toward the ticket purchase. You'll implement popular UI concepts like **list filters**, a **collapsing header view** and **floating action buttons**. Since this is an animations book, you'll also enhance them via various types of **transitions**, which you already got to briefly play with in the first chapter. You'll also get to roll up your sleeves and craft a custom transition.

Getting Started

You can continue working on the project from the previous chapter or use the starter project from this chapter's materials.

To pick up where you left off at the previous chapter, grab the **EventDetails** folder and the Asset catalog, **Assets.xcassets**, from this chapter's starter project and add them to your current project.

Since you'll work on several different components this time, append the following values inside your `Constants` enum, over at **Constants.swift**:

```
static let spacingS = 8.0
static let spacingM = 16.0
static let spacingL = 24.0
static let cornersRadius = 24.0
static let iconSizeS = 16.0
static let iconSizeL = 24.0

static let orange = Color("AccentColor")

static let minHeaderOffset = -80.0
static let headerHeight = 220.0
static let minHeaderHeight = 120.0

static let floatingButtonWidth = 110.0
```

If you're starting from the starter project, these files and values will already be part of your project.

Implementing Filter View

Head over to the already familiar **ContentView.swift**.

In the first iteration of the events screen, the navigation is somewhat cumbersome: the only way to find an event is to scroll to it, which can take a while. To make it more user-friendly, you'll implement a filtering functionality. For example, a user who only wants to see basketball can filter out all other games.

First, create a new SwiftUI file named **FilterView.swift**, and add the following properties to the generated struct:

```
@Binding var selectedSports: Set<Sport>
var isShown: Bool

private let sports = Sport.allCases
```

Before moving on, you'll fix the preview code so your code compiles. Replace the view in the preview code with:

```
FilterView(selectedSports: .constant([]), isShown: true)
```

Then, back in `FilterView`, below its `body`, add a method to build a view for each option:

```
func item(for sport: Sport) -> some View {
  Text(sport.string)
    .frame(height: 48)
    .foregroundColor(selectedSports.contains(sport) ? .white : .
primary)
    .padding(.horizontal, 36)
}
```

Now, you'll add a bit more style. Add the following `.background` modifier to the `Text` in `item(for:)`:

```
.background {
  ZStack {
    RoundedRectangle(cornerRadius: Constants.cornersRadius)
      .fill(
        selectedSports.contains(sport)
        ? Constants.orange
        : Color(uiColor: UIColor.secondarySystemBackground)
      )
      .shadow(radius: 2)
    RoundedRectangle(cornerRadius: Constants.cornersRadius)
      .strokeBorder(Constants.orange, lineWidth: 3)
  }
}
```

This code makes the item appear as a rounded rectangle outlined by an orange stroke. If `selectedSports` contains the sport the user picked, it paints the view orange to indicate it was selected.

Now, replace the view's body with a `ZStack` to hold all the sports options:

```
ZStack(alignment: .topLeading) {
  if isShown {
    ForEach(sports, id: \.self) { sport in
      item(for: sport)
        .padding([.horizontal], 4)
        .padding([.top], 8)
    }
  }
}
.padding(.top, isShown ? 24 : 0)
```

With the code above, you stack all the filtering items on top of each other. To build a grid out of them, you need to define each item's location relative to its neighbors.

Aligning Subviews With Alignment Guides

Using the `alignmentGuide(_:computeValue:)` view modifier, you can shift a component relative to the positions of its sibling views. Since you want to implement a grid, you'll adjust the item's horizontal and vertical alignment guides.

Computations like this require iterating over all the elements to accumulate the total values of the horizontal and vertical shift, so add the following variables above the `ZStack` you added in the previous step, at the top of the `body`:

```
var horizontalShift = CGFloat.zero
var verticalShift = CGFloat.zero
```

You'll start with the horizontal alignment.
Add `.alignmentGuide(_:computeValue:)` to the `item` below its padding:

```
// 1
.alignmentGuide(.leading) { dimension in
  // 2
  if abs(horizontalShift - dimension.width) >
UIScreen.main.bounds.width {
    // 3
    horizontalShift = 0
    verticalShift -= dimension.height
  }
  // 4
  let currentShift = horizontalShift
  // 5
  horizontalShift = sport == sports.last ? 0 : horizontalShift -
dimension.width
  return currentShift
}
```

Here's a step-by-step explanation:

1. First, you tell SwiftUI you want to make a computation to change the `.leading` alignment of a filter option. Inside the closure, you receive its dimensions, which will help calculate the alignment.
2. You check whether the current item still fits horizontally.

3. If it doesn't, you move it to the next "row" by setting the horizontal shift to 0, which places it at the left corner of the parent container. Additionally, you deduct the view's height from the vertical alignment to move the element down, forming a new row.
4. Then, you assign the current item's alignment value to a variable.
5. You deduct the current view's width from the alignment, which the *next* item in the loop will use.

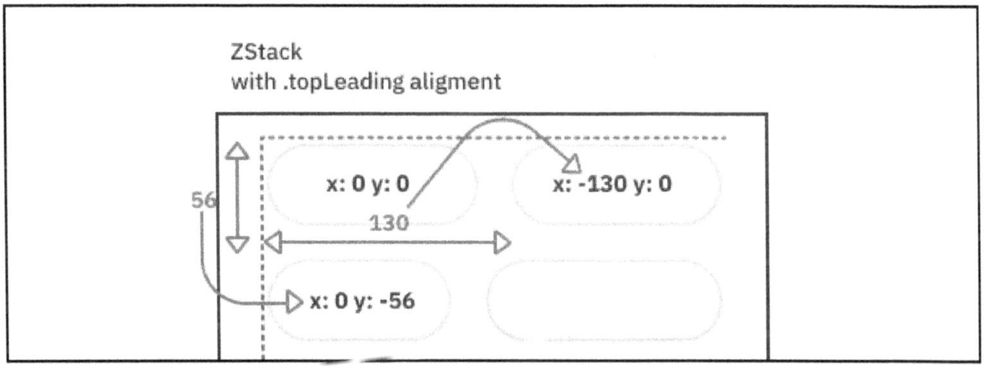

> **Note**: Although it may appear confusing at first, to move a view to the right, you need to move its horizontal alignment guide to the left. Therefore you deduct a view's width from the alignment value.Once the alignment guide moves to the left, SwiftUI **aligns** it with the alignment guides of the view's siblings by moving the view to the right.

Now, add `alignmentGuide(_:computeValue:)` to adjust the vertical alignment right below the previous one:

```
// 1
.alignmentGuide(.top) { _ in
  let currentShift = verticalShift
  // 2
  verticalShift = sport == sports.last ? 0 : verticalShift
  return currentShift
}
```

Here's a code breakdown:

1. This time, you adjust the `.top` alignment guide.
2. Unless the current element is the last one, assign the value calculated alongside the horizontal alignment above. Otherwise, reset the shift value to `0`.

Now you'll handle the user's selection. Add a new method to `FilterView`:

```
private func onSelected(_ sport: Sport) {
  if selectedSports.contains(sport) {
    selectedSports.remove(sport)
  } else {
    selectedSports.insert(sport)
  }
}
```

This code simply adds the sport to `selectedSports` or removes it if `selectedSports` already contains it.

Then, wrap your entire `item(for:)` with a `Button` and call your new `onSelected` method, so it looks similar to the following:

```
Button {
  onSelected(sport)
} label: {
  item(for: sport)
    // padding and alignment guide modifiers
}
```

Filtering List Content

To use your new component, you'll have to adapt `ContentView` a bit. Open **ContentView.swift** and add these new properties to it:

```
@State var filterShown = false // 1
@State var selectedSports: Set<Sport> = [] // 2
@State var unfilteredEvents: [Event] = [] // 3
```

Here's what you'll use each property for:

1. You'll use `filterShown` to toggle the visibility of `FilterView`.
2. `selectedSports` is a set where you'll keep the selected sports. Later, changing this property will filter the sports events.
3. To reset the filter, you'll keep the original array in `unfilteredEvents`.

Next, add a method to ContentView, which is responsible for filtering the events:

```
func filter() {
  events = selectedSports.isEmpty
    ? unfilteredEvents
    : unfilteredEvents.filter
{ selectedSports.contains($0.team.sport) }
}
```

To prevent the pull-to-refresh from breaking the filter functionality, replace the code inside update() with:

```
unfilteredEvents = await fetchMoreEvents(toAppend: events)
filter()
```

Add a toolbar item on the view's primary ScrollView, using the toolbar(content:) modifier:

```
.toolbar {
   // 1
  ToolbarItem {
    Button {
      // 2
      filterShown.toggle()
    } label: {
      Label("Filter", systemImage:
"line.3.horizontal.decrease.circle")
        .foregroundColor(Constants.orange)
    }
  }
}
```

Here's a code breakdown:

1. Inside .toolbar, you pass the toolbar items you want to display on top of the screen. You add only one primary action displayed as a filter icon.
2. Once a user taps it, you toggle filterShown.

To trigger the filter, you'll use the view modifier .onChange(of:) to listen to the changes to selectedSports. Add the following modifier to ScrollView:

```
.onChange(of: selectedSports) { _ in filter() }
```

Finally, wrap the `LazyVStack` holding the event views into another `VStack` and add `FilterView` on top so that the structure looks like this:

```
VStack {
  FilterView(selectedSports: $selectedSports, isShown:
filterShown)
     .padding(.top)
     .zIndex(1)
  LazyVStack { ... }
}
```

Make sure the `.animation` and the `.offset` modifiers are attached to the outer `VStack` so the filters and pull-to-refresh won't overlap.

Run the app, and tap the filter button in the navigation bar to see the new feature:

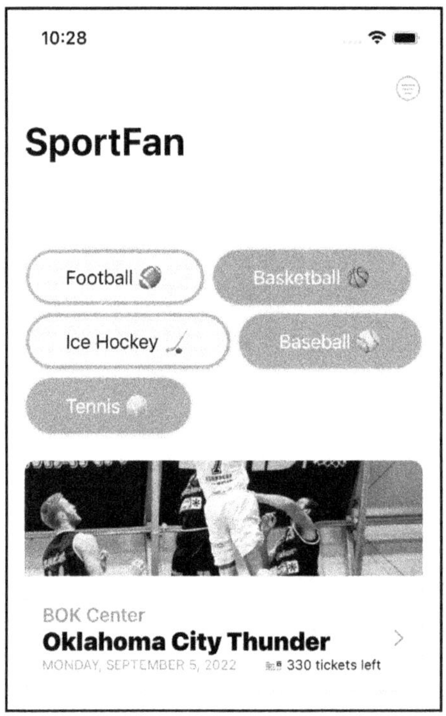

The functionality is there, but it's not very fun to use. The filter view abruptly moves the events container down, which doesn't look neat.

But it's a piece of cake to make it smooth with SwiftUI's transitions! Next, you'll add a basic transition to your component.

Applying Basic Transitions

In SwiftUI, a **transition** is a movement that occurs as you add or remove a view in the rendering tree. It animates only in the context of a SwiftUI's animation.

Since you already modify ContentView's layout by showing and hiding the filter view and updating the content of the events set, only two components are missing: transitions and animations.

Still inside **ContentView.swift**, wrap the contents of filter() with withAnimation(_:_:) and pass some bouncy animation there:

```
withAnimation(
  .interpolatingSpring(stiffness: 30, damping: 8)
  .speed(1.5)
) {
  events = selectedSports.isEmpty
    ? unfilteredEvents
    : unfilteredEvents.filter
{ selectedSports.contains($0.team.sport)
  }
}
```

Modifying the events value inside withAnimation lets SwiftUI animate every view's update that depends on the events property.

Next, inside ForEach, replace EventView with:

```
// 1
EventView(event: event)
// 2
  .transition(.scale.combined(with: .opacity))
```

Here, you:

1. Create the event view just as you did before.
2. Attach a *scale* transition to EventView and combine it with an opacity transition.

This changes the animation of EventView from *easing* into the view to scaling and slowly fading in.

Build and run, then filter by any sport to see the new transition.

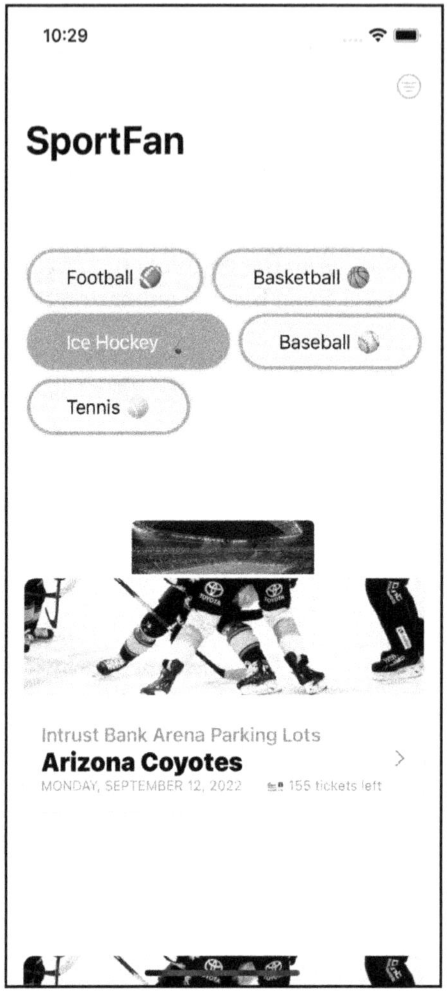

> **Note**: It's sometimes preferable using `VStack` instead of `LazyVStacks` for animated content, since the lazy nature of the latter means the elements you want to animate aren't necessarily available yet, which can cause the animation the look sloppy or stuck.

Crafting Custom Transitions

Your next goal is to animate `FilterView`, which gives you an opportunity to try out some more advanced transitions. With SwiftUI, you can create a custom modifier to animate the transition between the active and inactive (i.e. identity) states of your `FilterView`.

Back in **FilterView.swift**, add the following code to the bottom of the file:

```
struct FilterModifier: ViewModifier {
  // 1
  var active: Bool

  // 2
  func body(content: Content) -> some View {
    content
      // 3
      .scaleEffect(active ? 0.75 : 1)
      // 4
      .rotationEffect(.degrees(active ? .random(in: -25...25) :
0), anchor: .center)
  }
}
```

This code creates a struct named `FilterModifier` that conforms to `ViewModifier`. In the code above:

1. You add an `active` property so you can animate the change between it's `true` and `false` states.
2. For `FilterModifier` to conform to `ViewModifier`, you must implement `body(content:)`, where you apply the preferable transformations to the `content` you receive as a parameter.
3. You animate the change in scale between `0.75` and `1`.
4. Additionally, you make the view swing in a random direction and then get back to `0` degrees.

Now, add a new property in `FilterView` to keep the transition created with your view modifier:

```
private let filterTransition = AnyTransition.modifier(
  active: FilterModifier(active: true),
  identity: FilterModifier(active: false)
)
```

To apply the newly created transition, add the following modifier to the `Button` containing your filter item:

```
.transition(.asymmetric(
  insertion: filterTransition,
  removal: .scale
))
```

Typically, you apply the same transition to a view's entry and exit. Since you only want the filter options to bounce when they appear, you need to apply an **asymmetric** transition. This way, you define `insertion` and `removal` transitions separately.

To start the transition, you need to animate the `filterShown` value change.

Back inside **ContentView.swift**, find:

```
filterShown.toggle()
```

Replace it with:

```
withAnimation(filterShown
  ? .easeInOut
  : .interpolatingSpring(stiffness: 20, damping: 3).speed(2.5)
) {
  filterShown.toggle()
}
```

With this approach, you alternate between the plain `.easeInOut` and the bouncy `.interpolatingSpring` animations. Try it out. Run the app and tap the filter button.

Nice job! The filter view appears with a bouncy spring animation and disappears with an ease animation. How much cooler is that? Next, you'll improve the user experience on the event details screen.

Improving UX With Collapsible Header

To connect your `ContentView` to the new event details screen, wrap the `EventView` instance inside the `ForEach` with a `NavigationLink` as follows:

```
NavigationLink(destination: EventDetailsView(event: event)) {
  EventView(event: event)
}
```

Now, tapping on an event view cell in the container will navigate the user to the `EventDetailsView`. Try it out. Run the app to see what you've got to work on next.

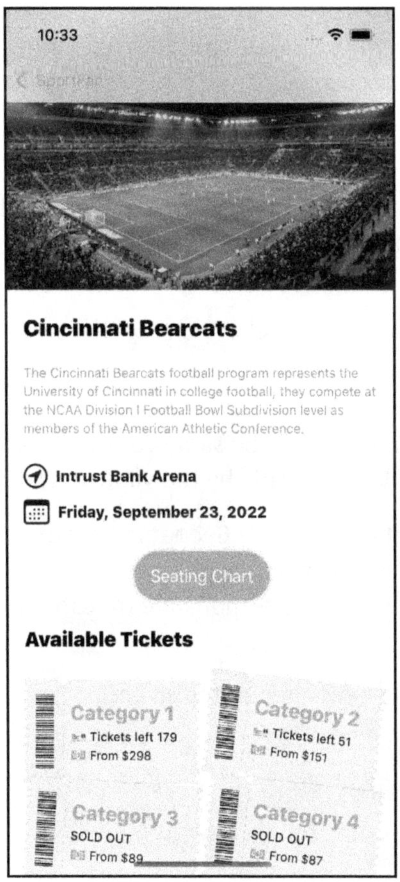

On the new details screen, you'll see all the relevant information on the specific event: the date, location, tickets available and the team's upcoming games. You'll also notice a button, **Seating Chart**. It doesn't do much right now, but soon it'll be a linking point to the component you'll craft in the fourth and fifth chapters. Sounds intriguing?

For now, you have a lot to do on this screen.

Although the event details screen looks fine and fulfills its designated purpose - displaying event info - a good animation can improve its usability drastically.

Notice that `EventDetailsView` contains many components. Some are essential, while others are less critical. When a user scrolls down to see all the upcoming events, the most vital information and functionality gets lost: the date and button to navigate to the seating chart to buy tickets. If too many events are already planned, it can take a while to scroll back to the important section.

There are multiple viable approaches to solving this problem. You could split the screen's functionality and, for example, show the upcoming games only on demand, thus making the details screen smaller and more manageable.

Alternatively, you could hide them completely, add a search bar on the events list screen and make users look for the stuff they need. You could also "pin" the crucial components to stay visible and accessible while a user scrolls down the screen's content, which is the strategy you'll take for this chapter.

Building a Collapsible Header With GeometryReader

To make a header view collapse with the same velocity as a user scrolls down content, you need to shrink it vertically by the value of the scroll view's offset.

Since you're now an expert on SwiftUI's `GeometryReader`, the first steps may already be clear to you: create a new SwiftUI view file and name it **HeaderGeometryReader.swift**. It's responsible for catching the offset value of your scroll view.

Add these properties to the newly generated struct:

```
@Binding var offset: CGFloat
@Binding var collapsed: Bool

@State var startOffset: CGFloat = 0
```

`EventDetailsView` is aware of the current offset and if the header is collapsed.

Before moving on, remove the generated `HeaderGeometryReader_Previews` because you won't need it for this specific view.

Then, replace `body`'s content with:

```
GeometryReader<AnyView> { proxy in
 // 1
  guard proxy.frame(in: .global).minX >= 0 else {
    return AnyView(EmptyView())
  }

  Task {
    // 2
    offset = proxy.frame(in: .global).minY - startOffset

    withAnimation(.easeInOut) {
      // 3
      collapsed = offset < Constants.minHeaderOffset
    }
  }

  return AnyView(Color.clear.frame(height: 0)
    .task {
      // 4
      startOffset = proxy.frame(in: .global).minY
    }
  )
}
```

In the code snippet above, you:

1. Verify that the frame of the proxy is valid as a safety measure. If you navigate to a different screen while some transitions are animating on the previous screen, the proxy's values may be off upon entering the screen. You ignore such values until the valid ones appear.

2. Calculate the *change* to the scroll view's offset by subtracting the starting value from the current offset, `minY` of the proxy's frame. This way, before a user interacts with the content, the value of `offset` is `0`.

3. The header should collapse if the offset gets below the minimum value. You wrap this change in `withAnimation` to allow seamless transitions between the collapsed and expanded states.

4. To fetch the starting value of the offset only once before the view appears, you attach a `.task` modifier and access the proxy's `minY` from within it.

Now, open **EventDetailsView.swift** and add the `offset` and `collapsed` properties:

```
@State private var offset: CGFloat = 0
@State private var collapsed = false
```

Next, wrap the content of your`ScrollView` with a `ZStack`, so it looks like so:

```
ScrollView {
  ZStack {
    VStack {...}
  }
}
```

> **Note**: You may find the **code folding ribbon** option particularly helpful while working on this chapter. With it, you can easily fold the code blocks when you need to wrap them into another component. To enable it, tap on the checkbox in **Xcode Preferences -> Text Editing -> Display -> Code Folding Ribbon.**

Then, add your `HeaderGeometryReader` inside the `ZStack` above the `VStack`:

```
HeaderGeometryReader(
  offset: $offset,
  collapsed: $collapsed
)
```

Before `EventDetailsView`'s `body` grows even further, create a new SwiftUI file and name it **HeaderView.swift**. This file is responsible for the views you'll pin to the top of the screen.

Add the following properties inside the struct:

```
var event: Event
var offset: CGFloat
var collapsed: Bool
```

Next, replace the content of `body` with:

```
ZStack {
  // 1
  AsyncImage(
    url: event.team.sport.imageURL,
    content: { image in
      image.resizable()
        .scaledToFill()
        .frame(width: UIScreen.main.bounds.width)
```

```
        // 2
        .frame(height: max(
          Constants.minHeaderHeight,
          Constants.headerHeight + offset
        ))
        .clipped()
    },
    placeholder: {
      ProgressView().frame(height: Constants.headerHeight)
    }
  )
}
```

Here's what's happening:

1. You add an `AsyncImage` from `EventDetailsView` to `HeaderView` and wrap it into a `ZStack`.
2. You use the new `headerHeight` for the height instead of the hardcoded one. This makes the image shrink as the user scrolls the content of `EventDetailsView` and updates the height of `AsyncImage` in `.frame` so that it changes alongside the offset but doesn't go below the minimum allowed value.

Now, below `clipped()`, add some shadow and round the corners of the image to make it appear elevated above the content:

```
.cornerRadius(collapsed ? 0 : Constants.cornersRadius)
.shadow(radius: 2)
```

Since you're going to display the title and date label in the header, you need to apply an overlay to the image to darken it and make the text more readable. Add an `.overlay` modifier to the end of `AsyncImage`:

```
.overlay {
  RoundedRectangle(cornerRadius: collapsed ? 0 :
Constants.cornersRadius)
    .fill(.black.opacity(collapsed ? 0.4 : 0.2))
}
```

Since you're building a custom header, namely a toolbar, you need to hide the system header. Head over to **EventDetailsView.swift** and add the two following modifiers on the root `ZStack` of `EventDetailsView`:

```
.toolbar(.hidden)
.edgesIgnoringSafeArea(.top)
```

You also use `edgesIgnoringSafeArea(_:)` to make the content of `EventDetailsView` move toward the top border of the screen.

Now, it's time to add the missing views in your `HeaderView`. Head back to **HeaderView.swift** and add a `VStack` below the `AsyncImage`. It'll be the container for the team's name and date labels and the back button because you need to replace the system one, which is now gone:

```
VStack(alignment: .leading) {

}
.padding(.horizontal)
.frame(height: max(
  Constants.minHeaderHeight,
  Constants.headerHeight + offset
))
```

Next, you'll want to dismiss the view once the user taps the back button. Add the following environment property to `HeaderView` above the `event` property:

```
@Environment(\.dismiss) var dismiss
```

> **Note**: SwiftUI provides several environment values which can come in handy, like color scheme and size class. You can access them using a keypath in the `@Environment` attribute.

Next, add a new `Button` inside the `VStack` together with the back button and the title label:

```
Button {
  // 1
  dismiss()
} label: {
  HStack {
    Image(systemName: "chevron.left")
      .resizable()
      .scaledToFit()
      .frame(height: Constants.iconSizeS)
      .clipped()
      .foregroundColor(.white)

    // 2
    if collapsed {
      Text(event.team.name)
        .frame(maxWidth: .infinity, alignment: .leading)
        .font(.title2)
```

```
        .fontWeight(.bold)
        .foregroundColor(.white)
    } else {
      Spacer()
    }
  }
  .frame(height: 36.0)
  // 3
  .padding(.top, UIApplication.safeAreaTopInset +
Constants.spacingS)
}
```

Here's a code breakdown:

1. You wrap an `HStack` inside a `Button` which triggers the `dismiss()` method when tapped.
2. You show the team's name alongside the back button image in case the header is collapsed. Otherwise, you replace it with the `Spacer`.
3. Since you make your header ignore the safe area insets via `edgesIgnoringSafeArea(_:)`, you need to account for this measurement yourself to prevent the notch of your iPhone from hiding the back button and title.

The only thing missing in the header is the date label. Add the following code right below the `Button` you added in the previous step:

```
// 1
Spacer()

// 2
if collapsed {
  HStack {
    Image(systemName: "calendar")
      .renderingMode(.template)
      .resizable()
      .scaledToFit()
      .frame(height: Constants.iconSizeS)
      .foregroundColor(.white)
      .clipped()

    Text(event.date)
      .foregroundColor(.white)
      .font(.subheadline)
  }
  .padding(.leading, Constants.spacingM)
  .padding(.bottom, Constants.spacingM)
}
```

Here's what you did:

1. You use a `Spacer` to keep the space when the header is expanded and prevent the back button from jumping along the y-axis between state changes.
2. If `collapsed` is `true`, you display a calendar icon and the date.

Finally, update `HeaderView_Previews`'s `Header` initializer:

```
HeaderView(
  event: Event(team: teams[0], location: "Somewhere",
ticketsLeft: 345),
  offset: -100,
  collapsed: true
)
```

Note: Check out the preview to see this view. Tweak the values of `HeaderView` in the preview to check its states.

Now, go back to **EventDetailsView.swift** and remove the `AsyncImage`. In its place, add `HeaderView` in the root `ZStack` above `ScrollView`:

```
HeaderView(
  event: event,
  offset: offset,
  collapsed: collapsed
)
.zIndex(1)
```

A few lines down, add a `Spacer` above the team name to prevent the header from overlapping the screen's content:

```
Spacer()
  .frame(height: Constants.headerHeight)
```

Updating EventLocationAndDate to Animate When Collapsed

Now, open **EventLocationAndDate.swift** and add the following property below the `event`:

```
var collapsed: Bool
```

Update the preview with:

```
EventLocationAndDate(
  event: makeEvent(for: teams[0]),
  collapsed: false
)
```

Inside the second `HStack`, wrap the calendar `Image` and the date `Text` into an `if` statement to remove them when the header collapses, leaving the `Spacer` outside of the condition:

```
if !collapsed {
  ...
}
```

Go back to **EventDetailsView.swift** and pass `collapsed` to the initializer of the `EventLocationAndDate`:

```
EventLocationAndDate(event: event, collapsed: collapsed)
```

Last but not least, hide the team's name label once the header collapses as well:

```
if !collapsed {
  Text(event.team.name)
    .frame(maxWidth: .infinity, alignment: .leading)
    .font(.title2)
    .fontWeight(.black)
    .foregroundColor(.primary)
    .padding()
}
```

Run the app or check the preview of `EventDetailsView`:

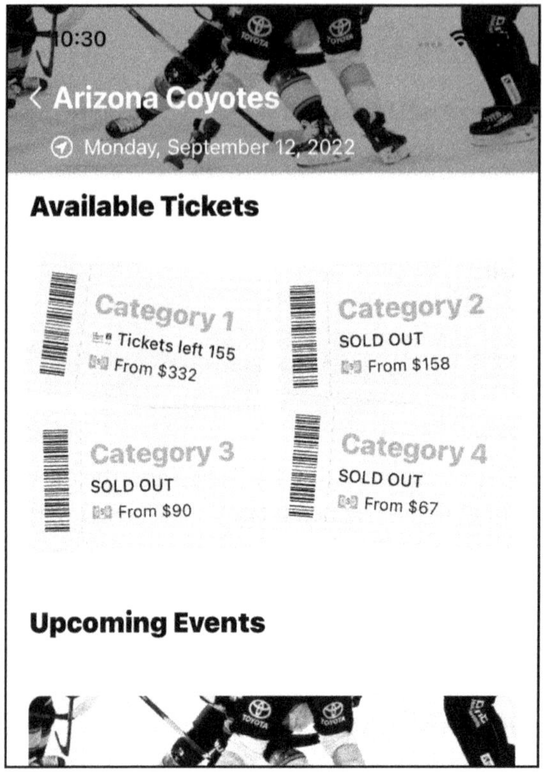

Synchronizing Geometry of Views With .matchedGeometryEffect

To make it appear as if you're "pinning" a label when it reaches the top of the screen, you need to align its disappearance in `EventDetailsView` and appearance in `HeaderView`. However, those are two different labels existing in two separate components!

It can seem challenging to implement this, but SwiftUI offers an out-of-the-box solution for this very problem — `matchedGeometryEffect`. This modifier matches two views by updating the frame of one view to match the frame of another.

SwiftUI recognizes which views it needs to adjust by their identifier in the common *namespace*.

Obtaining the animation namespace of a view is very straightforward. Simply add the following property to `EventDetailsView` above the `event` property:

```
@Namespace var namespace
```

Now that you have an animation namespace, you can add the `.matchedGeometryEffect` modifier to the team's name text below its padding:

```
.matchedGeometryEffect(
  id: "title",
  in: namespace,
  properties: .position
)
```

> **Note**: When linking two views with `.matchedGeometryEffect`, you can specify whether you want to align their sizes, positions or both. By default, it matches their frames, which works well for most use cases. When animating views containing text, you may want to use the `.position` option to prevent the text from being truncated while transitioning.

To make the title transition above the header, set its `zIndex` to move the label on top of the header:

```
.zIndex(2)
```

You need to share the same namespace ID between `EventDetailsView` and `HeaderView` to link their matched geometry together. Add a new property to `HeaderView` below the `dismiss` property:

```
var namespace: Namespace.ID
```

Then, add a matching `.matchedGeometryEffect` to the team name `Text` in `HeaderView`:

```
.matchedGeometryEffect(
  id: "title",
  in: namespace,
  properties: .position
)
```

To animate the transition for the calendar icon and the date label, add `.matchedGeometryEffect` to them as well:

```
.matchedGeometryEffect(id: "icon", in: namespace)
```

```
.matchedGeometryEffect(
  id: "date",
  in: namespace,
  properties: .position
)
```

To match them with the views inside `EventLocationAndDate`, follow the same steps as for `HeaderView`.

Go to `EventLocationAndDate` and:

1. Add `namespace` of type `Namespace.ID`.
2. Add `.matchedGeometryEffect` to the calendar icon, the date label with the `"icon"` and `"date"` identifiers, respectively:

```
.matchedGeometryEffect(id: "icon", in: namespace)
```

```
.matchedGeometryEffect(
  id: "date",
  in: namespace,
  properties: .position
)
```

If you want to have a preview of a view requiring a namespace, for example, `EventLocationAndDate` and `HeaderView`, you'll need to make `@Namespace` **static**:

```
struct EventLocationAndDate_Previews: PreviewProvider {
  @Namespace static var namespace
  static var previews: some View {
    EventLocationAndDate(
      namespace: namespace,
      event: makeEvent(for: teams[0]),
      collapsed: false
    )
  }
}
```

Finally, pass `namespace` from `EventDetailsView` to both `HeaderView`'s and `EventLocationAndDate`'s initializers:

```
HeaderView(
  namespace: namespace,
  event: event,
  offset: offset,
  collapsed: collapsed
)
```

```
EventLocationAndDate(
  namespace: namespace,
  event: event,
  collapsed: collapsed
)
```

Refresh the preview of `EventDetailsView` or run the app.

You've got the transitions working, but the button still goes out of sight when you scroll down to the upcoming games list. To keep it accessible to the user at all times, you'll implement the **floating action button** concept.

Implementing Floating Action Button

You'll wrap up this chapter by adding a Floating Action Button to order tickets for the event, and transition to it as the user scrolls - so the user has the order button right at their finger tips, wherever they are.

Inside `EventDetailsView`, wrap the button in an `if` statement:

```
if !collapsed {
  Button(action: {}) {
    ...
  }
}
```

Then, add `.matchedGeometryEffect` to the `Text` inside the button's label with a new identifier:

```
.matchedGeometryEffect(
  id: "button",
  in: namespace,
  properties: .position
)
```

To make the button shrink smoothly while scrolling, add a constant `.frame(width:)` to `RoundedRectangle`:

```
.frame(
  width: max( // 2
    Constants.floatingButtonWidth,
    min( // 1
      UIScreen.halfWidth * 1.5,
      UIScreen.halfWidth * 1.5 + offset * 2
    )
  )
)
```

1. The `min` function returns the smaller value out of the two parameters it receives. This ensures that as the `offset` value grows, the button's width doesn't go over `UIScreen.halfWidth * 1.5` or 75% of the screen width.
2. The `max` function does the exact opposite - it's helpful to ensure the bottom limit of a value. Once the `offset` value grows negatively, it caps the minimum value of the button's width to the `Constants.floatingButtonWidth`.

This way, although the button's width depends on the `offset`, you limit its possible values to the range between the `Constants.floatingButtonWidth` and 75% of the screen width.

Next, add a computed property inside `EventDetailsView` to store the collapsed representation of the button:

```
var collapsedButton: some View {
  HStack {
    Spacer()
    Button(action: { seatingChartVisible = true  }) {
      Image("seats")
        .resizable()
        .renderingMode(.template)
        .scaledToFit()
        .frame(width: 32, height: 32)
        .foregroundColor(.white)
        .padding(.horizontal)
        .background {
          RoundedRectangle(cornerRadius: 36)
            .fill(Constants.orange)
            .shadow(radius: 2)
            .frame(width: Constants.floatingButtonWidth, height:
48)
        }
        .matchedGeometryEffect(
          id: "button",
          in: namespace,
```

```
            properties: .position
          )
      }
      .padding(36)
    }
  }
```

In the collapsed state, you replace the label with an icon. And obviously we won't forget to link it to the original button with a `.matchedGeometryEffect` of the same `id`.

Finally, replace `HeaderView` in `EventDetailsView`'s `body` with the code below:

```
VStack {
  HeaderView(
    namespace: namespace,
    event: event,
    offset: offset,
    collapsed: collapsed
  )
  Spacer()
  if collapsed {
    collapsedButton
  }
}
.zIndex(1)
```

Time to run the app one more time!

Key Points

1. **Transitions** define the way a view appears and disappears from the screen.
2. You can combine your transitions with `.combined(with:)`.
3. Use `.matchedGeometryEffect` to align one view's frame to the other view's frame into a seamless animation.
4. A view will have different insertion and removal animations if you specify both via `.asymmetric(with:)`.
5. To implement a **custom transition**, you need to create a `ViewModifier` with the different transformations applied for the active and identity states.

Chapter 4: Drawing Custom Components

By Irina Galata

In the previous chapters, you got to use existing SwiftUI controls, like `Image`, `Button` or various stacks, to build an animated component. In many cases, if not the majority, they're sufficient to make an app engaging and valuable. But what about a non-trivial view requiring more intricate user interaction?

Avid basketball fans often have specific preferences regarding their seating. It's not enough to choose how many tickets they need for a game and have their credit card charged. They also want to choose *where* their seats are.

In this chapter, you'll build an interactive animated seating chart that lets users select their favorite seats quickly and conveniently. Considering the complexity of the shapes and their composition, drawing the various shapes from scratch is the way to go.

By the end of this chapter, your seating chart will look like this:

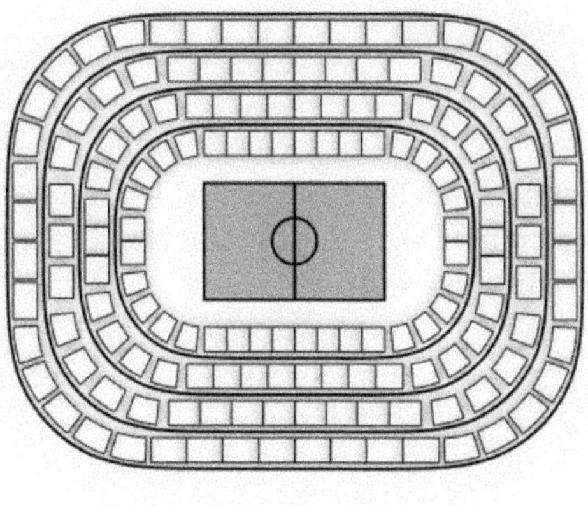

Outlining the Seating Chart View Using a Path

The seating chart you'll implement consists of a few key components: the field, which is that green rectangle in the middle, the sectors and the tribunes. You'll need to build two kinds of tribunes: rectangular ones located along a straight line and those placed in the corner areas of the stadium. You'll position corner tribunes along an arc, so you'll brush up on your trigonometry. :]

> **Note**: Some of the parts related to drawing and positioning the various stadium parts are a bit math-heavy, but no worries - we've got you covered! You can simply follow along the provided code snippets, or compare your code against the final project of this project's materials.

Open the starter project in this chapter's materials, or start working from the end of the previous chapter.

Start by creating a new SwiftUI view file that will contain all the above sub-components and name it **SeatingChartView.swift**. For now, place a `ZStack` in the `body` of the generated struct:

```
ZStack {

}
```

Immediately below `SeatingChartView`, create a new struct named `Stadium` and conform it to the `Shape` protocol:

```
struct Stadium: Shape {
  func path(in rect: CGRect) -> Path {
  }
}
```

In SwiftUI, `Shape` is a 2-dimensional drawn view, which can have a stroke and a fill. To implement a shape, you must create and manipulate a `Path` instance in the `path(in:)` method and return the result.

Drawing the Sectors

In this section, you'll create the sectors, which are the elliptical lines that separate the tribunes. When you're done, the seating chart will look like this:

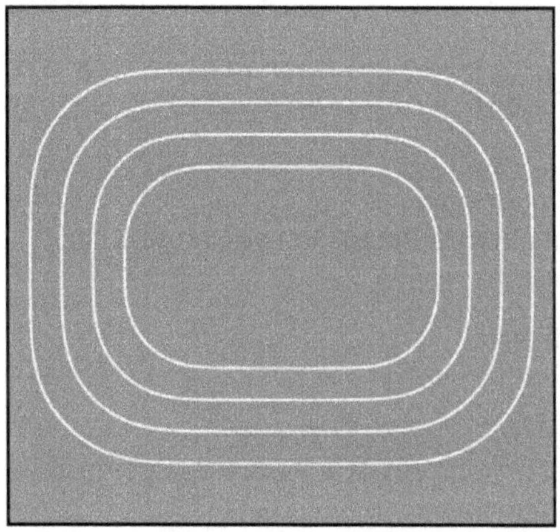

First, you'll declare the number of sectors your stadium contains. Add a new constant to your **Constants.swift** file:

```
static let stadiumSectorsCount = 4
```

To calculate sectors' frames based on the size of the stadium, add the following lines inside `Stadium`'s `path(in:)`:

```
// 1
Path { path in
  let width = rect.width

  let widthToHeightRatio = 1.3 // 2
  let sectorDiff = width /
(CGFloat(Constants.stadiumSectorsCount * 2)) // 3
}
```

Here's a code breakdown:

1. You initialize a new `Path` using a special initializer which hands you a `path` argument you can manipulate and draw the chart's main outlines onto.
2. To make the stadium appear elliptical, you need a width-to-height ratio different from `1.0`.
3. Since the sectors are different sizes, you need to calculate the size change value, vertically and horizontally, between the neighboring sectors.

Now, add a loop under the variables you just added to calculate frames for each sector, and draw a rounded rectangle for each:

```
(0..<Constants.stadiumSectorsCount).forEach { i in
  let sectionWidth = width - sectorDiff * Double(i) // 1
  let sectionHeight = width / widthToHeightRatio - sectorDiff *
Double(i) // 2
  let offsetX = (width - sectionWidth) / 2.0 // 3
  let offsetY = (width - sectionHeight) / 2.0

  let sectorRect = CGRect(
    x: offsetX, y: offsetY,
    width: sectionWidth, height: sectionHeight
  )

  path.addRoundedRect(
    in: sectorRect,
    cornerSize: CGSize(
      width: sectorRect.width / 4.0,
      height: sectorRect.width / 4.0
    ), // 4
    style: .continuous
  )
}
```

Here's a code breakdown:

1. Because a rectangle is defined by its origin (`x`, `y`) and size (`width`, `height`), you calculate those values based on the stadium's size, making sure to deduct a value of the `sectorDiff` each time to get the width of the next smaller sector.
2. In addition to the difference between the sectors, you must account for the width-to-height ratio to calculate the sector's height.
3. To calculate the offset of a sector's origin, you calculate the difference between the available width (or height) and the section width. You then divide it by two.
4. You draw a rounded rectangle into the `path` with corners a quarter of the sector's width.

To get the first preview of your component, add an instance of `Stadium` inside the `ZStack` in `SeatingChartView`:

```
Stadium()
  .stroke(.white, lineWidth: 2)
```

Now, open SeatsSelectionView and replace Text(Something is missing here!) with the SeatingChartView you just created:

```
SeatingChartView()
  .aspectRatio(1.0, contentMode: .fit)
  .padding()
```

You set the aspect ratio to 1 to give the view a squared area to draw the stadium.

Finally, back in **SeatingChartView.swift**, update your preview so it has a nice orange background which lets you see the white sectors:

```
struct SeatingChartView_Previews: PreviewProvider {
  static var previews: some View {
    SeatingChartView()
      .padding()
      .background(orange)
  }
}
```

Your SwiftUI preview should look like the screenshot in the beginning of this section.

Drawing the Field

In this section, you'll draw the field in the middle of the stadium. When you're done, it will look like this:

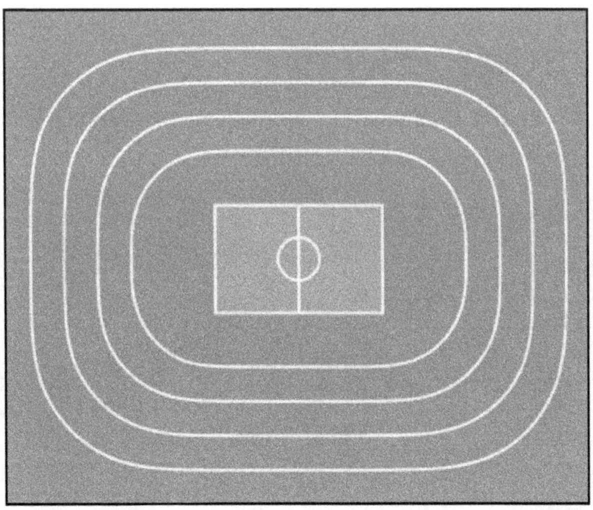

To animate the stadium field separately from the other components and fill it with a different color, you need to draw it separately.

Create a `@State` property `field` inside `SeatingChartView`:

```
@State private var field = CGRect.zero
```

Then, in the same file, add a `@Binding` variable of the same type in `Stadium` shape:

```
@Binding var field: CGRect
```

Pass it from `SeatingChartView` to `Stadium`'s initializer:

```
Stadium(field: $field)
```

To draw the field inside the smallest sector frame, add a new variable above the loop in `Stadium`:

```
var smallestSectorFrame = CGRect.zero
```

Once you calculate the rectangle for a sector inside the loop, assign it to the new variable. This will guarantee that when the loop finishes, the smallest sector `Rect` stores inside this variable. Add this below `let sectorRect = ...`:

```
smallestSectorFrame = sectorRect
```

The field needs to be half the size of the smallest sector. You'll calculate the exact field `Rect` with the help of some simple math.

Below the `path(in:)` method of `Stadium`, add a new method to calculate and update the `field` property:

```
private func computeField(in rect: CGRect) {
  Task {
    field = CGRect(
      x: rect.minX + rect.width * 0.25,
      y: rect.minY + rect.height * 0.25,
      width: rect.width * 0.5,
      height: rect.height * 0.5
    )
  }
}
```

Now, back in `path(in:)` and after the `forEach`, run `computeField` to assign the result of the computation to `field` :

```
computeField(in: smallestSectorFrame)
```

With these preparations in place, you're ready to draw the field. Below `Stadium`, add a new shape to describe the field:

```
struct Field: Shape {
  func path(in rect: CGRect) -> Path {
  }
}
```

Inside `path(in:)`, add the following manipulations:

```
Path { path in
  path.addRect(rect) // 1
  path.move(to: CGPoint(x: rect.midX, y: rect.minY)) // 2
  path.addLine(to: CGPoint(x: rect.midX, y: rect.maxY)) // 3
  path.move(to: CGPoint(x: rect.midX, y: rect.midX))
  path.addEllipse(in: CGRect( // 4
    x: rect.midX - rect.width / 8.0,
    y: rect.midY - rect.width / 8.0,
    width: rect.width / 4.0,
    height: rect.width / 4.0)
  )
}
```

Here's what you draw above:

1. First, you outline the rectangle of the field.
2. Then, you move the path to the top center of the rectangle.
3. You draw the line from there toward the bottom center to split the field in half.
4. From the center of the field, you draw a circle with a diameter of a quarter of the field's width.

Go back to `SeatingChartView` and on top of `Stadium` inside the `ZStack`, add:

```
Field().path(in: field).fill(.green)
Field().path(in: field).stroke(.white, lineWidth: 2)
```

Right now, a path can either have a stroke or a fill. To have both, you need to duplicate them. Run the app or check the preview to see how the field you just created looks.

Computing the Positions of the Rectangular Tribunes

Similar to the field, you'll draw the tribunes separately to ease the animation.When you're done, it'll look like this:

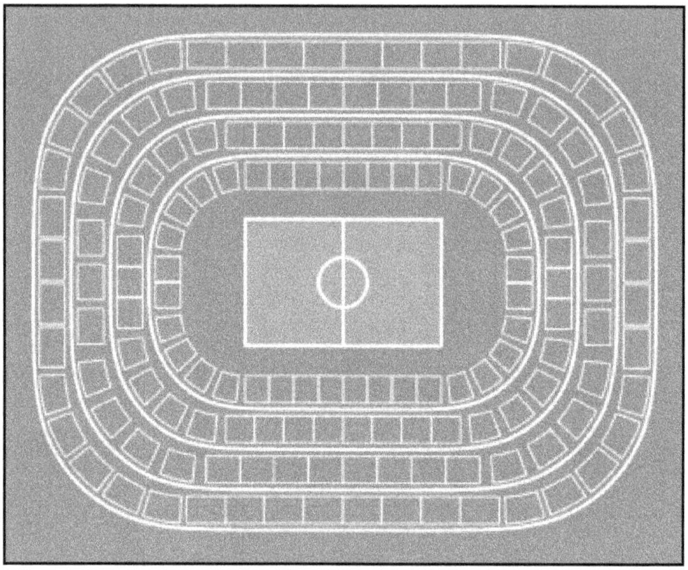

Create a new `struct` at the bottom of **SeatingChartView.swift**, which will represent both types of tribunes:

```
struct Tribune: Hashable, Equatable {
  var path: Path

  public func hash(into hasher: inout Hasher) {
    hasher.combine(path.description)
  }
}
```

Additionally, you'll need a `Shape` to draw the rectangular tribunes:

```
struct RectTribune: Shape {
  func path(in rect: CGRect) -> Path {
    Path { path in
      path.addRect(rect)
      path.closeSubpath()
    }
  }
}
```

Now, create a new property inside `SeatingChartView` to make it aware when the calculations of the tribunes are complete:

```
@State private var tribunes: [Int: [Tribune]] = [:]
```

You'll keep the tribunes as a dictionary of sector indices and the tribunes belonging to it.

Create the `@Binding` variable to mirror this state in `Stadium`:

```
@Binding var tribunes: [Int: [Tribune]]
```

Don't forget to pass it from `SeatingChartView`:

```
Stadium(field: $field, tribunes: $tribunes
  .stroke(.white, lineWidth: 2)
```

Then, to split the sectors-related computations from the general outline, create a new `Shape` for a sector:

```
struct Sector: Shape {
  @Binding var tribunes: [Int: [Tribune]] // 1
  var index: Int
  var tribuneSize: CGSize // 2
  var offset: CGFloat

  func path(in rect: CGRect) -> Path {
    Path { path in
      let corner = rect.width / 4.0

      path.addRoundedRect( // 3
        in: rect,
        cornerSize: CGSize(width: corner, height: corner),
        style: .continuous
      )
    }
  }
}
```

Here's what happens in the code above:

1. To update the `tribunes` value once you finish the computations, you create a `@Binding` in `Sector`, which you'll pass from `Stadium`.
2. `Sector` needs a few values to position the tribunes. Specifically, their size and the offset from the bounds of the current sector.
3. You move the drawing of the rounded rectangle from `Stadium` to `Sector`.

Now, go back to `Stadium`'s `path(in:)` and add the following variable above the loop:

```
let tribuneSize = CGSize(
  width: sectorDiff / 3,
  height: sectorDiff / 4.5
)
```

Based on the difference between the sector sizes, you need to decide on the height of a tribune. You divide the diff value by three to account for the vertical measurements of two rows of tribunes, top and bottom, and the top and bottom spacings for both of a quarter of a tribune's height: two tribunes + spacings of 0.25.

For the width, you'll use a ratio of 1:1.5, meaning fifty percent bigger than its height.

Then, replace the drawing of the rounded rectangle with the `Sector` shape you just created. Replace `path.addRoundedRect(...)` with:

```
let tribuneSize.widthOffset = (tribuneSize.width /
CGFloat(Constants.stadiumSectorsCount * 2)) * Double(i) // 1
path.addPath(Sector(
  tribunes: $tribunes,
  index: i,
  tribuneSize: CGSize(
    width: tribuneSize.width - tribuneSize.widthOffset,
    height: tribuneSize.height
  ),
  offset: (sec
```

Here's a breakdown:

1. Normally, the tribunes closer to the field are smaller than those on the borders. Therefore, depending on the index of the current sector, you deduct a part of the tribune width.
2. You divide the difference between the `sectorDiff` and the tribune's height in half to have equal top and bottom spacings for the tribune.

Now, to the tribunes. Create a new method inside the `Sector` struct:

```
private func computeRectTribunesPaths(at rect: CGRect, corner:
CGFloat) -> [Tribune] {
}
```

Since you place the rectangular tribunes only along a sector's straight segments, horizontal and vertical, you need to keep track of the width and height of such a segment.

Add them inside the method:

```
let segmentWidth = rect.width - corner * 2.0
let segmentHeight = rect.height - corner * 2.0
```

Then you need to know how many tribunes would fit horizontally or vertically:

```
let tribunesHorizontalCount = segmentWidth / tribuneSize.width
let tribunesVerticalCount = segmentHeight / tribuneSize.width
```

Notice that you divide the value in both cases by `tribuneSize.width`. In the sector's vertical segments, the tribunes rotate by 90 degrees, so you still need to operate with the width to know how many would fit vertically.

Define the spacings:

```
let spacingH = (segmentWidth - tribuneSize.width *
tribunesHorizontalCount) / tribunesHorizontalCount
let spacingV = (segmentHeight - tribuneSize.width *
tribunesVerticalCount) / tribunesVerticalCount
```

Finally, before computing each tribune, you need to add a helper function to create a `Tribune` instance out of a `RectTribune`. Add it right below `computeRectTribunesPaths(at:corner:)`:

```
private func makeRectTribuneAt(x: CGFloat, y: CGFloat, rotated:
Bool = false) -> Tribune {
  Tribune(
    path: RectTribune().path(
      in: CGRect( // 1
        x: x,
        y: y,
        width: rotated ? tribuneSize.height : tribuneSize.width,
// 2
        height: rotated ? tribuneSize.width : tribuneSize.height
      )
    )
  )
}
```

Here's what you just added:

1. You create an instance of `Tribune` and pass the path of `RectTribune`.
2. Depending on whether the tribune is rotated, you swap the width and height when building a `CGRect`.

Go back to `computeRectTribunesPaths(at:corner:)` and add the following code to compute the horizontal tribunes:

```
var tribunes = [Tribune]()
(0..<Int(tribunesHorizontalCount)).forEach { i in // 1
  let x = rect.minX + (tribuneSize.width + spacingH) *
CGFloat(i) + corner + spacingH / 2 // 2
  tribunes.append(makeRectTribuneAt(x: x, y: rect.minY +
offset)) // 3
  tribunes.append(makeRectTribuneAt(x: x, y: rect.maxY - offset
- tribuneSize.height)) // 4
}
```

Here's what you did:

1. You iterate over each tribune in a loop.
2. The `x` value for the top and bottom horizontal tribune is the same, so you calculate it beforehand, each time moving from left to right, by the width of the tribune and the horizontal spacing.
3. You add the top tribune. To offset it vertically, you add the value of the offset to the `minY` of the rectangle.
4. You place the bottom tribune by offsetting it from the bottom border of the rectangle. Since the origin of a `CGRect` refers to its *top* left corner, you must also deduct the tribune's height.

Now, calculate the positions for the vertical tribunes and return the result:

```
(0..<Int(tribunesVerticalCount)).forEach { i in
  let y = rect.minY + (tribuneSize.width + spacingV) *
CGFloat(i) + corner + spacingV / 2 // 1
  tribunes.append(makeRectTribuneAt(x: rect.minX + offset, y: y,
rotated: true)) // 2
  tribunes.append(makeRectTribuneAt(x: rect.maxX - offset -
tribuneSize.height, y: y, rotated: true)) // 3
}

return tribunes
```

Here's a code breakdown:

1. The y value is equal for the left and right vertical pair of tribunes. In this case, you move from top to bottom, starting from minY.
2. You add the left tribune by offsetting it from the rectangle's minX. You pass true as a rotated argument because the tribune is vertical.
3. You calculate the right tribune's position similar to the bottom horizontal one. You deduct the height value and offset from the maxX.

Now, assign the calculated result to the tribunes variable in the path(in:) method of Sector below the line drawing the rounded rectangle:

```
guard !tribunes.keys.contains(where: { $0 == index }) else { //
1
  return
}
Task {
  tribunes[index] = computeRectTribunesPaths(at: rect, corner:
corner) // 2
}
```

Here's what you did:

1. Since you want to calculate the tribunes' positions only once to improve the performance, you check whether the dictionary already contains them. They're not moving once installed, right? :]
2. You assign the calculated rectangular tribunes to the tribunes variable.

Finally, draw the tribunes in the SeatingChartView's body right below Stadium:

```
ForEach(tribunes.flatMap(\.value), id: \.self) { tribune in
  tribune.path
    .stroke(.white, style: StrokeStyle(lineWidth: 1,
lineJoin: .round))
}
```

Whew, that was a lot! But if you check out your preview, you'll see you've made some amazing progress. So close!

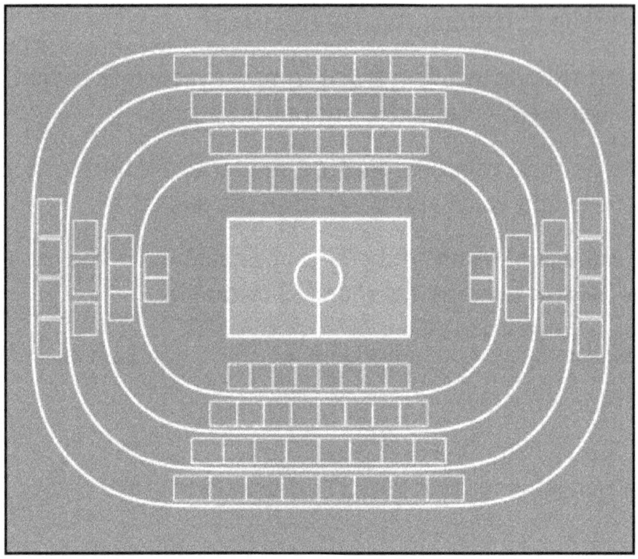

Applying Trigonometry to Position Views Along an Arc

To align the tribunes along an arc, you need to know some of the properties of the **circle** this arc belongs to.

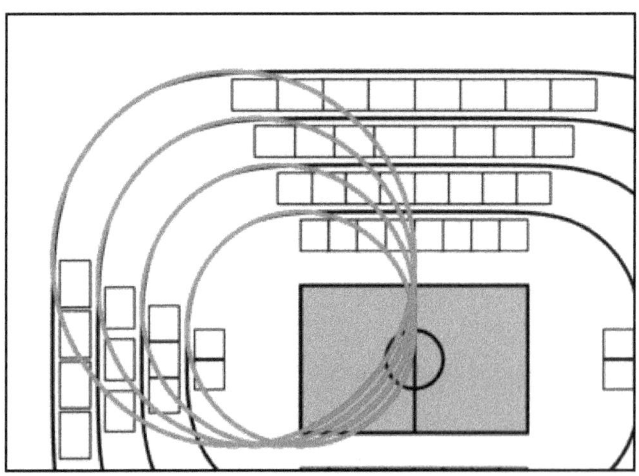

Look at the sectors you drew, and you'll notice that the corners are lying precisely on a circle with a radius the size of the corner of the rounded rectangle and the center in `(minX + corner, minY + corner)` for the top left corner. This information is sufficient to make further computations.

Create a new function below `computeRectTribunesPaths(at:corner:)`:

```
private func computeArcTribunesPaths(at rect: CGRect, corner:
CGFloat) -> [Tribune] {
}
```

As you build an arc tribune, you need to outline the arcs of two circles, one bigger and one smaller, and then connect them with straight lines.

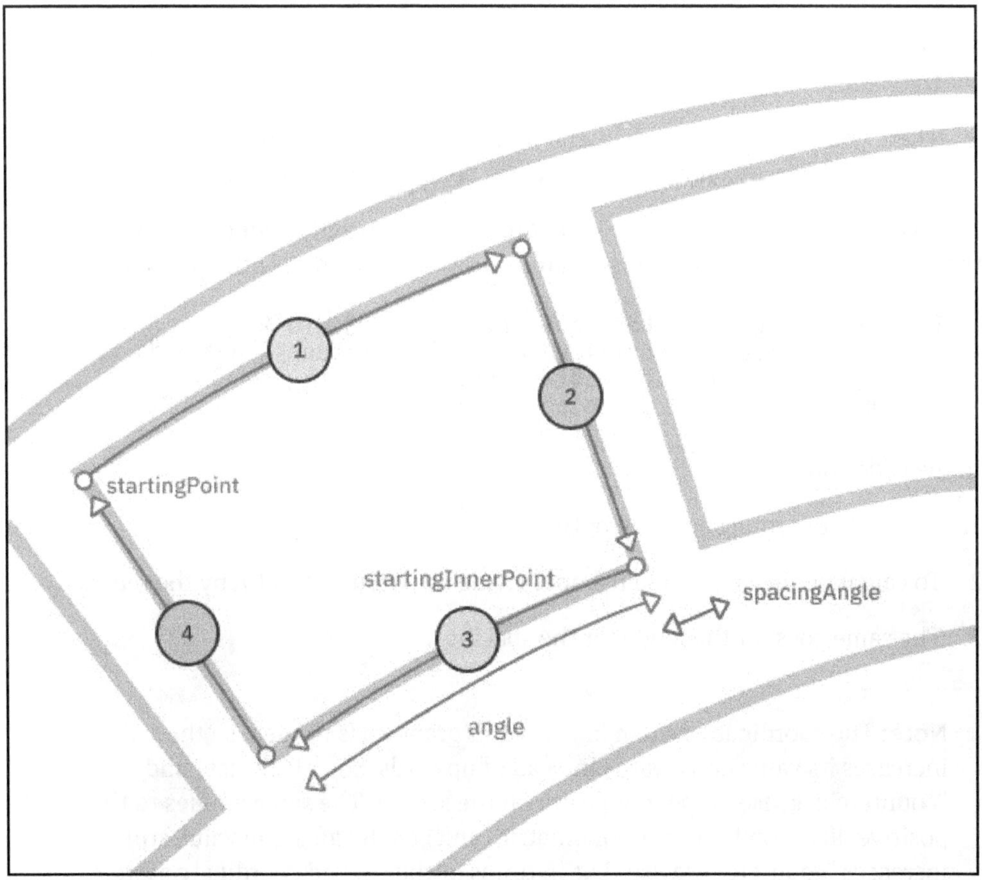

To calculate the radiuses of these circles, start by adding these variables inside the method:

```
let radius = corner - offset
let innerRadius = corner - offset - tribuneSize.height
```

Then, you'll need to calculate how many tribunes would fit into the arc. First, you obtain the length of the arc:

```
let arcLength = (.pi / 2) * radius // 1
let arcTribunesCount = Int(arcLength / (tribuneSize.width *
1.2)) // 2
```

Here's a code breakdown:

1. To calculate the arc length, you need to multiply the center angle in radians by the radius.
2. Then, you divide the length by the width of the tribune and an additional twenty percent of it to account for the spacings between the tribunes.

Now, you can calculate the angle of an arc needed for each tribune and an angle for the spacing. When moving along an arc, it's easier to operate with angles than sizes:

```
let arcSpacing = (arcLength - tribuneSize.width *
CGFloat(arcTribunesCount)) / CGFloat(arcTribunesCount + 1) // 1
let angle = tribuneSize.width / radius // 2
let spacingAngle = arcSpacing / radius // 3
```

In the code above, you:

1. Calculate the total spacing length.
2. To calculate the angle for a tribune, divide the tribune's width by the radius.
3. The same goes for the angle for the spacings.

> **Note**: The coordinate system in computer graphics is flipped, so the y-axis increases its value downwards instead of upwards. So, "clockwise" and "counterclockwise" appear opposite on the screen. The same applies to the positive direction for the trigonometric (unit) circle: an angle value still increases "counterclockwise" but in terms of the flipped coordinate system. From here onward, all the directions and angles will imply this system.

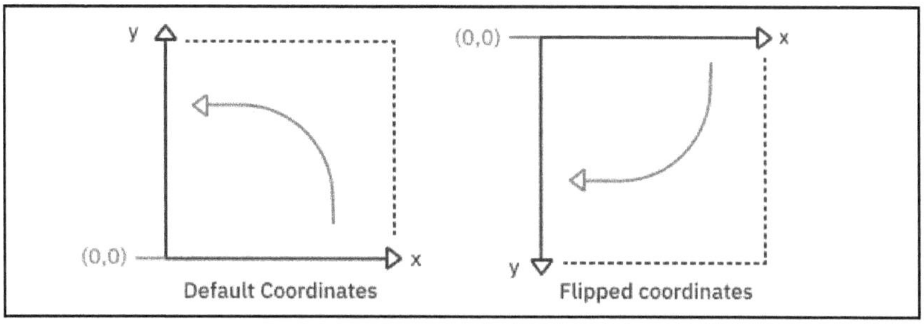

Now, you need to define an arc's starting angles and a circle's center for each corner of the sector. Make a dictionary to track them:

```
let arcs: [CGFloat: CGPoint] = [
  .pi: CGPoint(x: rect.minX + corner, y: rect.minY + corner), //
1
  3 * .pi / 2: CGPoint(x: rect.maxX - corner, y: rect.minY +
corner), // 2
  2 * .pi: CGPoint(x: rect.maxX - corner, y: rect.maxY -
corner), // 3
  5 * .pi / 2: CGPoint(x: rect.minX + corner, y: rect.maxY -
corner) // 4
]
```

Here's a code breakdown:

1. You start from the *top left* corner of the sector. Its arc will go from `.pi` to `3 * .pi / 2`.
2. The *top right* sector's arc starts at `3 * .pi / 2` and ends at `2 * .pi`.
3. The *bottom right* sector continues from `2 * .pi` until `5 * .pi / 2`.
4. Finally, the *bottom left* sector starts at `5 * .pi / 2`.

Now, you need to iterate over the dictionary and compute the `arcTribunesCount` amount of tribunes for each corner of the current sector. Add the following lines below the dictionary:

```
return arcs.reduce(into: [Tribune]()) { tribunes, arc in
  var previousAngle = arc.key
  let center = arc.value

  let arcTribunes = (0..<arcTribunesCount).map { _ in
    return Tribune(path: .init())
  }

  tribunes.append(contentsOf: arcTribunes)
}
```

You'll calculate the outer arc's starting point and the inner ones for each tribune. Add these calculations at the top of the inner `map`:

```
let startingPoint = CGPoint(
  x: center.x + radius * cos(previousAngle + spacingAngle),
  y: center.y + radius * sin(previousAngle + spacingAngle)
)
let startingInnerPoint = CGPoint(
  x: center.x + innerRadius * cos(previousAngle + spacingAngle +
angle),
  y: center.y + innerRadius * sin(previousAngle + spacingAngle +
angle)
)
```

To calculate the x-coordinate of a point on a circle, you need to use the following formula:

`x = x0 + r * cos(t)`, where `x0` is the x-coordinate of the circle's center, and `t` is the angle at the origin.

The formula for the y-coordinate is similar:

`y = y0 + r * sin(t)`

The `startingPoint` is the point from which you'll draw the outer arc *counterclockwise*. Then, you'll draw a straight line toward the `startingInnerPoint`. From there, draw an arc *clockwise*, then connect it to the `startingPoint` with a straight line again.

To implement this sequence, create a new shape at the bottom of **SeatingChart.swift**, `ArcTribune`, containing all the needed parameters:

```
struct ArcTribune: Shape {
  var center: CGPoint
  var radius: CGFloat
  var innerRadius: CGFloat
  var startingPoint: CGPoint
  var startingInnerPoint: CGPoint
  var startAngle: CGFloat
  var endAngle: CGFloat

  func path(in rect: CGRect) -> Path {
  }
}
```

To implement the idea mentioned above, inside `path(in:)`, add:

```
Path { path in
  path.move(to: startingPoint)
```

```
    path.addArc(
      center: center,
      radius: radius,
      startAngle: .radians(startAngle),
      endAngle: .radians(endAngle),
      clockwise: false
    )
    path.addLine(to: startingInnerPoint)
    path.addArc(
      center: center,
      radius: innerRadius,
      startAngle: .radians(endAngle),
      endAngle: .radians(startAngle),
      clockwise: true
    )
    path.closeSubpath()
  }
```

Go back to the map in `computeArcTribunesPaths(at:corner:)` and replace the `return` statement with:

```
let tribune = Tribune(
  path: ArcTribune(
    center: center,
    radius: radius,
    innerRadius: innerRadius,
    startingPoint: startingPoint,
    startingInnerPoint: startingInnerPoint,
    startAngle: previousAngle + spacingAngle,
    endAngle: previousAngle + spacingAngle + angle
  )
  .path(in: CGRect.zero)
)

previousAngle += spacingAngle + angle

return tribune
```

With this code, you add a new arc tribune on each iteration and continue moving counterclockwise.Add a new method in `Sector` to calculate both types of tribunes for the sector:

```
private func computeTribunes(at rect: CGRect, with corner:
CGFloat) -> [Tribune] {
  computeRectTribunesPaths(at: rect, corner: corner) +
  computeArcTribunesPaths(at: rect, corner: corner)
}
```

Finally, replace the closure of the Task in path(in:) of Sector with:

```
tribunes[index] = computeTribunes(at: rect, with: corner)
```

The most complicated part is over! You only need to add some bells and whistles to make the seating chart view shine. But for now, run the app!

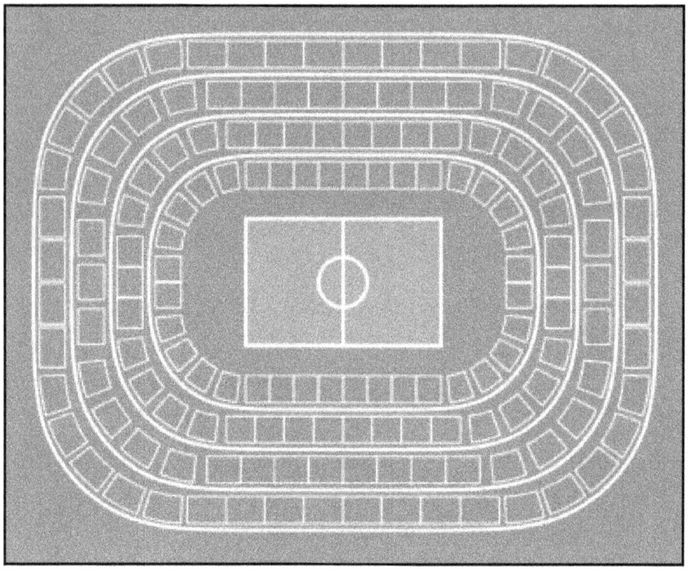

Animating Path Trimming

The Shape struct offers a method called trim(from:to:), which lets you define a range of the path SwiftUI will draw, cutting the other parts out. You can create a beautiful animated effect by animating the values passed to the method.

Create a new property inside SeatingChartView:

```
@State private var percentage: CGFloat = 0.0
```

Then, add .onChange on the ZStack element:

```
.onChange(of: tribunes) {
  guard $0.keys.count == Constants.stadiumSectorsCount else
{ return } // 1
  withAnimation(.easeInOut(duration: 1.0)) {
    percentage = 1.0 // 2
  }
}
```

Here's a breakdown:

1. You check whether the data is complete every time the `tribunes` count changes, for example, when you append a sector's tribunes.
2. If all the tribunes are ready, you trigger an animation.

Finally, you'll apply `.trim(from:to:)` to each shape you want to animate. In `SeatingChartView`'s `body`, add the following line to both `Field` shapes, `Stadium` and tribune inside the loop *before applying a stroke or a fill*:

```
.trim(from: 0.0, to: percentage)
```

Every time the view appears on the screen, SwiftUI will animate the chart.

To give it a final touch, add background to the tribune inside the loop, below the `.stroke` modifier:

```
.background(
  tribune.path
    .trim(from: 0.0, to: percentage)
    .fill(.blue)
)
```

Time to check out the result, run the app and see for yourself! ;]

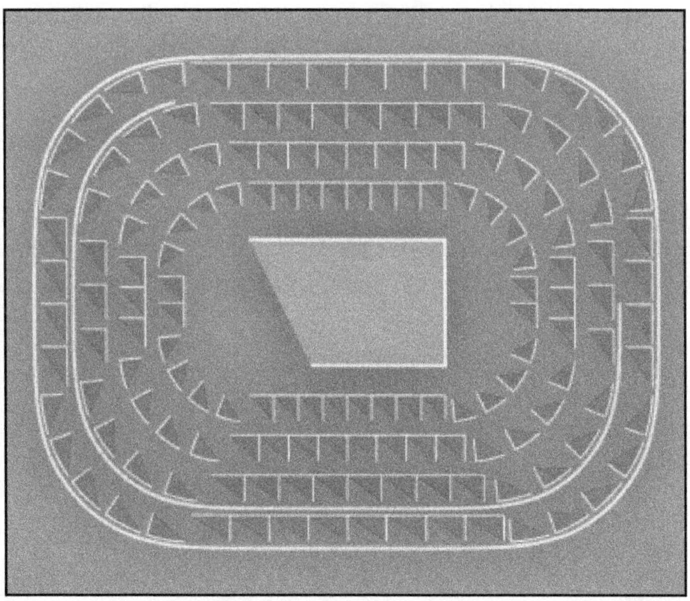

Basic Interaction With Path Objects

In the next chapter, you'll draw seats for each tribune and implement more complex gesture handling to ease the user's navigation. To prepare, you first must make it possible for a user to select a tribune.

Add a few new properties to `SeatingChartView`:

```
@State private var selectedTribune: Tribune? = nil
@State private var zoom = 1.25
@State private var zoomAnchor = UnitPoint.center
```

Once the user selects a tribune, you'll zoom the chart with the chosen tribune as an anchor.

To do this, add a `scaleEffect(:anchor:)` modifier to the `ZStack`. Additionally, rotate the seating chart to make it bigger and easier to interact with:

```
.rotationEffect(.radians(.pi / 2))
.coordinateSpace(name: "stadium")
.scaleEffect(zoom, anchor: zoomAnchor)
```

Since every view defines its own coordinate system, the touch gestures have coordinates in the context of the view where the gesture occurred. In the current case, you want to receive touch events from each specific tribune but apply the zoom anchor toward a bigger container. You need to operate in the same coordinate space to make it possible.

The anchor of a scale effect is defined by its `UnitPoint`. Its x and y values lay in the range of [0...1]. For example, the `.center` `UnitPoint` is `(x: 0.5, y: 0.5)`. This way, to translate normal coordinates into a `UnitPoint`, you need to divide them by the width and height of the coordinate space's owner, `ZStack`. To obtain its size, you need to wrap the `ZStack` in a `GeometryReader` and fetch the value from its proxy:

```
var body: some View {
  GeometryReader { proxy in
      ZStack { ... }
  }
}
```

Now, go to the `ForEach` in `SeatingChartView` iterating the tribunes and add an `.onTapGesture` modifier below `.background`:

```
.onTapGesture(coordinateSpace: .named("stadium")) { tap in // 1
  let unselected = selectedTribune == tribune // 2
  withAnimation(.easeInOut(duration: 1)) {
    selectedTribune = unselected ? nil : tribune // 3
    zoomAnchor = unselected
      ? .center
      : UnitPoint(
          x: tap.x / proxy.size.width,
          y: tap.y / proxy.size.height
        ) // 4
    zoom = unselected ? 1.25 : 12.0 // 5
  }
}
```

Here's a step-by-step explanation of the code:

1. First, you define the coordinate space in the context in which you want to receive a touch event's coordinates. You use the same name you used for the `ZStack`.
2. If `selectedTribune` equals the current tribune, a user unselected the tribune.
3. Inside `withAnimation`, you assign the tribune to `selectedTribune`.
4. You create an instance of `UnitPoint`, pass the translated values to its initializer and assign it to `zoomAnchor` if the user selects a tribune.
5. Finally, if the user selects a tribune, you increase the scale effect. Otherwise, you decrease to the normal value and shift the zoom anchor toward the center of `ZStack`.

Last but not least, to indicate that a tribune is selected, update its background fill. Replace `.fill(.blue)` with:

```
.fill(selectedTribune == tribune ? .white : .blue)
```

Run the app:

Linking Animations

Right now, the selected tribune goes out of sight for a moment when zooming in, which can feel somewhat confusing for a user. It would make sense to shift the anchor and zoom the selected tribune so that a user doesn't feel lost while the animation is ongoing. When the tribune is deselected, the opposite would work better - zoom out, then shift the anchor.

There are a few ways to chain the animations in SwiftUI, but no direct method. To implement this API yourself, create a new **Swift** file named `LinkedAnimation` and add:

```
import SwiftUI

struct LinkedAnimation { // 1
  let type: Animation
  let duration: Double
  let action: () -> Void

  static func easeInOut(for duration: Double,
                        action: @escaping () -> Void) ->
LinkedAnimation {
    return LinkedAnimation(type: .easeInOut(duration: duration),
                           duration: duration,
                           action: action) // 2
  }
}
```

Here's a breakdown:

1. First, you create a struct representing an `Animation`, which would be linkable to another animation. It has a type, such as `easeIn` or `linear`, duration and closure to execute.

2. You create a helper function to quickly initialize the most commonly used `easeInOut` type of linkable animation.

Now, add the `link` method to `LinkedAnimation`:

```
func link(to animation: LinkedAnimation, reverse: Bool) {
  withAnimation(reverse ? animation.type : type) {
    reverse ? animation.action() : action() // 1
  }

  withAnimation(reverse ? type.delay(animation.duration) :
                          animation.type.delay(duration)) { // 2
    reverse ? action() : animation.action()
  }
}
```

Here you create an easy-to-use method that lets you link two animations in regular or reverse order:

1. In case of the reverse order, you start with the second animation, pass it to the `withAnimation` and execute its action inside the closure.
2. Right after, you execute the next animation but delay it for the duration of the previous one.

Back in `SeatingChartView`, replace the code inside `.onTapGesture`:

```
let unselected = tribune == selectedTribune
let anchor = UnitPoint(
  x: tap.x / proxy.size.width,
  y: tap.y / proxy.size.height
)

LinkedAnimation
  .easeInOut(for: 0.7) { zoom = unselected ? 1.25 : 12 }
  .link(
    to: .easeInOut(for: 0.3) {
      selectedTribune = unselected ? nil : tribune
      zoomAnchor = unselected ? .center : anchor
    },
    reverse: !unselected
  )
```

With this code, you alternate the order of the zooming and anchor animations depending on whether a user selected a tribune.

Run your app one more time, select and deselect some seats, and give yourself a hard-earned pat on the back for some incredible work. Well done!

Key Points

1. To create a custom `Shape`, you need to create a struct conforming to the protocol and implement `path(in:)`, which expects you to return the shape's path.
2. Apple uses a flipped coordinate system, which results in a flipped unit circle: angle value increases downward from the positive x-axis direction.
3. Use `trim(from:to:)` to animate the stroke or fill of a `Shape` instance.
4. `UnitPoint` represents an anchor in SwiftUI, its x- and y-values are in the range of 0.0 and 1.0. To convert those values to their normal, you must divide them by a view's width and height, respectively.
5. To ease the use of the coordinates across different views, you can define a common coordinate space for them, using `.coordinateSpace(name:)` together with `.onTapGesture(count:coordinateSpace:perform)`.

Chapter 5: Applying Complex Transformations & Interactions

By Irina Galata

In the previous chapter, you learned how to draw a custom seating chart with tribunes using SwiftUI's `Path`. However, quite a few things are still missing. Users must be able to preview the seats inside a tribune and select them to purchase tickets. To make the user's navigation through the chart effortless and natural, you'll implement gesture handling, such as dragging, magnifying and rotating.

As usual, fetch the starter project for this chapter from the materials, or continue where you left off in the previous chapter.

Open **SportFan.xcodeproj** and head straight to `SeatingChartView`.

Manipulating SwiftUI Shapes Using CGAffineTransform

You need two things to display seats for each tribune: a `Shape` containing the `Path` drawing the seat and a `CGRect` representing its bounds. To accomplish the former, create a new `struct` named `SeatShape`:

```
struct SeatShape: Shape {
  func path(in rect: CGRect) -> Path {
    Path { path in

    }
  }
}
```

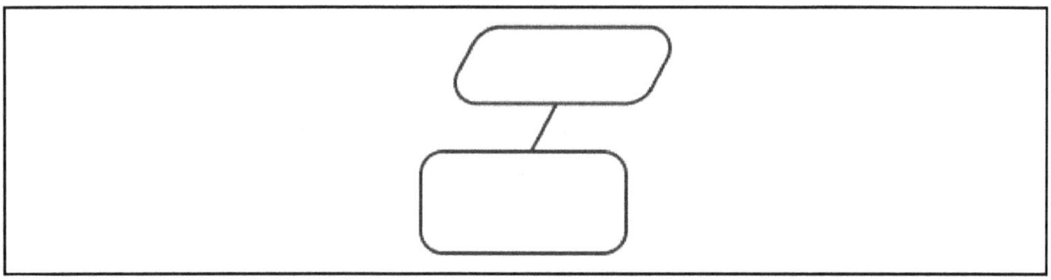

The shape you're about to draw consists of a few parts: the seat's back, squab, and rod connecting them. Start by defining a few essential properties right below inside the `Path`'s trailing closure:

```
let verticalSpacing = rect.height * 0.1
let cornerSize = CGSize(
  width: rect.width / 15.0,
  height: rect.height / 15.0
)
let seatBackHeight = rect.height / 3.0 - verticalSpacing
let squabHeight = rect.height / 2.0 - verticalSpacing
let seatWidth = rect.width
```

To emulate the top-to-bottom perspective, you calculate the seat back rectangle as slightly shorter vertically than the squab.

Then, right below these variables, define the `CGRect`'s for the back and squab and draw the corresponding rounded rectangles:

```
let backRect = CGRect(
  x: 0, y: verticalSpacing,
  width: seatWidth, height: seatBackHeight
```

```
)
let squabRect = CGRect(
  x: 0, y: rect.height / 2.0,
  width: seatWidth, height: squabHeight
)

path.addRoundedRect(in: backRect, cornerSize: cornerSize)
path.addRoundedRect(in: squabRect, cornerSize: cornerSize)
```

Now, draw the rod:

```
path.move(to: CGPoint(
  x: rect.width / 2.0,
  y: rect.height / 3.0
))
path.addLine(to: CGPoint(
  x: rect.width / 2.0,
  y: rect.height / 2.0
))
```

You still have a long way to go before looking at the seat's shape as part of a tribune. To get a quick preview for the time being, create a new `struct` called `SeatPreview`:

```
struct SeatPreview: View {
  let seatSize = 100.0
  var body: some View {
    ZStack {
      SeatShape().path(in: CGRect(
        x: 0, y: 0,
        width: seatSize, height: seatSize
      ))
      .fill(.blue) // 1

      SeatShape().path(
        in: CGRect(
          x: 0, y: 0,
          width: seatSize, height: seatSize
        ))
        .stroke(lineWidth: 2) // 2
    }
    .frame(width: seatSize, height: seatSize)
  }
}
```

This process is similar to the shapes you've drawn in the previous chapter:

1. Inside a `ZStack`, you use one instance of `SeatShape` as a background with `.blue` fill.

2. You use the second shape's instance to draw the seat's stroke.

Finally, you must make Xcode show the `SeatPreview` in the previews window. Create a new `PreviewProvider`:

```
struct Seat_Previews: PreviewProvider {
  static var previews: some View {
    SeatPreview()
  }
}
```

Your seat preview should look like this, for the time being:

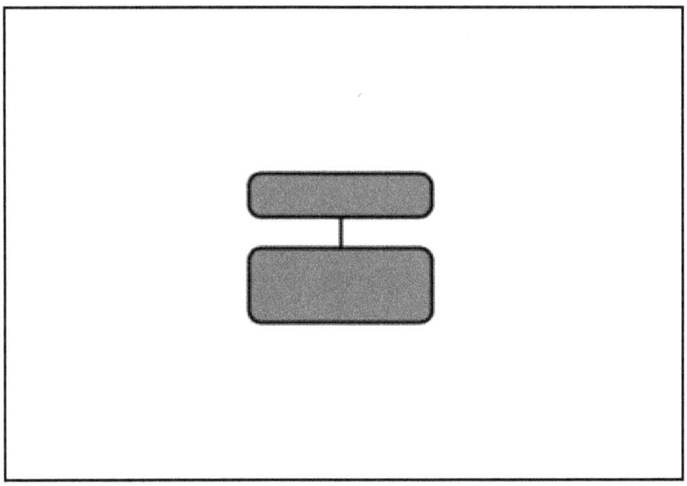

The seat is there but looks relatively flat. You'll skew it back to give it a slightly more realistic perspective. Don't forget that you drew the tribunes all around the stadium field, which means the seats should always face the center of the field. Head to the next section to learn how to transform shapes!

Matrices Transformations

Check `Path`'s API, and you'll notice there are many methods, such as `addRoundedRect` or `addEllipse`, accepting an argument of type `CGAffineTransform` called `transform`. Via just one argument, you can manipulate a subpath in 2D space in several ways: rotate, skew, scale or translate.

As you might have guessed from its prefix, `CGAffineTransform` is part of Apple's **Core Graphics** framework, which still comes in handy in SwiftUI.

`CGAffineTransform` is essentially a 3x3 matrix:

$$\begin{bmatrix} a & b & 0 \\ c & d & 0 \\ t_x & t_y & 1 \end{bmatrix}$$

You'll work with the parameters `a`, `b`, `c`, `d`, `tx` and `ty`. The third column stays unchanged regardless of the transformations you apply - `0`, `0` and `1`.

An **identity** matrix is one that SwiftUI applies to a subpath by default. It performs no transformations when multiplying to another matrix:

$$\begin{bmatrix} 1 & 0 & 0 \\ 0 & 1 & 0 \\ 0 & 0 & 1 \end{bmatrix}$$

When you want to apply an offset to an object, you need a **translation** matrix, where `tx` represents the shift along the x-axis, and `ty` moves the object along the y-axis:

$$\begin{bmatrix} 1 & 0 & 0 \\ 0 & 1 & 0 \\ t_x & t_y & 1 \end{bmatrix}$$

A **scaling** operation is similar as well, having only two defining parameters, `sx` and `sy`:

$$\begin{bmatrix} S_x & 0 & 0 \\ 0 & S_y & 0 \\ 0 & 0 & 1 \end{bmatrix}$$

You do, however, need to use `a`, `b`, `c` and `d` to make a **rotation** matrix to rotate an object counterclockwise by angle `a`:

$$\begin{bmatrix} \cos a & \sin a & 0 \\ -\sin a & \cos a & 0 \\ 0 & 0 & 1 \end{bmatrix}$$

Finally, **skewing** an object requires applying the `b` or `c` parameters of a transformation matrix, where `b` skews the subpath along the y-axis, and `c` affects the x-axis:

$$\begin{bmatrix} 1 & S_y & 0 \\ S_x & 1 & 0 \\ 0 & 0 & 1 \end{bmatrix}$$

Now, knowing all the transformation possibilities matrices offer you, you can sketch out your action plan:

1. First, skew the seat back along the x-axis.
2. Then rotate the entire seat's shape by an angle it accepts from the outside to face the stadium field.
3. Finally, translate the seat's shape to negate the translation effect from previously rotating it since SwiftUI rotates a subpath around its `(minX, minY)` point. The shape will appear to rotate around its center point without shifting sideways.

Applying the Skewing Operation

Back in `SeatShape`'s `Path`, find the `seatWidth` you previously added, and add the following line above it:

```
let skewAngle = .pi / 4.0
```

Next, you need to calculate how much further along the x-axis the seat back goes after being skewed. You'll account for this measurement when defining `seatWidth`, thus making the whole shape fit into `rect`. Add the following variable right below `skewAngle`:

```
let skewShift = seatBackHeight / tan(skewAngle)
```

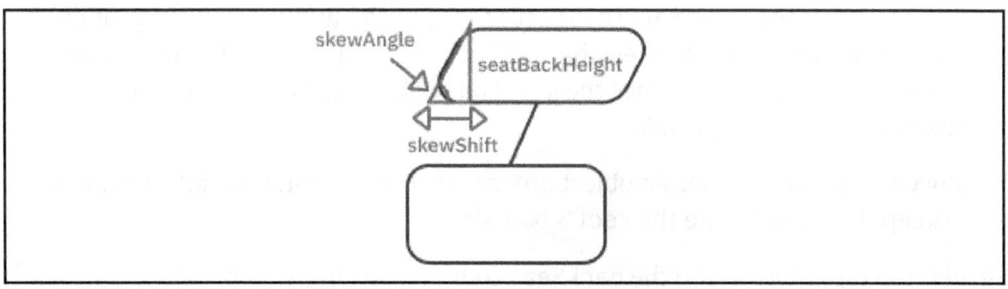

To calculate the value of `skewShift`, you use a mathematical formula to find the adjacent in the right triangle by the angle's tangent.

Now, update seatWidth:

```
let seatWidth = rect.width - skewShift
```

Next, update the rod's final point to connect it to the center of the squab. Replace:

```
path.addLine(to: CGPoint(
  x: rect.width / 2.0,
  y: rect.height / 2.0
))
```

With:

```
path.addLine(to: CGPoint(
  x: rect.width / 2.0 - skewShift / 2,
  y: rect.height / 2.0
))
```

Here comes the exciting part! Above the addRoundedRect invocations, create a matrix to skew the seat back:

```
let skew = CGAffineTransform(
  a: 1, b: 0, c: -cos(skewAngle), // 1
  d: 1, tx: skewShift + verticalSpacing, ty: 0
) // 2
```

Here are two crucial points:

1. You use CGAffineTransform(a:b:c:d:tx:ty:) to build a matrix on your own. You update the c value to skew the seat back along the x-axis. The minus in front of the cos of the angle defines the *direction* of skewing. You set it to skew the object towards the right side.

2. Since SwiftUI transforms an object around its origin point, you shift the x value to keep the shape inside the rect's bounds.

Finally, add the transform to the backSeat rounded rectangle. Replace:

```
path.addRoundedRect(in: backRect, cornerSize: cornerSize)
```

With:

```
path.addRoundedRect(
  in: backRect,
  cornerSize: cornerSize,
  transform: skew
)
```

Take a look at the Seat preview:

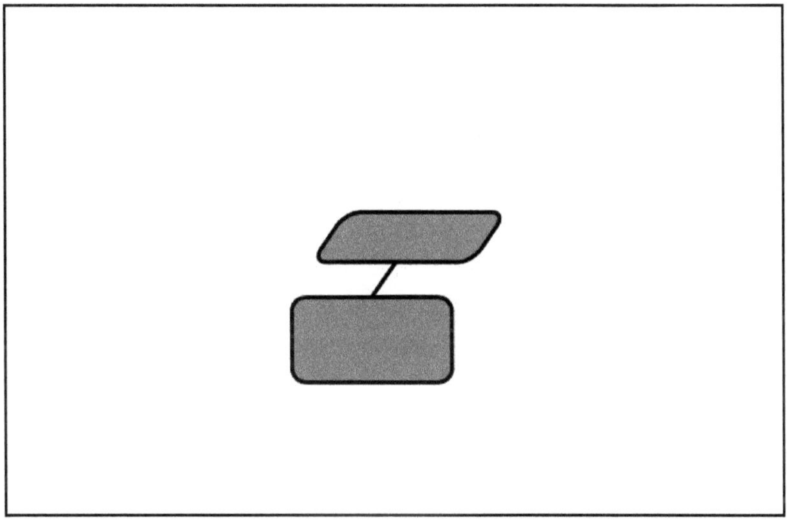

Rotating the Seat

To allow SeatShape to rotate, add a new property to the struct:

```
let rotation: CGFloat
```

To verify the rotation functionality in the preview, add a rotation property to SeatPreview:

```
@State var rotation: Float = 0.0
```

Pass the rotation value to the initializers of both shapes:

```
SeatShape(rotation: CGFloat(-rotation))
```

Then, wrap the root view in the preview's body into a VStack. Then add a Slider and a Text:

```
VStack {

  // ZStack with SeatShape's

  Slider(value: $rotation, in: 0.0...(2 * .pi), step: .pi / 20)
  Text("\(rotation)")
}.padding()
```

Now, return to SeatShape and apply a rotation matrix to the path by mutating the existing final path:

```
path = path.applying(CGAffineTransform(rotationAngle: rotation))
```

Well, that was easy, wasn't it? Check out the preview and play around with the rotation slider:

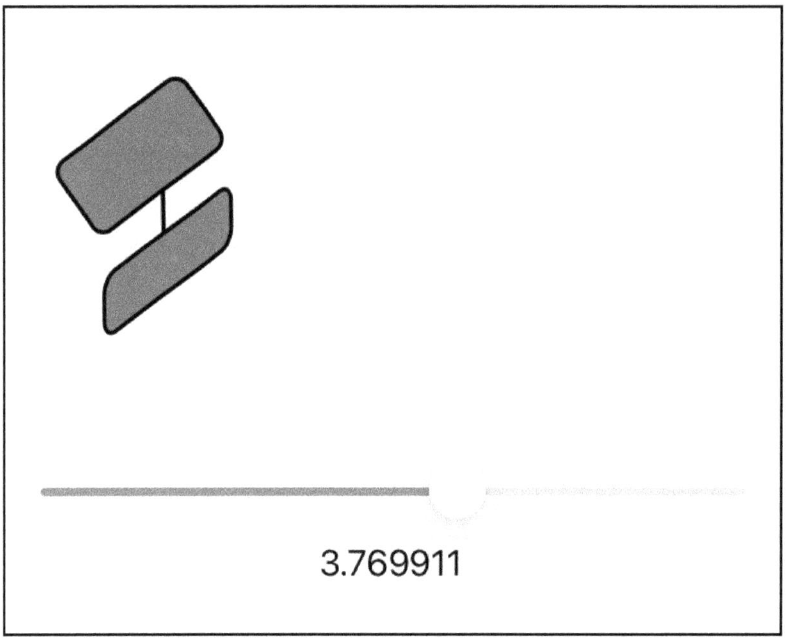

Oh, it shouldn't fly around, though! :]

Rotating an Object Around an Arbitrary Point

Applying a rotation matrix rotates an object around its origin (minX, minY). To perform the transformation around an arbitrary point like its center, you first need to shift the object to that point, perform the rotation and then translate the object back.

First, define the rotation point by adding the following variable at the very bottom of `Path { }` before applying the rotation transformation:

```
let rotationCenter = CGPoint(x: rect.width / 2, y: rect.height /
2)
```

Now, create the first translation matrix to shift the seat to the rotation point:

```
let translationToCenter = CGAffineTransform(
  translationX: rotationCenter.x,
  y: rotationCenter.y
)
```

Additionally, you need a translation matrix to move the seat inside the `rect`'s bounds:

```
let initialTranslation = CGAffineTransform(
  translationX: rect.minX,
  y: rect.minY
)
```

Now, apply the transformations step-by-step. Create a variable to keep the result of the first multiplication:

```
var result = CGAffineTransformRotate(translationToCenter,
rotation)
```

Instead of directly multiplying the `translationToCenter` and the rotation matrix, you use `CGAffineTransformRotate` to apply a transformation on the `translationToCenter` matrix and get the result.

To translate the seat back, use `CGAffineTransformTranslate` as follows:

```
result = CGAffineTransformTranslate(result, -rotationCenter.x,
-rotationCenter.y)
```

Finally, apply the result of multiplying `initialTranslation` and `result` to the path, and assign it to the path by replacing the last line:

```
path = path.applying(result.concatenating(initialTranslation))
```

Pay attention to the order of the matrices concatenation. In terms of matrices, `a * b != b * a`!

Check out the preview and move the slider's knob around a bit to make sure the seat rotates around its center:

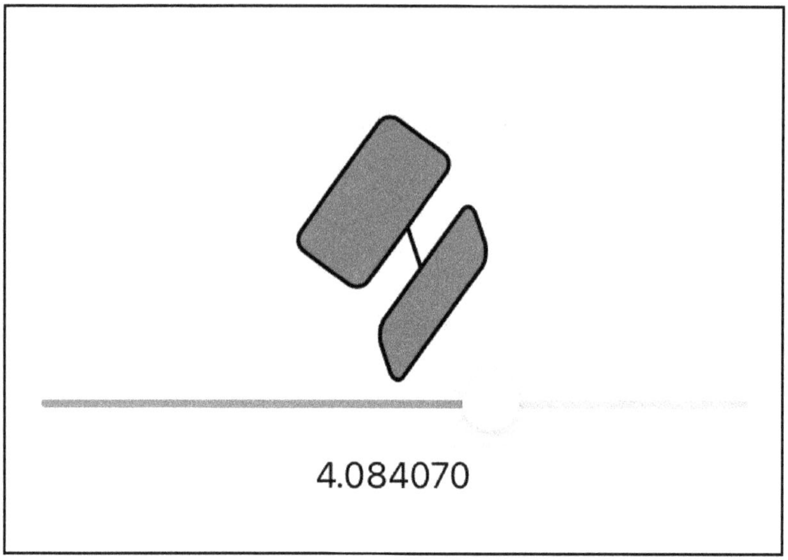

That was a bit of a challenge. Great job! Next, to calculate the bounds for each seat in all the rectangular tribunes.

Locating Rectangular Tribunes' Seats

With your animation's performance in mind, you'll ensure the seat locations are computed only once, assigned to the respective tribune and drawn only when a user picks a specific tribune. Otherwise, it would be a waste to draw each one when they're barely visible due to the scale of the seating chart.

Create a new struct to hold a seat's path:

```
struct Seat: Hashable, Equatable {
  var path: Path

  public func hash(into hasher: inout Hasher) {
    hasher.combine(path.description)
  }
}
```

You conform `Seat` to `Hashable` to iterate over a tribune's seats to display them. Later, you'll enable users to pick a specific seat, so being `Equatable` will also come in handy.

Go to the `Sector` shape and create a new method:

```
private func computeSeats(for tribune: CGRect, at rotation:
CGFloat) -> [Seat] {
  var seats: [Seat] = []

  // TODO

  return seats
}
```

This method will eventually calculate the bounds for the seats based on the `CGRect` of the tribune and the rotation.

Start by defining all the necessary values, such as size, the number of horizontal and vertical seats and spacings. Add these lines in the `// TODO` above:

```
let seatSize = tribuneSize.height * 0.1
let columnsNumber = Int(tribune.width / seatSize)
let rowsNumber = Int(tribune.height / seatSize)
let spacingH = CGFloat(tribune.width - seatSize *
CGFloat(columnsNumber)) / CGFloat(columnsNumber)
let spacingV = CGFloat(tribune.height - seatSize *
CGFloat(rowsNumber)) / CGFloat(rowsNumber)
```

Below the variables you've just added, create two loops to iterate over all the seats:

```
(0..<columnsNumber).forEach { column in
  (0..<rowsNumber).forEach { row in

  }
}
```

Inside the inner loop, calculate the origin points for each seat and build a `CGRect`:

```
let x = tribune.minX + spacingH / 2.0 + (spacingH + seatSize) *
CGFloat(column)
let y = tribune.minY + spacingV / 2.0 + (spacingV + seatSize) *
CGFloat(row)

let seatRect = CGRect(
  x: x, y: y,
  width: seatSize, height: seatSize
)
```

Finally, create a `SeatShape`, pass the rotation to it and append `Seat` to the array:

```
seats.append(Seat(
  path: SeatShape(rotation: rotation)
    .path(in: seatRect)
  )
)
```

Displaying the Seats

To access each tribune's seats when rendering the seating chart, add a new property to `Tribune`:

```
var seats: [Seat]
```

Now, find `makeRectTribuneAt(x:y:rotated:)` and update its declaration to include a `rotation` parameter.

```
private func makeRectTribuneAt(
  x: CGFloat, y: CGFloat,
  vertical: Bool, rotation: CGFloat
) -> Tribune {
```

Note that you also removed the default value for `vertical`, so you'll need to provide this in all invocations, or the compiler will throw an error. You'll handle that shortly.

Now, create a variable for the tribune's `CGRect` inside the method:

```
let rect = CGRect(
  x: x,
  y: y,
  width: vertical ? tribuneSize.height : tribuneSize.width,
  height: vertical ? tribuneSize.width : tribuneSize.height
)
```

Use `rect` to instantiate `Tribune` and calculate the seats by updating the `return` statement:

```
return Tribune(
  path: RectTribune().path(in: rect),
  seats: computeSeats(for: rect, at: rotation)
)
```

Now, the compiler will be unhappy about some missing arguments. To sort it out, pass an empty array as the last parameter to the arc tribune initializer.

At the bottom of `computeArcTribunesPaths(at:corner:)`:

```
tribunes.append(Tribune(path: ArcTribune(
  /* arc tribune's properties */
).path(in: CGRect.zero), seats: []))
```

Then, pass the correct rotations to the `makeRectTribuneAt` invocations in `computeRectTribunesPaths(at:corner:)`. You compute the top and bottom horizontal tribunes in the `(0..<tribunesNumberH).forEach` loop, so pass `0` and `-.pi` as `rotation` respectively:

```
tribunes.append(makeRectTribuneAt(
  x: x,
  y: rect.minY + offset,
  vertical: false,
  rotation: 0
))
tribunes.append(makeRectTribuneAt(
  x: x, y: rect.maxY - offset - tribuneSize.height,
  vertical: false,
  rotation: -.pi
))
```

For the vertical tribunes, pass `-.pi / 2.0` and `3.0 * -.pi / 2.0`:

```
tribunes.append(makeRectTribuneAt(
  x: rect.minX + offset,
  y: y,
  vertical: true,
  rotation: -.pi / 2.0
))
tribunes.append(makeRectTribuneAt(
  x: rect.maxX - offset - tribuneSize.height,
  y: y,
  vertical: true,
  rotation: 3.0 * -.pi / 2.0
))
```

Finally, you can display the selected tribune's seats! Go to `SeatingChartView`'s `body` and add the following code after the tribunes `ForEach`:

```
if let selectedTribune {
  ForEach(selectedTribune.seats, id: \.self) { seat in
    ZStack {
      seat.path.fill(.blue)
      seat.path.stroke(.black, lineWidth: 0.05)
    }
  }
}
```

Run the app and select any of the non-arced tribunes:

Next, you'll work on the arc tribune's seats!

Computing Positions of the Arc Tribune's Seats

Calculating the bounds of an arc tribune's seats is similar to building an arc tribune's `Path`. Since you move along an arc, not a straight line, you operate with angles. You used an angle value for a tribune and another for the spacing. In the same way, you'll calculate the angle needed for a seat and the spacing between neighboring seats.

To implement it, create a new method inside `Sector`:

```
private func computeSeats(for arcTribune: ArcTribune) -> [Seat]
{
  var seats: [Seat] = []
```

```
    // TODO

    return seats
}
```

An arc tribune has seat columns of the same size, but the rows shrink toward the stadium field. So, define the "static" variables right away in the method, instead of the `// TODO` mark:

```
let seatSize = tribuneSize.height * 0.1
let rowsNumber = Int(tribuneSize.height / seatSize)
let spacingV = CGFloat(tribuneSize.height - seatSize *
CGFloat(rowsNumber)) / CGFloat(rowsNumber)
```

Now, add the outer loop to iterate over the rows:

```
(0..<rowsNumber).forEach { row in

}
```

Inside the loop, add variables that will dynamically change depending on the row:

```
let radius = arcTribune.radius - CGFloat(row) * (spacingV +
seatSize) - spacingV - seatSize / 2.0 // 1
let arcLength = abs(arcTribune.endAngle - arcTribune.startAngle)
* radius // 2
let arcSeatsNum = Int(arcLength / (seatSize * 1.1)) // 3
```

Here's a code breakdown:

1. For each row, you calculate the radius of a circle. You'll place the row's seats along an arc of this circle, just as you did when drawing the arc tribunes' outlines.
2. You multiply the difference between the tribune's `endAngle` and `startAngle` by the radius to produce the length of the corresponding arc.
3. Based on the length of the arc, you calculate the number of seats in the row. You multiply `seatSize` by `1.1` to give a slight spacing between the seats.

Now, add some more variables:

```
let arcSpacing = (arcLength - seatSize * CGFloat(arcSeatsNum)) /
CGFloat(arcSeatsNum) // 1
let seatAngle = seatSize / radius // 2
let spacingAngle = arcSpacing / radius // 3
var previousAngle = arcTribune.startAngle + spacingAngle +
seatAngle / 2.0 // 4
```

Here's a code breakdown:

1. To calculate the spacing, you deduct the sum of all seat sizes from the arc length and divide the result by the number of seats.
2. Dividing `seatSize` by `radius` gives you the angle needed for each seat. Although `seatSize` is the measurement of a seat along a straight line, you need an arc measurement for the formula. The difference between them is negligible in this case.
3. Applying the same formula, you calculate the angle needed for the spacing between the seats.
4. `previousAngle` contains the latest offset along the arc, and you'll update it after each seat's calculations.

Create an inner loop below the variables:

```
(0..<arcSeatsNum).forEach { _ in

}
```

Inside the inner loop, calculate the "center" of each seat based on `previousAngle`:

```
let seatCenter = CGPoint(
  x: arcTribune.center.x + radius * cos(previousAngle),
  y: arcTribune.center.y + radius * sin(previousAngle)
)
```

With the approach above, you'll iteratively move along the arc, centering the seats precisely on the arc.

Knowing the seat's center, you can calculate its origin and bounds:

```
let seatRect = CGRect(
  x: seatCenter.x - seatSize / 2,
  y: seatCenter.y - seatSize / 2,
  width: seatSize,
  height: seatSize
)
```

Create a `Seat` and append it to the array:

```
seats.append(
  Seat(
    path: SeatShape(rotation: previousAngle + .pi / 2)
      .path(in: seatRect)
  )
)
```

Since the seats' angles are perpendicular to the angle of the tribune, meaning you drew tribunes from left to right, but you draw the seats from the tribune's top to bottom, you need to add `.pi / 2` to `previousAngle`.

Right below, update `previousAngle`:

```
previousAngle += spacingAngle + seatAngle
```

Finally, back in `computeArcTribunesPaths(at:corner:)`, find the code where you insantiate the `Tribune` (i.e. `let tribune = ...`) and update it with your new `computeSeats(for:)` method, like so:

```
let arcTribune = ArcTribune(
  center: center,
  radius: radius,
  innerRadius: innerRadius,
  startingPoint: startingPoint,
  startingInnerPoint: startingInnerPoint,
  startAngle: previousAngle + spacingAngle,
  endAngle: previousAngle + spacingAngle + angle
)

let tribune = Tribune(
  path: arcTribune.path(in: CGRect.zero),
  seats: computeSeats(for: arcTribune)
)
```

Run the app and try to pick a tribune:

Nice! It's now time to let the user actually interact with the seats.

Processing User Gestures

Navigating through the seating chart is somewhat cumbersome and extremely limited right now. Users should be as free with gestures as possible to speed up a tribune and seat selection.

SwiftUI offers a variety of gesture handlers, most of which are valuable for the seating chart.

Dragging

To obtain the offset value from the user's drag gesture, you'll use SwiftUI's `DragGesture`. First, add these new properties to `SeatingChartView`:

```
@GestureState private var drag: CGSize = .zero
@State private var offset: CGSize = .zero
```

`@GestureState` is a property wrapper that keeps `drag` up-to-date when the gesture that is ongoing and will reset it to its initial state once the user is done. The `offset` property keeps the latest value between the gestures to avoid resetting it.

Since `CGSize` is the measurement for a drag gesture, add a handy extension to ease `CGSizes` concatenation:

```
extension CGSize {
  static func +(left: CGSize, right: CGSize) -> CGSize {
    return CGSize(width: left.width + right.width, height:
left.height + right.height)
  }
}
```

Add one more property to `SeatingChartView`:

```
var dragging: some Gesture {
  DragGesture()
    .updating($drag) { currentState, gestureState, transaction
in // 1
      gestureState = currentState.translation
    }
    .onEnded { // 2
      offset = offset + $0.translation
    }
}
```

Here's a code breakdown:

1. SwiftUI invokes the `.updating` callback repeatedly while the gesture is in progress. `currentState` contains the latest `translation` value, and changing `gestureState` updates the `drag` property.
2. Once the gesture is over, `.onEnded` is invoked. There you update the `offset` property to ensure the chart stays in place once the user lifts their finger.

Then, below `.rotationEffect` of `SeatingChartView`, add `.offset`:

```
.offset(offset + drag)
```

Finally, right below `.offset`, attach the drag gesture handler using `.simultaneousGesture`:

```
.simultaneousGesture(dragging)
```

SwiftUI can handle multiple gestures at the same time. Use `.simultaneousGesture` to indicate that you'd like to enable more than one gesture giving them equal priority.

Currently, you have two gesture handlers: `dragging` and the tap gesture handler for the tribunes. You'll add a few more soon. Now, when you run the app, the chart is easily draggable:

Zooming

Like `DragGesture`, you can use `MagnificationGesture` to obtain the current gesture's scale.

Add a new property to `SeatingChartView`:

```
@GestureState private var manualZoom = 1.0
```

Then, create a gesture handler:

```
var magnification: some Gesture {
  MagnificationGesture()
    .updating($manualZoom) { currentState, gestureState,
transaction in
      gestureState = currentState
    }
    .onEnded {
      zoom *= $0
    }
}
```

Now, update `.scaleEffect` and move it above `.rotationEffect`:

```
.scaleEffect(manualZoom * zoom, anchor: zoomAnchor)
```

Finally, attach the gesture handler below `dragging`:

```
.simultaneousGesture(magnification)
```

Run the app and try to zoom the chart.

If you run it on a simulator, hold the **Option (⌥)** key and drag the chart with your mouse to emulate a magnification gesture.

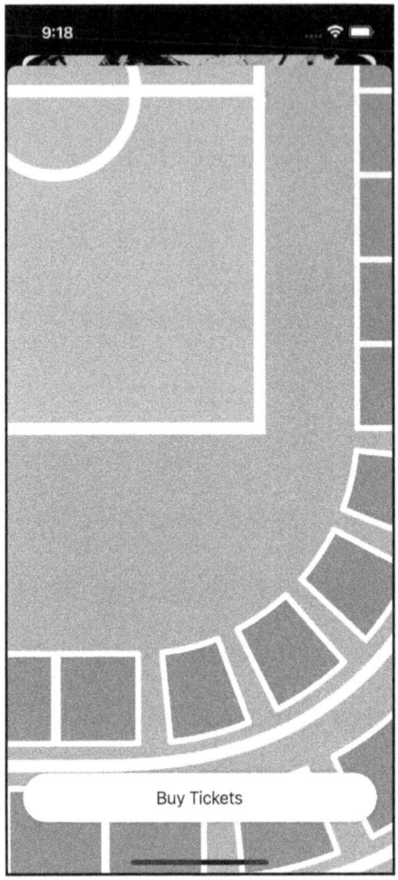

Rotating

The 2D rotating gesture is as easily implemented in SwiftUI as the others. You know what to do! Add another `@GestureState` property, and add a `rotation` property keep track of the applied rotation:

```
@GestureState private var currentRotation: Angle = .radians(0.0)
@State var rotation = Angle(radians: .pi / 2)
```

Don't forget about the corresponding gesture handler:

```
var rotationGesture: some Gesture {
  RotationGesture()
```

```
    .updating($currentRotation) { currentState, gestureState,
transaction in
      gestureState = .radians(currentState.radians)
    }
    .onEnded {
      rotation += $0
    }
}
```

Update `.rotationEffect` of `SeatingChartView`:

```
.rotationEffect(rotation + currentRotation, anchor: zoomAnchor)
```

Last but not least, add the gesture handler below the two previous ones:

```
.simultaneousGesture(rotationGesture)
```

That was a piece of cake, right? :] Next, you'll implement seat selection and add some bells and whistles.

Handling Seat Selection

To keep track of the selected seats, add a new property to SeatingChartView:

```
@State private var selectedSeats: [Seat] = []
```

A tap gesture to pick a tribune and one to pick a seat should be mutually exclusive: they can't co-occur. Therefore, it makes sense to handle both in one gesture handler and decide which one should occur depending on the coordinates of the touch.

Remove .onTapGesture from the tribune, and add a new .onTapGesture to the ZStack above .scaleEffect:

```
.onTapGesture { tap in
  if let selectedTribune, selectedTribune.path.contains(tap) {
    // TODO pick a seat
  } else {
    // TODO pick a tribune
  }
}
```

Now, if a user has already selected a tribune and the touch occurred inside its bounds, it's safe to assume the user tapped a seat. Otherwise, they've chosen a tribune.

To handle seat selection, create a new method in SeatingChartView:

```
private func findAndSelectSeat(at point: CGPoint, in
selectedTribune: Tribune) {
  guard let seat = selectedTribune.seats
    .first(where: { $0.path.boundingRect.contains(point) }) else
{
    return
  } // 1

  withAnimation(.easeInOut) {
    if let index = selectedSeats.firstIndex(of: seat) { // 2
      selectedSeats.remove(at: index)
    } else {
      selectedSeats.append(seat)
    }
  }
}
```

Here's a breakdown:

1. First, you search for a seat containing the coordinates of the touch among the selected tribune's seats. If there is none, you return immediately.
2. Finally, you select or deselect the seat depending on whether the seat is present in `selectedSeats`.

Now, add another method to handle a tribune selection:

```
private func findAndSelectTribune(at point: CGPoint, with proxy:
GeometryProxy) {
  let tribune = tribunes.flatMap(\.value)
    .first(where: { $0.path.boundingRect.contains(point) })
  let unselected = tribune == selectedTribune
  let anchor = UnitPoint(
    x: point.x / proxy.size.width,
    y: point.y / proxy.size.height
  )

  LinkedAnimation.easeInOut(for: 0.7) {
    zoom = unselected ? 1.25 : 25
  }
  .link(
    to: .easeInOut(for: 0.3) {
      selectedTribune = unselected ? nil : tribune
      zoomAnchor = unselected ? .center : anchor
      offset = .zero
    },
    reverse: !unselected
  )
}
```

Like the seat selection, you first search for the tribune containing the needed coordinates. After that, you proceed the way you have since the previous chapter, except the `offset` is reset to `.zero` when zooming in or out.

Update `.onTapGesture` to invoke the newly created methods:

```
if let selectedTribune, selectedTribune.path.contains(tap) {
  findAndSelectSeat(at: tap, in: selectedTribune)
} else {
  findAndSelectTribune(at: tap, with: proxy)
}
```

Now update a seat's `.fill` depending on whether the user has selected it. Replace:

```
seat.path.fill(.blue)
```

With:

```
seat.path.fill(selectedSeats.contains(seat) ? .green : .blue)
```

As the last step, remove `.coordinateSpace` from the `ZStack`. Now all touch events occur in the same view, so there's no need to convert the coordinate space.

Check the preview or run the app:

You're *so close* to the finish line with only a few things left to polish.

Final Animating Touches

Since a seat is essentially a `Path`, just like a tribune, it's pretty easy to animate it by trimming it. Add a new property of type `CGFloat` to `SeatingChartView`:

```
@State private var seatsPercentage: CGFloat = .zero
```

Find `seat.path` and trim the seat's stroke and fill:

```
seat.path
  .trim(from: 0, to: seatsPercentage)
  .fill(selectedSeats.contains(seat) ? .green : .blue)
```

```
seat.path
  .trim(from: 0, to: seatsPercentage)
  .stroke(.black, lineWidth: 0.05)
```

Go back to `findAndSelectTribune` and add the following line below `anchor`:

```
seatsPercentage = selectedTribune == nil || !unselected ? 0.0 :
1.0
```

Now, the animation will reset every time you select a new tribune.

Additionally, update `seatsPercentage` in the first of the two linked animations, right below `zoom`:

```
seatsPercentage = unselected ? 0.0 : 1.0
```

Check it out:

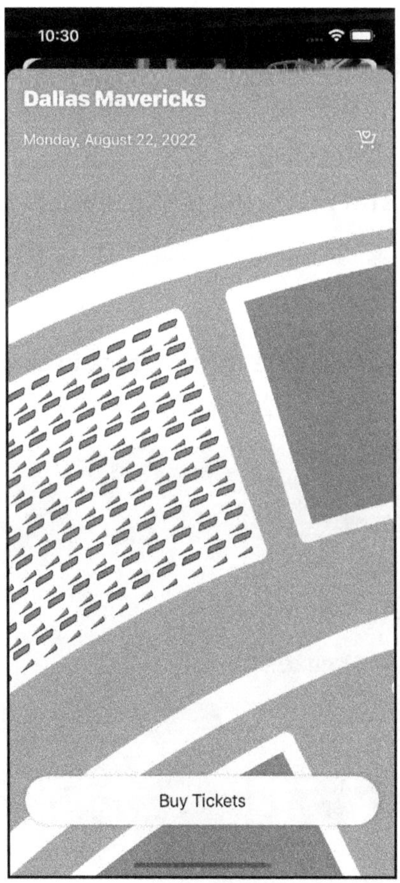

To make SeatsSelectionView aware of the changes happening in SeatingChartView, add the following @Binding properties to SeatingChartView:

```
@Binding var zoomed: Bool
@Binding var selectedTicketsNumber: Int
```

Increment or decrement selectedTicketsNumber in findAndSelectSeat(at:in:) inside withAnimation accordingly:

```
if let index = selectedSeats.firstIndex(of: seat) {
  selectedTicketsNumber -= 1
  selectedSeats.remove(at: index)
} else {
  selectedTicketsNumber += 1
  selectedSeats.append(seat)
}
```

Then, update zoomed in MagnificationGesture's .onEnded callback. Add this code below zoom *= $0:

```
withAnimation {
  zoomed = zoom > 1.25
}
```

In findAndSelectTribune(at:with:) in the first linked animation, add:

```
zoomed = !unselected
```

Then, to zoom out and reset the chart, if zoomed gets updated from SeatsSelectionView, add .onChange to the ZStack in SeatingChartView:

```
.onChange(of: zoomed) {
  if !$0 && zoom > 1.25 {
    LinkedAnimation.easeInOut(for: 0.7) {
      zoom = 1.25
      seatsPercentage = 0.0
    }
    .link(
      to: .easeInOut(for: 0.3) {
        selectedTribune = nil
        zoomAnchor = .center
        offset = .zero
      },
      reverse: false
    )
  }
}
```

Update the preview of `SeatingChartView` to include the new initializer arguments:

```
SeatingChartView(
  zoomed: Binding.constant(false),
  selectedTicketsNumber: Binding.constant(5)
)
```

Finally, return to `SeatSelectionView`, and add these `@State` properties:

```
@State private var stadiumZoomed = false
@State private var selectedTicketsNumber: Int = 0
@State private var ticketsPurchased: Bool = false
```

Update `SeatingChartView`'s initializer:

```
SeatingChartView(
  zoomed: $stadiumZoomed,
  selectedTicketsNumber: $selectedTicketsNumber
)
```

Now, wrap the inner `VStack` containing the team name and the cart icon into the `if-statement`, and add a `.transition`:

```
if !stadiumZoomed {
  VStack { ... }
    .transition(.move(edge: .top))
}
```

Now when a user zooms on the chart, the title and icon go out of sight to make the screen less cluttered.

To indicate the number of selected tickets, wrap the cart icon in a `ZStack`, and add a label:

```
ZStack(alignment: .topLeading) {
  /* cart icon */
  if selectedTicketsNumber > 0 {
    Text("\(selectedTicketsNumber)")
      .foregroundColor(.white)
      .font(.caption)
      .background {
        Circle()
          .fill(.red)
          .frame(width: 16, height: 16)
      }
      .alignmentGuide(.leading) { _ in -20}
      .alignmentGuide(.top) { _ in 4 }
  }
}
```

Using the alignment guides, you adjust the label to appear on the top right corner of the icon.

To reset the gestures quickly, add a zoom-out button below the **Buy Tickets** button and wrap both into an `HStack`:

```
HStack {
  /* Buy Tickets button */

  if stadiumZoomed {
    Button {
      withAnimation {
        stadiumZoomed = false
      }
    } label: {
      Image("zoom_out")
        .resizable()
        .scaledToFit()
        .frame(width: 48, height: Constants.iconSizeL)
        .clipped()
        .background {
          RoundedRectangle(cornerRadius: 36)
            .fill(.white)
            .frame(width: 48, height: 48)
            .shadow(radius: 2)
          }
          .padding(.trailing)
    }
  }
}
```

Update the action of the **Buy Tickets** button:

```
if selectedTicketsNumber > 0 {
  ticketsPurchased = true
}
```

Finally, you need to show a pop-up to tell the user that the purchase was successful. Add `.confirmationDialog` to the root view, right below `background(Constants.orange, ignoresSafeAreaEdges: .all)`:

```
.confirmationDialog(
  "You've bought \(selectedTicketsNumber) tickets.",
  isPresented: $ticketsPurchased,
  actions: { Button("Ok") {} },
  message: { Text("You've bought \(selectedTicketsNumber)
tickets. Enjoy your time at the game!")}
)
```

Ta-da! You've done it! Run the app to see the final result:

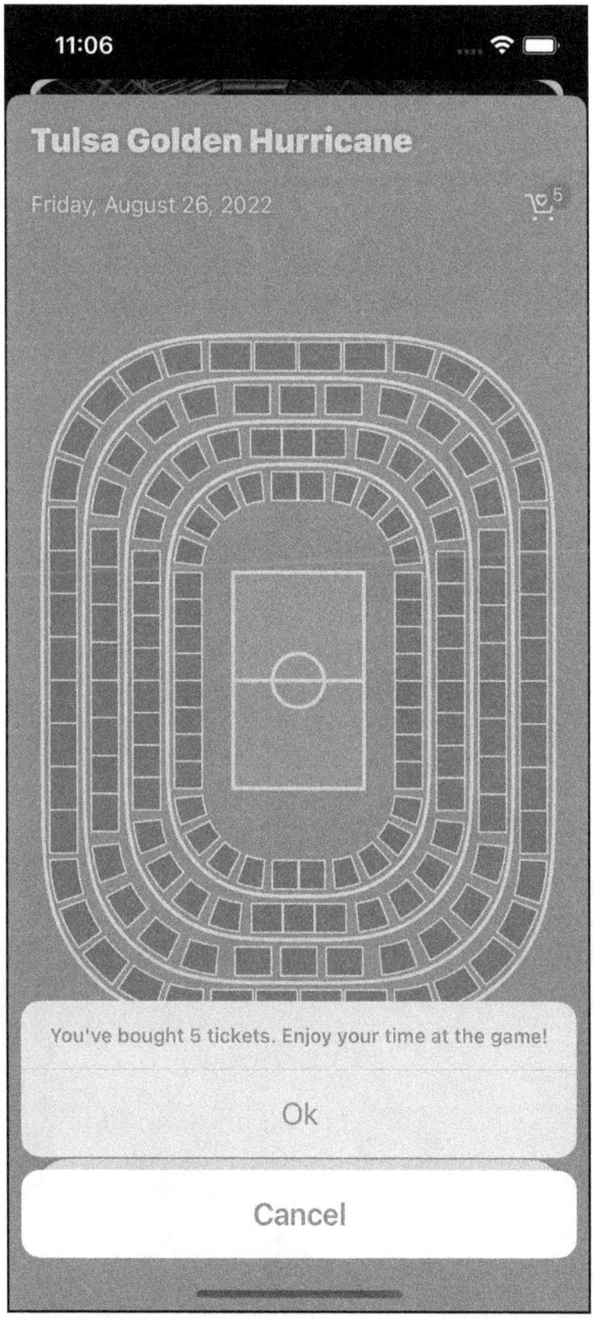

Key Points

1. `CGAffineTransform` represents a transformation matrix, which you can apply to a subpath to perform rotation, scaling, translating or skewing.
2. A transformation matrix in 2D graphics is of size 3x3, where the first two columns are responsible for all the applied transformations. The last one is constant to preserve the matrices' concatenation ability.
3. An object rotates around its **origin** when manipulated by a rotation matrix. To use a different point as an anchor, move the object towards that point first, apply the desired rotation and then shift it back.
4. SwiftUI can process multiple gestures, like `DragGesture`, `MagnificationGesture`, `RotationGesture` or `TapGesture`, simultaneously when you attach them with the `.simultaneousGesture` modifier.

Where to Go From Here?

Transformation matrices are still universally used in computer graphics regardless of the programming language, framework or platform. Learning them once will be handy when working with animations outside the Apple ecosystem.The Wikipedia article on the topic (https://en.wikipedia.org/wiki/Transformation_matrix) offers a good overview of transformation matrices as a mathematical concept, also in the context of 2D or 3D computer graphics.

Additionally, if matrices don't scare but excite you, and you want to dive deep into Metal, Apple's low-level computer graphics framework, Metal by Tutorials (https://www.kodeco.com/books/metal-by-tutorials/v2.0) can guide you step-by-step along your journey.

Chapter 6: Intro to Custom Animations

By Bill Morefield

In this book, you've explored many ways SwiftUI makes animation simple to achieve. By taking advantage of the framework, you created complex animations with much less effort than previous app frameworks required. For many animations, this built-in system will do everything that you need. However, as you attempt more complex animations, you'll find places where SwiftUI can't do what you want without further assistance.

Fortunately, the animation support in SwiftUI includes protocols and extensions that you can use to produce animation effects beyond the basics while still having SwiftUI handle *some* of the work. This support lets you create more complex animations while still leveraging SwiftUI's built-in animation capabilities.

In this chapter, you'll start by adding a standard SwiftUI animation to an app. Then you'll learn to implement animations beyond the built-in support while having SwiftUI handle as much as possible.

Animating the Timer

Open the starter project for this chapter. You'll find an app that helps users brew and prepare tea. Build and run the app and tap any of the provided teas.

The app lists several types of tea and provides suggestions on water temperature and the amount of tea leaves needed for the desired amount of water. It also provides a timer that counts down the time needed to steep the tea.

You'll see information for brewing the tea you selected. Adjust the amount of water, and it'll update the needed amount of tea leaves to accommodate the change. It also lets you start and stop a timer for steeping the tea. When you start the brewing timer, it begins a countdown until your steeping completes.

Once it finishes, a view tells you your tea is ready to drink.

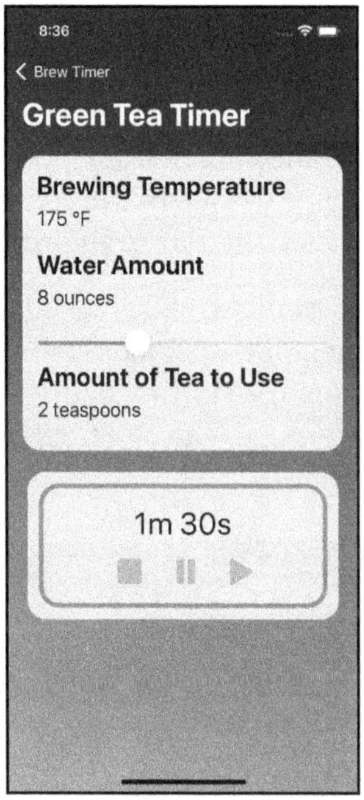

While it works, the app lacks energy and excitement. You'll add some animations that give it more energy and help users in their quest for the best tea.

First, the ring around the timer turns blue when you start the timer. While the color change does show the timer is running, it doesn't attract the eye. To do so, you'll animate the timer's border as a better indicator of a running timer.

Open **TimerView.swift**, and you'll see the code for this view. The `CountingTimerView` used in this view contains the control for the timer. It currently uses `overlay(alignment:content:)` to add a rounded rectangle with the color provided by the `timerBorderColor` computed property. You'll add a special case to display an animated border when the timer is running.

After the existing state properties, add the following new property:

```
@State var animateTimer = false
```

You'll use this property to control and trigger the animation by toggling its value. The animation here will animate the border around the timer display and controls. You'll animate the border so it appears to move in a circle around the digits and controls. To do this, you'll create an **angular gradient** or conic gradient.

Unlike the more common linear gradient, which blends colors based on the distance from a starting point, an angular gradient blends colors as it sweeps around a central point. Instead of the distance from the starting point determining the color, the angle from the central point determines the color. All points along a line radiating from the center will share the same color.

Add the following code after the existing computed properties to create the angular gradient:

```
var animationGradient: AngularGradient {
  AngularGradient(
    colors: [
      Color("BlackRussian"), Color("DarkOliveGreen"),
Color("OliveGreen"),
      Color("DarkOliveGreen"), Color("BlackRussian")
    ],
    center: .center,
    angle: .degrees(animateTimer ? 360 : 0)
  )
}
```

You specify the gradient will begin as a dark shade of black, transition to olive green at the midpoint, and then back to the same shade of black at the end. You set the gradient to use the center of the view as its origin. To allow animation, you set the angle by multiplying `animateTimer` by 360 degrees.

Toggling `animaterTimer` to `true` will rotate the gradient in a complete revolution. Note that the gradient will transition through a complete circle since you only specify a single angle. SwiftUI positions the start of the gradient at that angle and sweeps through the full rotation to the final color. It'll provide a circular shift from nearly black through olive green around the circle and then back to nearly black, where the gradient started.

Now find the `overlay` modifier on `CountingTimerView` and replace its contents with:

```
switch timerManager.status {
  case .running:
    RoundedRectangle(cornerRadius: 20)
      .stroke(animationGradient, lineWidth: 10)
  default:
    RoundedRectangle(cornerRadius: 20)
      .stroke(timerBorderColor, lineWidth: 5)
}
```

While the timer runs, you apply a different style to `stroke(_:lineWidth:)` that uses the gradient you just added. You also widen the line to draw the eye and provide more space for the animation to show, and add another visual indicator that something has changed.

Now, build and run the app. Tap any tea and then start the timer. The border takes on the new broader gradient but doesn't animate yet. You'll do that in the next section.

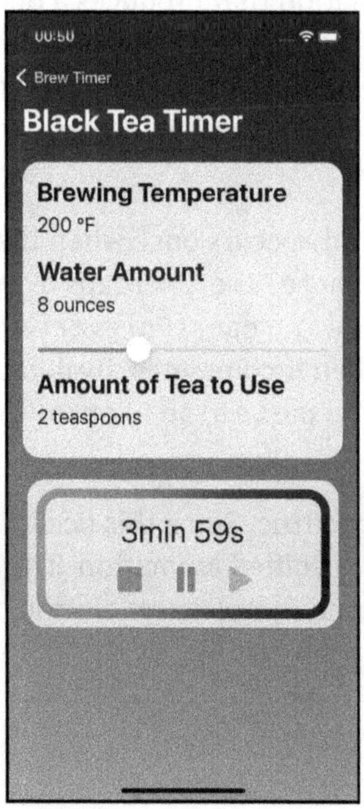

Animating the Gradient

Still in **TimerView.swift**, find `onChange(of:perform:)` on `NavigationStack`. This modifier monitors changes to the timer's `status`. Currently, it only checks for the `.done` state on the timer. Add a new `case` to the existing switch statement:

```
case .running:
  // 1
  withAnimation(
    .linear(duration: 1.0)
    // 2
    .repeatForever(autoreverses: false)
  ) {
    // 3
    animateTimer = true
  }
```

Here's what you did:

1. You create an explicit animation that produces a one-second linear animation. Using a linear animation produces constant motion that matches the flow of time. Setting the length to one second matches the rate at which the numbers in the timer change. Keeping the animation in sync with the number changes helps visually tie the two together.

2. By default, the animation only occurs once when the state changes. You could do a continuous change of `animateTimer`, perhaps by tying it directly to the elapsed time. Still, there's an easier way. `repeatForever(autoreverses:)` tells SwiftUI to restart the animation when it completes. By default, the animation would reverse before repeating. You pass `false` to `autoreverses` to skip the reversing of the animation.

3. You change `animateTimer` to true. Since this occurs in the closure, it'll animate the state change using the specified animation. The state changes cause the angular gradient to rotate one complete revolution, which will be animated.

Run your app, select any tea and start the timer. You'll see the gradient rotates while the timer counts down.

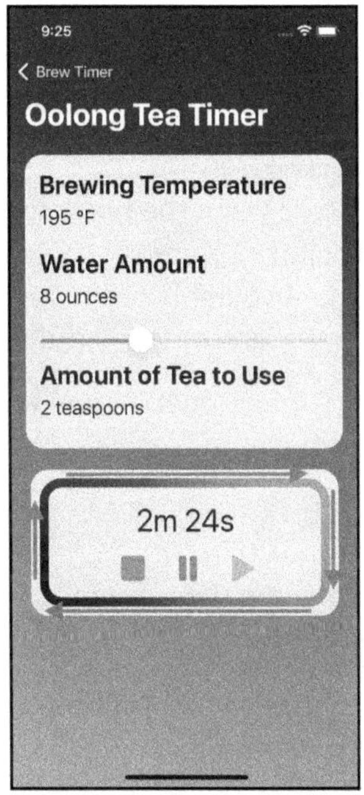

Next, you'll look at a similar animation using opacity to produce a pulsing effect when the user pauses the timer.

Animating the Pause State

You'll also add an animation when the user pauses the time. First, add the following state property after the existing ones:

```
@State var animatePause = false
```

You'll change this state property to trigger the animation when the user pauses the timer.

Now find `overlay(alignment:content:)` on `CountingTimerView` and add a new case for the `.paused` state:

```
case .paused:
  RoundedRectangle(cornerRadius: 20)
    .stroke(.blue, lineWidth: 10)
    .opacity(animatePause ? 0.2 : 1.0)
```

You added a new option for the case when the timer reaches the `paused` state. As with the others, you apply a `stroke(_:lineWidth:)`, in this case, a blue line the same width as when running. You then apply `opacity(_:)` using `animatePause` to change it between 0.2 (almost transparent) to 1.0 (fully opaque).

Now find the `onChange(of:perform:)` modifier you worked in earlier. Add the following line right at the beginning of the `.running` case:

```
animatePause = false
```

This code resets the property when the timer begins running. It's essential to ensure the animation is ready if triggered again.

Now you need to handle the new paused state. Still in `onChange(of:perform:)`, add a new case to handle the `.paused` state:

```
case .paused:
  // 1
  animateTimer = false
  // 2
  withAnimation(
    .easeInOut(duration: 0.5)
    .repeatForever()
  ) {
    animatePause = true
  }
```

And replace the `break` in the `default` case with:

```
// 3
animateTimer = false
animatePause = false
```

Here's what this code does:

1. When your time switches to the `paused` state, you set `animateTimer` to false. Setting `animateTimer` back to its original state prepares it if the user starts the timer again.
2. You use an explicit animation when setting `animatePause` to **true**. Recall this will change the opacity from 0.2 to 1.0. You apply an ease-in-out animation lasting one half-second. You also apply `repeatForever(autoreverses:)` using the default parameter for `autoreverses`, which will reverse the animation before repeating it. As a result, the animation will cycle from dim to bright and back once per second.
3. If the timer status changes to any other state, then neither animation should be active, and you set both state properties to **false**.

Run your app, select any tea and start the timer. After a few seconds, pause the timer. You'll see the border of the timer pulse.

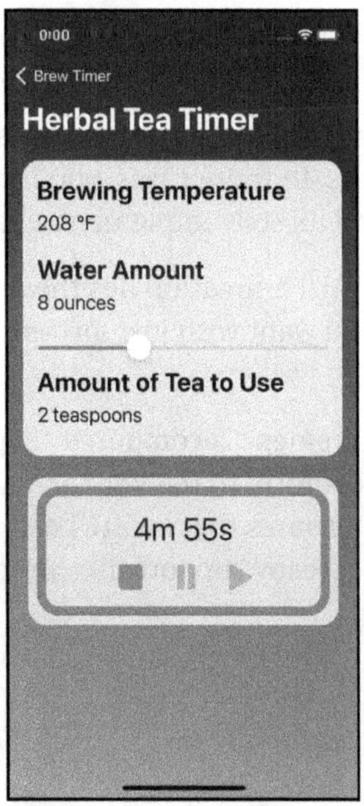

These two animations work like many others you've seen, taking advantage of SwiftUI automatically handling the animation for a `Bool` value such as `animateTimer`. In the next section, you'll learn how to handle more complex cases when SwiftUI can't handle the animation for you. It's time to look into the `Animatable` protocol.

Making a View Animatable

As mentioned in **Chapter 1: Introducing SwiftUI Animations**, an animation is a series of static images changing rapidly and providing the illusion of motion. When SwiftUI animates a shape, it rapidly draws the view many times. The type of animation and the elements that change determine how the views change. In the previous section, you changed the angle of the angular gradient and SwiftUI animated the result of that change.

SwiftUI can't manage a change to a `Path` or a shift in the text shown in a `Text` view. In these cases, you can conform to the `Animatable` protocol and manage the animation yourself.

In this section, you'll use `Animatable` to implement a text view that can animate the transition between two numbers. In these cases, you'll turn to the underlying structure you've been using and directly implement what you need.

Behind the scenes of every SwiftUI animation lies the `Animatable` protocol. You turn to it when you can't do what you want with just `animation(_:)` or `withAnimation(_:_:)`.

This protocol has a single requirement, a computed property named `animatableData` which must conform to the `VectorArithmetic` protocol. A value that conforms to this protocol ensures that SwiftUI can add, subtract and multiply the value. Many built-in types already support this protocol, including `Double`, which you'll use in this chapter.

These two protocols allow SwiftUI to provide a changing value to animate independent of how the view implements the animation. SwiftUI calculates the new `animatableData` values based on the kind of animation used. Your view needs to handle the values that SwiftUI sends to it. It lets you produce a single view that can handle any animation without worrying about the differences between linear or spring animations.

Create a new SwiftUI View file named **NumberTransitionView.swift** and open it. Update the definition of the generated struct to:

```
struct NumberTransitionView: View, Animatable {
```

Adding the Animatable protocol lets you provide direct control of the animated values. Next, add the following code to the top of the struct:

```
var number: Int
var suffix: String

var animatableData: Double {
  get { Double(number) }
  set { number = Int(newValue) }
}
```

Here, you create a property to hold the number the view will display as an `Int`. You'll also let the user pass in a string to append to the number.

You then implement the `animatableData` required by the `Animatable` protocol as a computed property. This computed property gets or sets the value of `number` while converting between `Int` and `Double` as needed. In this case, given the range of values you'll animate, you don't need the extra resolution provided by the double.

Update the view's `body` to:

```
Text(String(number) + suffix)
```

You display the number and append the passed suffix to the end. Finally, update the preview to provide a number and the suffix by changing it to:

```
NumberTransitionView(number: 5, suffix: " °F")
```

If you look at the preview, you won't see much difference between this view and a regular text view showing a number.

The difference will only show when you animate the view. You'll do that in the next section.

Using an Animatable View

Open **BrewInfoView.swift**. You'll add a bit of animation to the brewing temperature that appears on the view. Add the following new property after the existing state properties:

```
@State var brewingTemp = 0
```

You'll use this property to change the value displayed. Initially, you set it to zero, so you can change it when the view appears. Now attach the following modifier to the `VStack` before `padding(_:_:)`:

```
.onAppear {
  withAnimation(.easeOut(duration: 0.5)) {
    brewingTemp = brewTimer.temperature
  }
}
```

You set the state property to the temperature passed into this view. You wrap this change inside an explicit call to `withAnimation(_:_:)` and specify an ease-out animation that lasts one half-second.

You choose the ease-out animation because the fast initial change of this type of animation makes the interface seem speedy. The short duration also gives the user enough time to see the animation while remaining quick enough so they don't grow impatient.

Before implementing the animation, you'll change the view so you can better compare it to the final animation. Find the line in the view that reads `Text("\(brewTimer.temperature) °F")` and change it to:

```
Text("\(brewingTemp) °F")
```

This change shows the new property instead of the brewing temperature passed into the view. So, the value will initially be zero and change to the final temperature.

Run the app and select any tea. When the view appears, you'll see what you probably expected. The initial view showing the zero fades out, and the new view showing the desired temperature fades in. SwiftUI doesn't know how to animate text changing from zero to a temperature, so it uses a view transition.

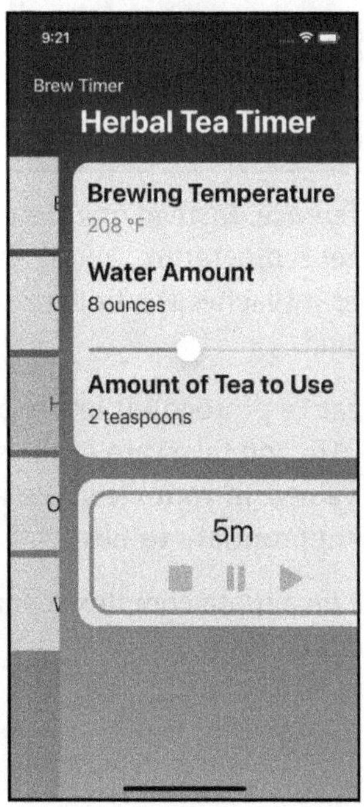

Change the text line to use your new view. Replace the view showing the brewing temperature with:

```
NumberTransitionView(number: brewingTemp, suffix: " °F")
```

Run the app and select any tea.

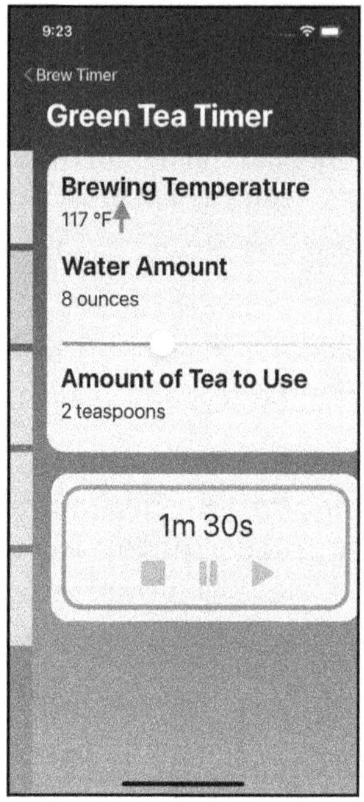

You'll notice an immediate difference. Instead of a view transition, the number counts up from zero to the target temperature. You'll also see the number change quickly at first before slowing as it reaches the final temperature. It gets to that final temperature after one half-second.

That's the power of the `Animatable` protocol! It lets you make almost anything you can imagine animate with SwiftUI. You take care of the state change as before and let SwiftUI calculate the changed values. In your view, you accept the changing values through the protocol and show appropriate values.

In the next section, you'll work on a more complex scenario to produce a better animation for the timer as it counts down.

Creating a Sliding Number Animation

Open **CountingTimerView.swift**. On the first line of the `VStack`, you'll see the timer currently displays a string from `timerManager`. This string shows the remaining time formatted using a `DateComponentsFormatter` that shows only the minutes and seconds. The result provides the information, but it's a bit plain.

Before digital timers, clocks often used mechanical movements that moved printed numbers to show time. In this section, you'll create an animated version of this type of display for the steeping timer as it counts down. You'll begin by creating a new view that shows each timer digit in a separate view.

Create a new SwiftUI View file named **TimerDigitsView.swift**. Add this new property to the top of the view:

```
var digits: [Int]
```

You'll pass in the digits of the timer as an array of `Int` values. The first two store the minutes, and the last two values in the array store the seconds. This change will display these values individually and make each digit easier to animate. Add this code below the `digits` property:

```
var hasMinutes: Bool {
  digits[0] != 0 || digits[1] != 0
}
```

This computed property will return false only when both digits of the minutes are zero. You'll use this to help format the numbers in this view. Now change the body of the view to:

```
HStack {
  // 1
  if hasMinutes {
    // 2
    if digits[0] != 0 {
      Text(String(digits[0]))
    }
    // 3
    Text(String(digits[1]))
    Text("m")
```

```
    }
    // 4
    if hasMinutes || digits[2] != 0 {
      Text(String(digits[2]))
    }
    // 5
    Text(String(digits[3]))
    Text("s")
  }
```

Here's what this view does:

1. You check the computed property and see if the time contains minutes. If not, then you skip displaying information about the minutes.
2. When minutes exist, you display the first digit as long as it's not zero.
3. You always show the second digit of the minutes followed by the letter **m** to indicate this value shows minutes.
4. If the first seconds digit is zero or if you had minutes, you show the first seconds digit. This condition will display a leading zero only when the time contains minutes.
5. You always show the seconds digit and an **s** string to indicate these show seconds.

Update the preview to pass in digits. Change the preview to:

```
TimerDigitsView(digits: [1, 0, 0, 4])
```

Open **CountingTimerView.swift** and look for the code that reads `Text(timerManager.remaingTimeAsString)`. Replace it with:

```
TimerDigitsView(digits: timerManager.digits)
```

Now you use this new view to show the time. The `digits` property of `timerManager` formats an array with the desired data based on the remaining time.

Run the app, select a tea and start the timer. The view looks similar to the original, except now, each digit is a separate view instead of a single `Text` view showing a formatted string.

Visually, the most noticeable difference is more spacing between the letters and numbers indicating the time.

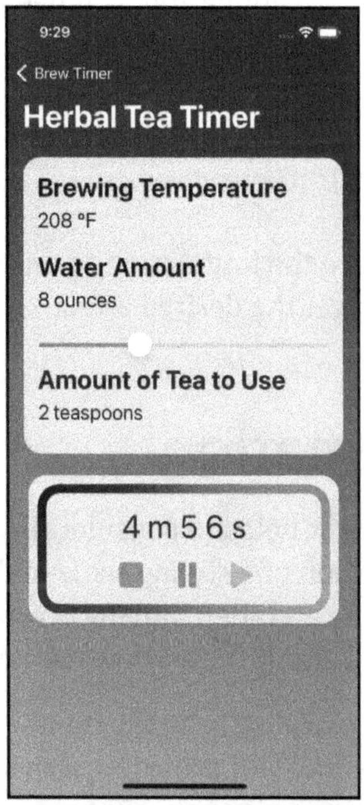

Now you'll build a view to animate these individual digits. Create a new SwiftUI View file named **SlidingNumber.swift**. Open the new view and change the definition of the struct to:

```
struct SlidingNumber: View, Animatable {
```

As a reminder, adding Animatable tells SwiftUI that you'll make this view support animation. As before, you implement the `animatableData` required by the protocol. Add this code to the top of the struct:

```
var number: Double

var animatableData: Double {
  get { number }
  set { number = newValue }
}
```

You store the value sent by SwiftUI in a `Double` property named `number`. You might wonder why you need a `Double` here instead of the `Int` you used in the last section, even though you'll only display single integer digits.

The reason comes down to the granularity of the data. In the previous section, you produced animation between far apart integers. Here, you'll change between adjacent digits. To create a smooth animation, you need the fractional values between the two numbers.

Update the preview to read:

```
SlidingNumber(number: 0)
```

With this view in place, you have the foundation to animate the timer. In the next section, you'll examine how to get the desired effect.

Building an Animation

When developing an animation, it helps to consider the visual effect you want to achieve. Go back to the inspiration of a sliding scale of digits. You'll implement a strip of numbers starting at nine and then moving down through zero. When the digit changes, the strip of numbers shifts to show the new value.

In SwiftUI terms, you want a vertical strip of the numbers around the new value. When the number changes, SwiftUI will provide a series of values between the original and new number through `animatableData`.

Look at this example where `number` begins at four and changes to three.

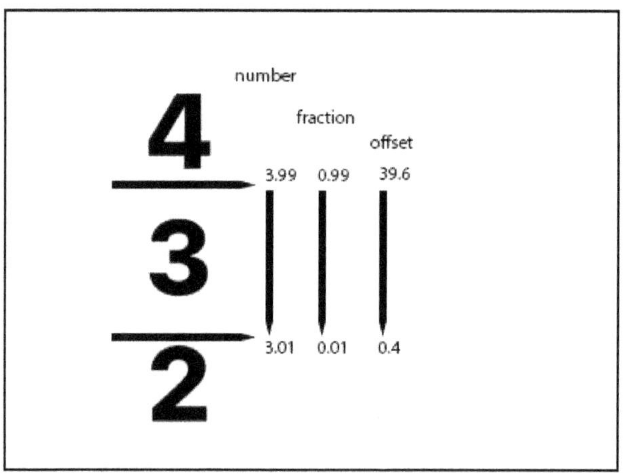

The series provided through `animatableData` begins at four and will decrease to three though the exact values will vary depending on the type of animation. The first value is slightly below four. The fractional part of the number indicates how far you're through the change in the digit and begins as near one and approaches zero.

As that fractional part decreases, you shift the number upward toward the new number.

Once the number reaches the new value of three, the view resets so that the central value is that new number. The cycle can then repeat when the number changes again. With that background, you can now implement it in SwiftUI in the next section.

Implementing Sliding Numbers

First, you need a vertical strip of numbers. Delete the existing `Text` view inside the body, and add the following code at the top of the view body:

```
// 1
let digitArray = [number + 1, number, number - 1]
  // 2
  .map { Int($0).between(0, and: 10) }
```

This code calculates the numbers to show:

1. You create an array of the number after the current number, the current number and the numbers below the current number. If `number` is four, the array would contain **[5, 4, 3]**. This array lets the animation flow in both directions.
2. You use `map` on the array to convert the values to integers and remove that fractional amount from the `Double`. You also use `between(:and)` from **IntegerExtensions.swift** to handle the edge cases. The value below zero is nine, and the value above nine is zero.

Add the following code below what you just added:

```
let shift = number.truncatingRemainder(dividingBy: 1)
```

You use `truncatingRemainder(dividingBy:)` to get only the fractional part of the `Double`. As mentioned in the last section, this indicates how far through the animation you are. Next, add:

```
// 1
VStack {
  Text(String(digitArray[0]))
  Text(String(digitArray[1]))
  Text(String(digitArray[2]))
}
// 2
```

```
.font(.largeTitle)
.fontWeight(.heavy)
// 3
.frame(width: 30, height: 40)
// 4
.offset(y: 40 * shift)
```

This code implements the steps discussed in the last section. Here's how each part creates part of the animation:

1. To create the strip of digits, you use a `VStack` showing the integers you stored in `digitArray`.
2. You apply the `.largeTitle` font with a heavy weight to let the digits stand out.
3. You set the frame for the view to 30 points wide and 40 points tall. The height matches the distance between digits in the `VStack`.
4. You take the `shift` you calculated earlier as the portion of the height that the view should shift for the current point in the animation. You multiply it by 40, the distance between digits in the stack. That converts the `shift` into an amount of vertical movement for the view.

Now you need to use this new view. Open **TimerDigitsView.swift** and change the body to:

```
HStack {
  if hasMinutes {
    if digits[0] != 0 {
      SlidingNumber(number: Double(digits[0]))
    }
    SlidingNumber(number: Double(digits[1]))
    Text("m")
  }
  if hasMinutes || digits[2] != 0 {
    SlidingNumber(number: Double(digits[2]))
  }
  SlidingNumber(number: Double(digits[3]))
  Text("s")
}
```

This code replaces the `Text` views from earlier with your new `SlidingNumber` view. Run the app, select any tea and start the timer.

In this state, you'll see the entire strip of digits. As it animates, note that the strip shifts and how new numbers appear and vanish as the animation progresses.

Use the **Slow Animations** option in the simulator to help.

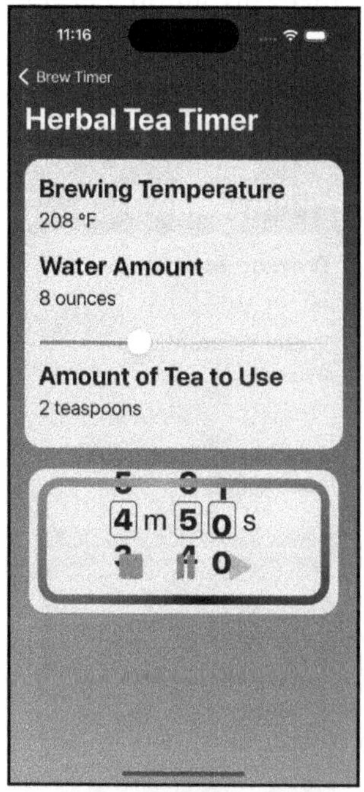

Once you watch the animation, you'll finish cleaning up the view. Open **SlidingNumber.swift**. Add two more modifiers after `offset(x:y:)`:

```
// 1
.overlay {
  RoundedRectangle(cornerRadius: 5)
    .stroke(lineWidth: 1)
}
// 2
.clipShape(
  RoundedRectangle(cornerRadius: 5)
)
```

Here's what these do:

1. You give the digit a thin frame using `stroke(lineWidth:)` applied to a `RoundedRectangle`.

2. While there is a strip of numbers, you only want to show a single number at a time. You do this using `clipShape(_:style:)` with `RoundedRectangle` that matches the one used to produce the frame in step two. This shape fills the frame and clips to the frame you applied to the view. Clipping removes any elements outside that space and hides the extra digits in the `VStack`.

Run the app and start a steeping timer. You'll see only a single digit that animates as the timer changes. It also has a nice surrounding border that helps each number stand out.

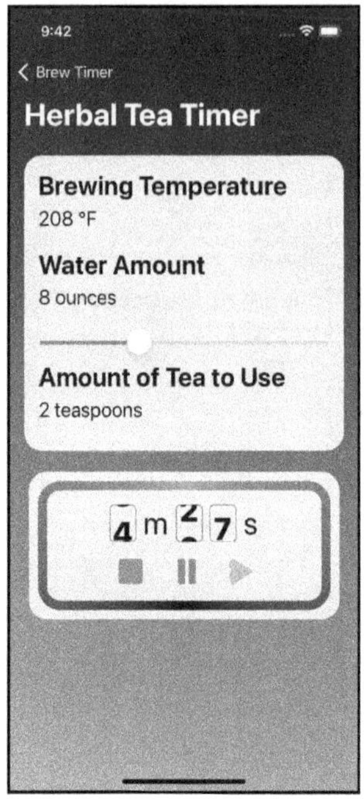

Challenge

Using what you've learned in this chapter, adjust the timer animation so the digits slide in the opposite direction and the numbers slide downward. As a hint, recall that in SwiftUI, a decrease in offset will cause a shift upward. How can you make that move down instead?

Check the challenge project in the materials for this chapter for one solution.

Key Points

- An angular gradient shifts through colors based on the angles around a central point.
- The **Animatable** protocol provides a method to help you handle the animation within a view yourself. You only need to turn to it when SwiftUI can't do things for you.
- When using the **Animatable** protocol, SwiftUI will provide the changing value to your view through the `animatableData` property.
- When creating custom animations using the **Animatable** protocol, begin by visualizing what you want the finished animation to look like.
- Take advantage of SwiftUI's ability to combine elements. In many cases, breaking an animation into smaller components will make it easier. You'll find it easier to animate individual digits instead of trying to animate an entire display of numbers.

Where to Go From Here?

- You can read more about angular gradients in Apple's Documentation (https://developer.apple.com/documentation/swiftui/angulargradient).
- You can find other examples of using the **Animatable** protocol in Getting Started with SwiftUI Animations (https://www.kodeco.com/5815412-getting-started-with-swiftui-animations).
- You'll also explore the **Animatable** protocol more in the next section, including learning how to deal with animations involving multiple elements.

Chapter 7: Complex Custom Animations

By Bill Morefield

By now, you can see that creating more complex animations in SwiftUI relies on understanding how the SwiftUI protocols and animation engine work. Done correctly, your custom animations still use SwiftUI to handle as much work as possible.

To create more complex animations, you often need to combine several elements working together. One way to produce a more complex animation is to combine view transitions with animated state changes. Animating the appearance and removal of a view while animating a state change can make a view stand out and clarify the relationship between new elements on a view.

In the previous chapter, you worked on adding animations to your custom views. Up to this point, your animations were limited to relying on a single property, but SwiftUI also supports animating multiple property changes within the same view. In this chapter, you'll create a view that supports *five* independently animated values.

First, you'll look at how to combine transitions and animations to produce a unified animation.

Adding a Popup Button

Open the starter project for this chapter. You'll see the tea brewing app you worked with in the previous chapter with a few added features. Since tastes in tea can vary, the app now lets users customize the brew settings. They can also record their review of the results of each brew to help them find the perfect process to match their taste for each tea.

Open **TimerView.swift**. You'll see the timer is now at the top of the view to make it easier to see. The timer also adds a slider to let the user adjust the brewing length.

Further down, you'll see the familiar information showing the suggested brewing temperature and a slider that lets the user adjust the amount of water so the app can provide a suggested amount of tea. You'll now add a button so the user can adjust the suggested ratio of tea to water.

Create a new SwiftUI view file inside the **Timer** folder named **PopupSelectionButton.swift**. Add the following properties to the generated view:

```
@Binding var currentValue: Double?
var values: [Double]
```

These properties provide a binding that passes the selection back from the view. It also allows passing in an array of `Double` values that can be selected. Replace the preview body with:

```
PopupSelectionButton(
  currentValue: .constant(3),
  values: [1.0, 1.5, 2.0, 2.5, 3.0, 4.0, 5.0]
)
```

This code provides the view sample settings. Update the view's body to:

```
Group {
  if let currentValue {
    Text(currentValue, format: .number)
      .modifier(CircledTextToggle(backgroundColor:
Color("Bourbon")))
  } else {
    Text("\(Image(systemName: "exclamationmark"))")
      .modifier(CircledTextToggle(backgroundColor: Color(.red)))
  }
}
```

This code attempts to unwrap the `currentValue` binding property. If successful, the value will display using the color bourbon for the background. If not, the view will show an exclamation mark with a red background. You wrap the conditional inside a `Group` so you can apply additional modifiers to the two view states without repeating code. The `CircledTextToggle` view modifier is identical to the `CircledText` view modifier, except it applies a fixed frame to the Text. Without adding this frame, the changing size of the `Text` view when transitioning from text to a system image would cause the view to shift.

Since you provided the preview a value of 3, you'll now see the result, which shows the numeral three with the bourbon color background.

Basic button

Your button shows the value but doesn't let the user change it. You'll implement that in the next section.

Adding Button Options

Add the following property after `values`:

```
@State private var showOptions = false
```

This state property stores whether the view should show the options. To toggle it, add the following modifier to `Group`:

```
.onTapGesture {
  showOptions.toggle()
}
```

When the user taps the view, you toggle showOptions. Now you need to show the user the options. You'll lay out the options in an arc starting above the button. Add the following methods after the body:

```
private func xOffset(for index: Int) -> Double {
  // 1
  let distance = 180.0
  // 2
  let angle = Angle(degrees: Double(90 + 15 * index)).radians
  // 3
  return distance * sin(angle) - distance
}

private func yOffset(for index: Int) -> Double {
  let distance = 180.0
  let angle = Angle(degrees: Double(90 + 15 * index)).radians
  return distance * cos(angle) - 45
}
```

Here's how these two methods create the arc layout:

1. You set distance to 180 for the radius of a circle. You'll lay the buttons along this circle.

2. You want each button rotated 15 degrees from the previous one, so you multiply the index by 15. You then add 90 to this value which rotates the element's location a quarter turn counter-clockwise. Note this difference from SwiftUI rotations. In a SwiftUI rotation, an increase in the angle rotates further clockwise. You then convert the angle from degrees to radians.

3. Then you multiply the distance by the sine of the angle. The Swift sin function expects the angle in radians, which you converted to in the previous step. You then subtract the distance from this value which shifts the circle's center to the left. As a result, the x offsets start in line with the button and then decrease as the angle increases.

The vertical offset calculation works the same, except you use a cosine since you're dealing with the y value. You subtract 45 to shift the circle's center to just above the button. With those methods to calculate each view's position, you can now show the options in the view.

Wrap the current Group inside a ZStack by holding down **Command** and clicking the Group view. Then select **Embed in ZStack** from the menu. A ZStack overlays its views, with each view lying above the previous views in the stack. Since you want to overlay these options, this is perfect.

Now add the following code to the start of the Group:

```
// 1
if showOptions {
  // 2
  ForEach(values.indices, id: \.self) { index in
    // 3
    Text(values[index], format: .number)
      .modifier(CircledText(backgroundColor:
Color("OliveGreen")))
      // 4
      .offset(
        x: xOffset(for: index),
        y: yOffset(for: index)
      )
      // 5
      .onTapGesture {
        currentValue = values[index]
        showOptions = false
      }
  }
  Text("\(Image(systemName: "xmark.circle"))")
    .transition(.opacity.animation(.linear(duration: 0.25)))
    .modifier(CircledTextToggle(backgroundColor: Color(.red)))
}
```

Here's what this code does:

1. You'll only show the options when `showOptions` is `true`.
2. You iterate through the `indices` property of the `values` array to get the index of each element in the array.
3. Then, you show the value using the initializer `Text` that allows passing a format. Using the `number` format also displays the value concisely with only the minimum digits needed to reflect the value.
4. You offset each option vertically using the methods you just added to the view.
5. When the user taps one of the options, you set the `currentValue` binding to the value and then set `showOptions` to `false` to hide the options.

You now have an implementation you can use in your app. Open **BrewInfoView.swift**, which contains the view showing the suggested amount of tea for a given amount of water. Find the last `Text` element in the `VStack` and replace it with the following:

```
HStack(alignment: .bottom) {
  Text("\(teaToUse.formatted()) teaspoons")
```

```
      .modifier(InformationText())
    Spacer()
    PopupSelectionButton(
      currentValue: $waterTeaRatio,
      values: [1.0, 1.5, 2.0, 2.5, 3.0, 4.0, 5.0]
    )
  }
```

You added the new `PopupSelectionButton` view to let the user select the desired ratio and provide several options between 1.0 and 5.0.

Now run the app. Select any tea, tap the button and change the ratio. Observe how the suggested amount of tea changes to match the new ratio. Adjust the amount of water and observe that the tea adjusts to fit.

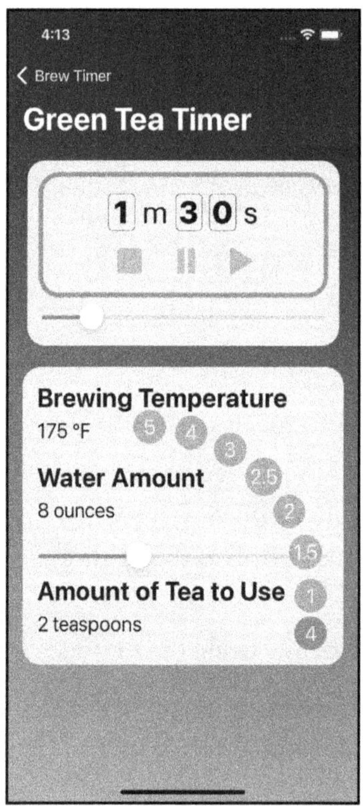

While the buttons show, they appear suddenly. In the next section, you'll animate the appearance of the options.

Animating the Options

Since an animation requires a state change, your first thought might be to animate using the showOptions already in place. If you try that, you'll find a problem. Changing showOptions causes SwiftUI to add or remove views. If you recall, you need a special type of animation called a transition to animate the appearance or removal of views.

You might consider triggering the animation based on the same state change, but that can be complicated. Instead, you'll introduce a new property to manage the animation.

Back in PopupSelectionButton, add the following new property after the existing ones:

```
@State private var animateOptions = false
```

You'll use this property to manage the view appearance and removal independently of each other. Now update your offset(x:y:), under comment four, to:

```
.offset(
  x: animateOptions ? xOffset(for: index) : 0,
  y: animateOptions ? yOffset(for: index) : 0
)
```

Now you only offset the views when animateOptions is true. Otherwise, they would remain hidden under the main button since they appear earlier in the ZStack. Changing animateOptions animates the buttons so they appear behind the main button and move to their final positions.

Next, update the code inside the outer onTapGesture attached to the Group to:

```
// 1
withAnimation(.easeOut(duration: 0.25)) {
  animateOptions = !showOptions
}
// 2
withAnimation { showOptions.toggle() }
```

You'll run two animations separately based on the current value of showOptions.

Here's how the code manages these changes:

1. You wrap the change of `animateOptions` inside `withAnimation(_:_:)` using the ease-out animation with a duration of 0.25 seconds. You set `animationOptions` to the opposite of `showOptions` — if `showOptions` is currently true, it means you need to hide the options, and vice-versa.
2. You use a separate `withAnimation(_:_:)` to toggle `showOptions`. You do not specify an animation since this will trigger a transition applied to the view.

Recall that you also hide the options when the user selects an option. You need to update that code to match these changes. Replace the `onTapGesture` closure inside the `ForEach` loop with:

```
.onTapGesture {
  currentValue = values[index]
  withAnimation(.easeOut(duration: 0.25)) {
    animateOptions = false
  }
  withAnimation { showOptions = false }
}
```

You're using the same code you did earlier, except you know you're hiding the options. As the last step, you'll add a transition to the view.

Go to the `Text` view at the top of the `ForEach` loop. Add the following modifier after the view and before all the other modifiers:

```
.transition(.scale.animation(.easeOut(duration: 0.25)))
```

By default, the scale animation scales from and to a vanishing point at the center of the view. You apply an ease-out animation with a duration of 0.25 seconds to the transition, which matches the animation used with the change of offset position. Using the same animation keeps the two in sync, so they act as a single combined animation instead of separate animations.

Run the app, select a tea and tap the button.

Now you'll see the options slide out from under the original button.

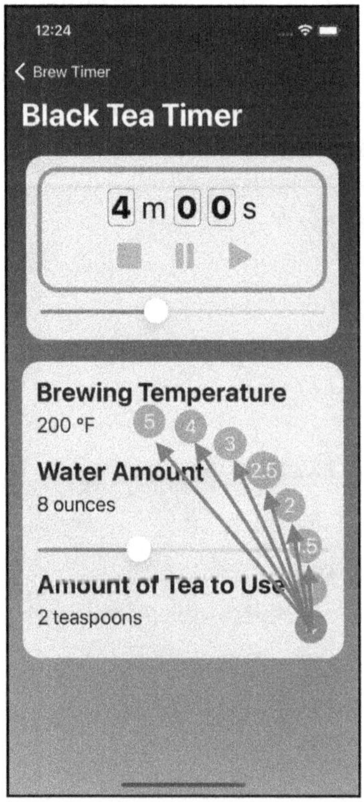

You've created an animated popup button combining transitions and state animation. As with most animations, it only animates a single element, the position. In the next section, you'll learn about animating a view with multiple properties.

Animating Multiple Properties

In **Chapter 6: Intro to Custom Animations**, you learned about the `Animatable` protocol and used it to produce views that could handle animations beyond what SwiftUI can handle by default. The changing number and sliding number animations you built in those chapters only dealt with a single changing value. In this section, you'll create a view with five parameters that are fully animated.

The app shows you the past ratings of your brews. While the list shows the information, it would be nice to provide a visualization to help clarify the relationships between the different settings and the results. To do this, you'll create a radar chart: a visualization to compare the characteristics of multiple values by plotting the data as a polygon, with each corner of the polygon representing one value. A radar chart looks like this:

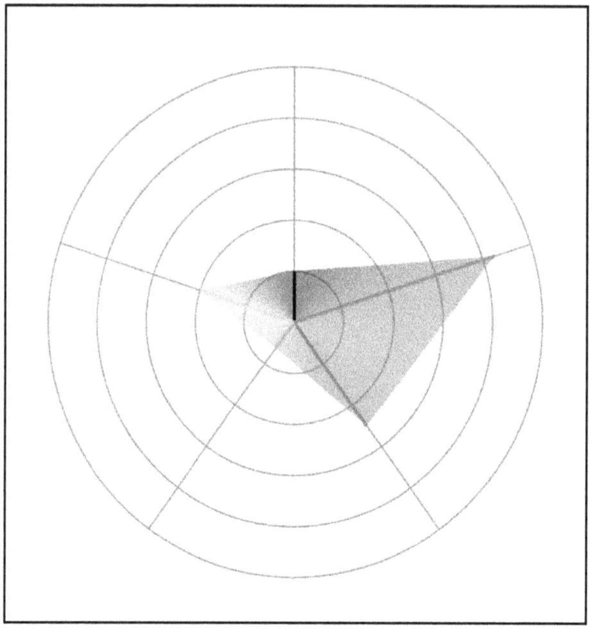

Run the app and select **Green Tea** or **Oolong Tea**, which already have ratings. At the bottom of the view, you'll see the ratings listed. Tap anywhere in that window, and you'll see a sheet showing the first rating. You can quickly swipe between the ratings.

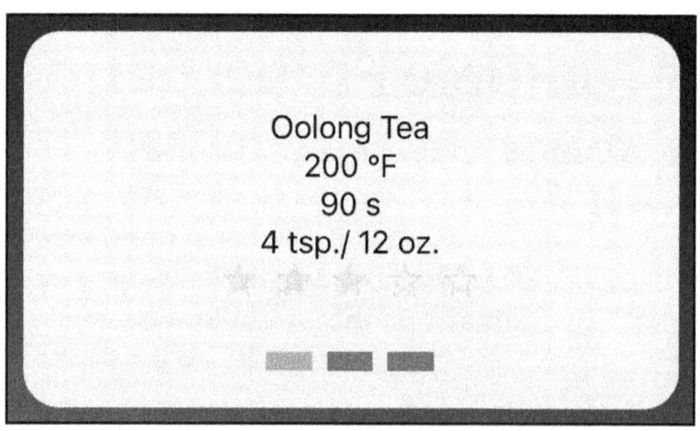

You'll now create a visualization that reflects the values in these ratings.

Creating a Radar Chart

Create a new SwiftUI view file named **AnimatedRadarChart.swift** under the **RadarChart** group. Add the following properties to the new view:

```
var time: Double
var temperature: Double
var amountWater: Double
var amountTea: Double
var rating: Double
```

These are the five properties that your radar chart will show. For greater precision during the animation, you use a `Double` type for each. Now update the preview to provide the values. Change the body of the preview to:

```
AnimatedRadarChart(
  time: Double(BrewResult.sampleResult.time),
  temperature: Double(BrewResult.sampleResult.temperature),
  amountWater: BrewResult.sampleResult.amountWater,
  amountTea: BrewResult.sampleResult.amountTea,
  rating: Double(BrewResult.sampleResult.rating)
)
```

Now add the following computed property to the view:

```
var values: [Double] {
  [
    time / 600.0,
    temperature / 212.0,
    amountWater / 16.0,
    amountTea / 16.0,
    rating / 5.0
  ]
}
```

This computed property takes the individual values, turns them into an array you can loop over and handles the problem of scaling the chart by dividing each value by the maximum expected value. This step turns each value into a fraction between zero and one and ensures that charts from different measurements are comparable.

Now you'll work on the chart to show these values. Replace the body of the view with:

```
// 1
ZStack {
  // 2
  GeometryReader { proxy in
```

```
      // 3
      let graphSize = min(proxy.size.width, proxy.size.height) /
2.0
      let xCenter = proxy.size.width / 2.0
      let yCenter = proxy.size.height / 2.0
    }
  }
```

This code makes some calculations you need to match the size of the chart to the size of the view. Here's what it does:

1. You'll add more to this chart later in this chapter, so you build the view within a `ZStack`, which overlays child views.
2. Using a `GeometryReader` causes the views in the closure to take up as much space as possible and allows you access to information about the view's size. You'll use this information to scale the chart within the view.
3. You can calculate some values you'll use later from the `GeometryProxy` passed to the closure of the `GeometryReader`. You determine which is smaller: the view's vertical or horizontal size. Then you divide it by two to determine the number of points to display when a value is at the maximum value. To help center the chart within the view, you calculate the center points in each position by dividing the width and height by two.

Now add the following code to the end of the `GeometryReader`:

```
// 4
ForEach(0..<5 id: \.self) { index in
  Path { path in
    path.move(to: .zero)
    path.addLine(to: .init(x: 0, y: -graphSize * values[index]))
  }
  // 5
  .stroke(.black, lineWidth: 2)
  // 6
  .offset(x: xCenter, y: yCenter)
  // 7
  .rotationEffect(.degrees(72.0 * Double(index)))
}
```

Here's what the code does:

4. You loop between 0 and 4, since `values` has 5 elements. Remember, `values` contains a scaled value between zero and one for each item to show on the chart. You then create a path that begins at the zero point and adds a line from that point. In SwiftUI, a negative value indicates a position upward in the view. To create a vertical upward line, you multiply the negative of the `graphSize` value computed earlier by the fraction of the current point.
5. You draw the path on the view using `stroke(_:lineWidth:)`, which draws a black line of width two.
6. The origin of a drawing in a SwiftUI view is at the leading top corner by default. To shift this to the center of the view, you apply `offset(x:y:)`, passing the center locations you calculated in step three.
7. You want to produce five equally spaced lines around the center point. You divide the 360 degrees of a full circle by five to find that you should rotate each line 72 degrees from the previous one. Since an increased number rotates clockwise in SwiftUI, succeeding lines will appear clockwise from the first.

You'll see the plotted values in the preview.

With the basics in place, you'll fill out the rest of the chart in the next section.

Adding Grid Lines

Now you'll add a guide to each value. Inside the `ForEach` loop, in front of the existing `Path`, add:

```
Path { path in
  path.move(to: .zero)
  path.addLine(to: .init(x: 0, y: -graphSize))
}
.stroke(.gray, lineWidth: 1)
.offset(x: xCenter, y: yCenter)
.rotationEffect(.degrees(72.0 * Double(index)))
```

This code is identical to the previous code, except it doesn't scale the height of the line so that it's the entire length. You also stroke the line in gray and one point wide. Since it occurs before plotting the value, the plotted value will overlay it.

Add the following code after the assignment of `yCenter` and before the current `ForEach`:

```
// 1
let chartFraction = Array(stride(
  from: 0.2,
  to: 1.0,
  by: 0.2
))
ForEach(chartFraction, id: \.self) { fraction in
  // 2
  Path { path in
    path.addArc(
      center: .zero,
      radius: graphSize * fraction,
      startAngle: .degrees(0),
      endAngle: .degrees(360),
      clockwise: true
    )
  }
  // 3
  .stroke(.gray, lineWidth: 1)
  .offset(x: xCenter, y: yCenter)
}
```

This code produces grid lines for the chart that help the reader interpret the values.

Here's what the lines do:

1. You loop through a set of fractions that evenly divide the chart into five sections. SwiftUI will pass the value to the closure as `fraction`.
2. For each value, you create a path and add an arc to the path. This arc will sweep around the center of the view with a radius of `graphSize` multiplied by the current `fraction`. You turn the arc into a circle by setting the start and end angles to sweep the full 360 degrees. This loop will draw a series of larger arcs as SwiftUI iterates over the values.
3. You stroke each path as a gray line with a width of one point. As before, you use `offset(x:y:)` to set the center point to the center of the view.

Look at your chart in the preview. Adding the grid lines makes it easier to interpret each value.

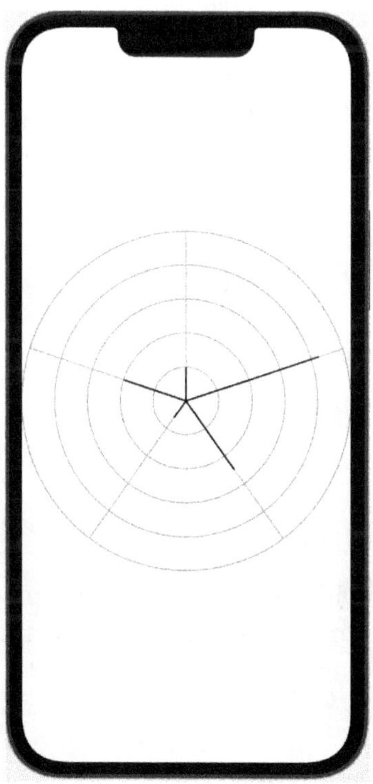

In the next section, you'll add a bit of color to the graph and add it to the app.

Coloring the Radar Chart

The chart looks a little dull in shades of gray. To add some color, add the following code before the body of the view:

```
let lineColors: [Color] = [.black, .red, .blue, .green, .yellow]
```

This constant defines a set of colors in an array. If you take them in the same order as the values in the chart, you'll notice the colors relate to the measurements: black for the time, red for temperature, blue for the amount of water, green for the amount of tea and yellow for the rating.

With this array, you can add color to the chart's values. Look for the line that reads `.stroke(.black, lineWidth: 2)` under comment five and change it to:

```
.stroke(lineColors[index], lineWidth: 2)
```

Now you draw each line in a unique color. To finish the radar chart, you'll draw the polygon connecting the ends of each measurement line. Since this view is a bit more complicated, add the following code to the end of the current file:

```
struct PolygonChartView: View {
  var values: [Double]
  var graphSize: Double
  var colorArray: [Color]
  var xCenter: Double
  var yCenter: Double

  var body: some View {
    Path { path in
    }
  }
}
```

You created a new view that will encapsulate the polygon part of the view. Separating this into a separate view will improve readability while reducing clutter and problems with the SwiftUI compiler.

Now add the following new code to PolygonChartView after the properties:

```
var gradientColors: AngularGradient {
  AngularGradient(
    colors: colorArray + [colorArray.first ?? .black],
    center: .center,
    angle: .degrees(-90)
  )
}
```

You create an AngularGradient and pass your colorArray while appending the first color to its end. You do this to match the start and end colors of the angular gradient. Since the gradient starts toward the right, you set the angle property to -90 degrees to rotate the gradient by a one-quarter revolution so it starts upward.

Now fill in the Path closure in the view's body with the following code:

```
// 1
for index in values.indices {
  let value = values[index]
  // 2
  let radians = Angle(degrees: 72.0 * Double(index)).radians
  // 3
  let x = sin(radians) * graphSize * value
  let y = cos(radians) * -graphSize * value
  // 4
  if index == 0 {
    path.move(to: .init(x: x, y: y))
  } else {
    path.addLine(to: .init(x: x, y: y))
  }
}
// 5
path.closeSubpath()
```

Here's how this code works:

1. Since you're inside a Path closure, you use the standard Swift for in loop instead of ForEach. You then get the value for the current iteration.

2. When plotting the values, you determine the angle of this measurement. You use the same 72 degrees angle and convert it to radians as you did before, since both sin and cos expect radian values.

3. Earlier, you let SwiftUI rotate the lines, but you need to do it yourself in this view. To calculate the x and y values for a point of a specific length at a specified angle, you multiply the sine of the angle by the distance to calculate `x`. You multiply the cosine of the angle by the length to calculate `y`. You use a negative value for y because trigonometric functions assume y increases upward and in a counter-clockwise direction while in SwiftUI angles increase clockwise and y increases going down the view.

4. The first time through the loop, you need to use `move(to:)` to start the path. For the remainder of the shape, you call `addLine(to:)` to add the new point with a line back to the previous point.

5. To finalize the path, you call `closeSubpath()` on the `Path`. This method draws a line back to the start of the path to close the polygon.

Now you'll let SwiftUI handle the offset and apply the gradient. Add the following code as modifiers to the `Path` you just added:

```
.offset(x: xCenter, y: yCenter)
.fill(gradientColors)
.opacity(0.5)
```

The first modifier offsets the `Path`, so the center lies at the center of the view. You then apply the gradient and reduce the opacity, so the gradient colors don't overwhelm the chart.

Finally, use `PolygonChartView` in `AnimatedRadarChart` by adding this piece of code at the end of the `GeometryReader`:

```
PolygonChartView(
  values: values,
  graphSize: graphSize,
  colorArray: lineColors,
  xCenter: xCenter,
  yCenter: yCenter
)
```

Your preview will now show the final chart using the sample data.

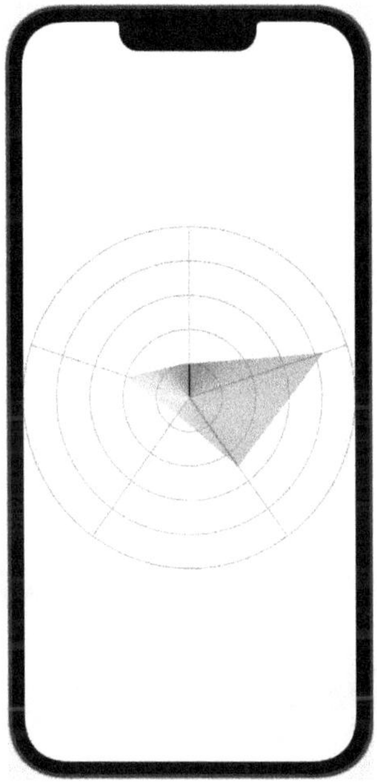

Now it's time to integrate the new chart into your app.

Using the Radar Chart

Open **TeaRatingsView.swift**. Now add the following code at the end of the `ZStack` in place of the comment reading `// Add Radar Chart Here`:

```
AnimatedRadarChart(
  time: Double(ratings[selectedRating].time),
  temperature: Double(ratings[selectedRating].temperature),
  amountWater: ratings[selectedRating].amountWater,
  amountTea: ratings[selectedRating].amountTea,
  rating: Double(ratings[selectedRating].rating)
)
.aspectRatio(contentMode: .fit)
.animation(.linear, value: selectedRating)
.padding(20)
.background(
  RoundedRectangle(cornerRadius: 20)
    .fill(Color("QuarterSpanishWhite"))
)
```

You add the radar chart below the swipeable area. It'll display the chart for the current rating through the `selectedRating` index.

Run the app and select either **Green Tea** or **Oolong Tea**. Tap the **Ratings** area, and the app will show the radar chart. Change between them by swiping or tapping the indicator squares, and you'll see the chart changes to match.

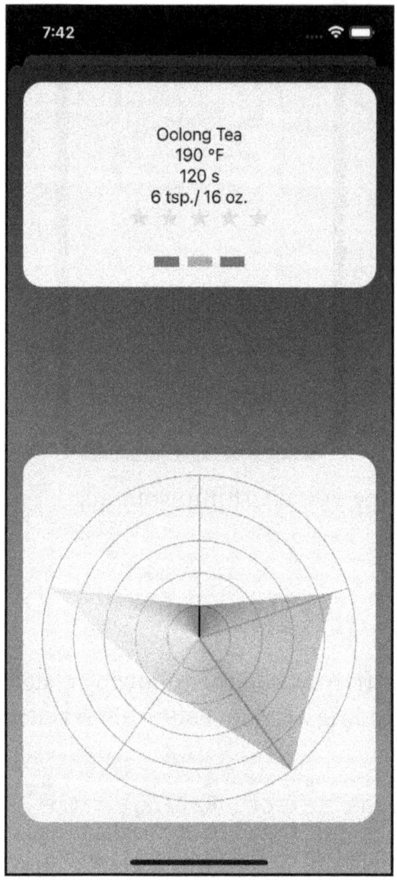

You might've noticed that despite the implicit animation applied when `selectedRating` changes, there's no animation. In the next section, you'll learn how to animate a view with multiple properties using `AnimatablePair`.

Animating the Radar Chart

When you need to animate a single value, you conform to the `Animatable` protocol. This protocol uses a property named `animatableData` that SwiftUI uses to pass the changing value into your view. In **Chapter 6: Intro to Custom Animations**, you set `animatableData` to a `Double`. So how can you manage five `Doubles`?

SwiftUI provides `AnimatablePair` especially for these cases. As the name implies, it supports two values instead of a single value. For example, the following code would expect two animated values for a view:

```
AnimatablePair<Double, Double>
```

So how would you handle the five values needed in this view? By nesting `AnimatablePairs`. Update the definition of `AnimatedRadarChart` to:

```
struct AnimatedRadarChart: View, Animatable {
```

Now add the following code after the properties for the view:

```
// 1
var animatableData: AnimatablePair<
  // 2
  AnimatablePair<Double, Double>,
  // 3
  AnimatablePair<
    // 4
    AnimatablePair<Double, Double>,
    // 5
    Double
  >
>
```

This code looks more complicated than it actually is. Here's how this block of code lets SwiftUI pass in animated values:

1. You begin by defining the `animatableData` property required by the Animatable protocol as a type of `AnimatablePair`. You then specify two values for the pair.
2. For the first element of the pair, you define another `AnimatablePair`, which takes two `Double` values. Each `AnimatablePair` has two properties named `first` and `second` used to access their elements. This means that `animatableData.first` now consists of an `AnimatablePair` with elements you can access by ``animatableData.first.firstandanimatableData.first.second`.

3. For the second element of the top level `AnimatablePair`, which you access through `animatableData.second`, you define another `AnimatablePair`.

4. The first element of this new `AnimatablePair` consists of another `AnimatablePair` of two `Doubles` as the first element.

5. The second element of that last `AnimatablePair` is a `Double`. As you can see, this gives you a total of the five `Double` values that you need.

This diagram shows how the elements flow from each other and how to access each element. You can continue this pattern if needed, but as you can see, it's pretty complicated at five values.

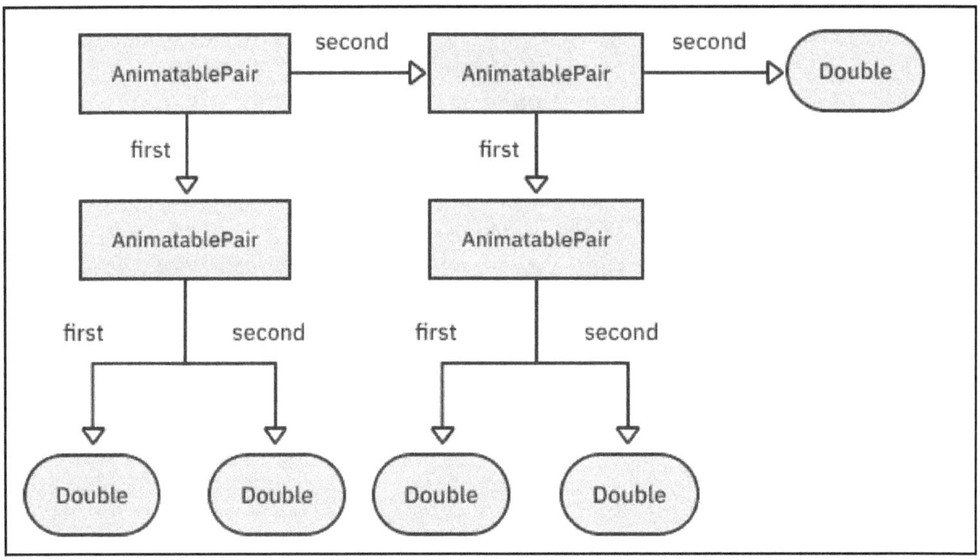

Next you'll need to assign each of the values in the nested `AnimatablePairs` to a property in the view. You want the first property in the view to match the first value in `animatableData`.

Here's a diagram showing how the design ties to specific values:

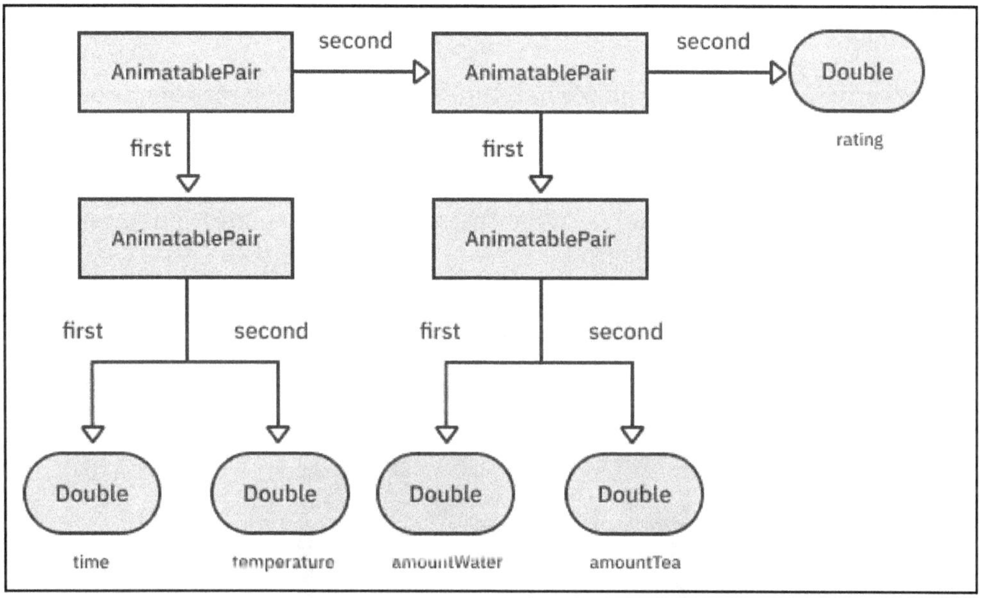

The getter and setter for the property then need to translate between these elements of the nested structures and the properties on the view. Add the following code directly after the declaration of `animatableData`. The first line replaces the lone closing > symbol in the last code block:

```
> {
  get {
    // 1
    AnimatablePair(
      AnimatablePair(time, temperature),
      AnimatablePair(
        AnimatablePair(amountWater, amountTea),
        rating
      )
    )
  }
  set {
    // 2
    time = newValue.first.first
    temperature = newValue.first.second
    amountWater = newValue.second.first.first
    amountTea = newValue.second.first.second
    rating = newValue.second.second
  }
}
```

Follow the diagram, and you'll see how the data structure for the `AnimatablePair` maps to the properties and the structure's properties. Here are the specifics for the two methods:

1. The getter for the property needs to return a value matching the complicated structure you defined earlier. You create a series of nested `AnimatablePair` types with the values set as shown in the diagram.
2. Setting the view's properties from the `AnimatablePair` requires you to navigate the `first` and `second` properties.

While complicated, this code wraps up everything needed to animate the view. Run the app and select either **Green Tea** or **Oolong Tea**. Tap the **Ratings** area, and the radar chart shows each rating when selected. As you change between the ratings, you'll see the view now animates between the charts.

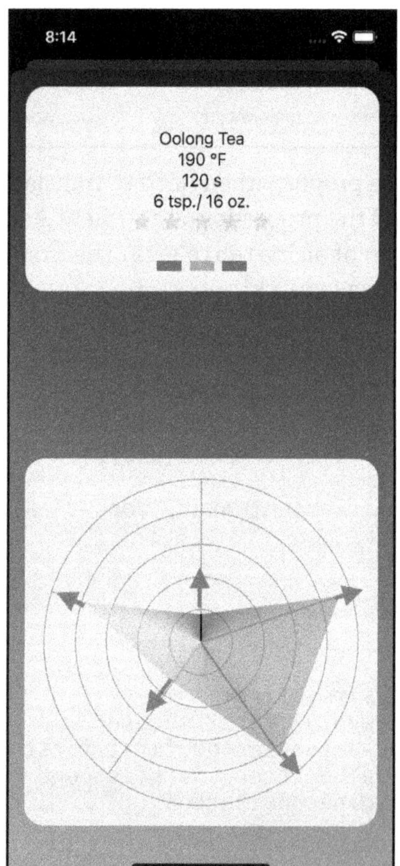

Key Points

- Transitions are a type of animation. When combining transitions, you'll find it easier to use different state changes to control each individually.
- You can apply an animation to a transition that will set the transition's animation curve and duration.
- A radar chart provides a way to visualize the relationship between multiple related values.
- You can use the `AnimatablePair` type when you need to animate multiple values in a view that conforms to the `Animatable` protocol.
- If you need to animate more than two values, you can nest multiple `AnimatablePair` structures within each other. While this can quickly become complicated, it'll let you support many values.

Where to Go From Here?

- For more about the relationship between angles and trigonometric methods, see Core Graphics Tutorial: Arcs and Paths (https://www.kodeco.com/349664-core-graphics-tutorial-arcs-and-paths).
- The new Swift Charts API (https://developer.apple.com/documentation/charts) handles many cases and supports animation, though not the radar chart used here.
- For more examples of creating charts in SwiftUI without the Swift Charts API, see SwiftUI Tutorial for iOS: Creating Charts (https://www.kodeco.com/6398124-swiftui-tutorial-for-ios-creating-charts).

Chapter 8: Time-Based Animations

By Bill Morefield

Using SwiftUI effectively requires adapting an app's UI based on its state. The animations you've used in the app for the last few chapters all animate based on state changes. The timer view you created in **Chapter 6: Intro to Custom Animations** used Combine to create a timer and publish events your view used to trigger changes to the timer. In earlier versions of SwiftUI, if you wanted to update a view at regular intervals, like a timer, then you had to use this method.

Then `TimelineView` arrived. Instead of providing layout or control, `TimelineView` acts only as a container that redraws its content at scheduled points in time, regardless of any state changes. The same version of SwiftUI also added the `Canvas` view, which provides a way to produce efficient 2D graphics inside a SwiftUI view. In this chapter, you'll combine these elements to create an animated analog timer for your tea brewing app.

Exploring the TimelineView

Open the starter project for this chapter, and you'll see the Brew Timer app from the past few chapters. Open **AnalogTimerView.swift** under the **Timer** group. Don't worry about all the commented code. You'll use it in a minute.

Now replace the view's body with:

```
TimelineView(.periodic(
  from: .now,
  by: 1.0
)) { context in
  Text(context.date.formatted(
    date: .omitted,
    time: .complete
  ))
}
```

The argument to the Timeline view provides a schedule that SwiftUI uses to update its content. Here you use the `periodic(from:by:)` schedule to specify the view should start updating immediately and refresh once per second.

The `context` provided to the closure provides the date that triggered in its `date` property. You use `formatted(date:time:)` to show only the time component of the property. In the preview, you'll see that you built a functional clock in just three lines of code.

Simple text based clock.

Note that the view contains no state information and updates without any state to change. That's the power of the TimelineView. It lets you create a view that updates based on time, not state.

Now add the following code to the top of the view:

```
@State var timerLength = 0.0
@State var timeLeft: Int?
@State var status: TimerStatus = .stopped
@State var timerEndTime: Date?
```

You will later set the initial value of timerLength to the value of the passed in timer and add a control letting the user adjust it. The other three properties will track the status and remaining time for the timer when active.

Next, uncomment the three methods in the view by selecting them and selecting **Editor ▸ Structure ▸ Comment Selection**, or pressing **Command-/**. These methods calculate the amount of time remaining on the timer based on the status and timerEndTime of the timer. Go to **AnalogTimerView.swift** and replace its body:

```
VStack {
  // 1
  Slider(value: $timerLength, in: 0...600, step: 15)
  // 2
  TimerControlView(
    timerLength: timerLength,
    timeLeft: $timeLeft,
    status: $status,
    timerEndTime: $timerEndTime,
    timerFinished: $timerFinished
  )
  .font(.title)
  // Place timeline here
}
.onAppear {
  // 3
  timerLength = Double(timer.timerLength)
}
```

Here's how the start of your timer works:

1. You provide a Slider so the user can adjust the default timer length. Note that the value bound to the slider must be a Double though you'll convert it to an Int when used.

2. You use the already provided TimerControlView, which manages the state of the timer and provides buttons to control it.

3. When the VStack first appears, you set the timerLength. Notice the need to convert to a Double as mentioned in step one.

Next, add the new timer view in place of // Place timeline here:

```
TimelineView(.periodic(
  from: .now,
  by: 1
)) { context in
  let timeString = timeLeftString(timeLeftAt(context.date))
  Text(timeString)
    .font(.title)
}
```

This TimelineView updates once per second. Within the view, you use the timeLeftAt(_:) uncommented earlier to get the number of seconds remaining on the timer and then convert that to a formatted string using timeLeftString(_:). It then displays the string on the view.

Notice that you include only the part of the view affected by time change inside the closure. Since SwiftUI updates *all* views contained inside the closure of a TimelineView, including views that don't change decreases performance without adding any benefit.

Run the app, and you'll see it already uses the new AnalogTimerView. Start the timer. It works much like before and displays the remaining time as text.

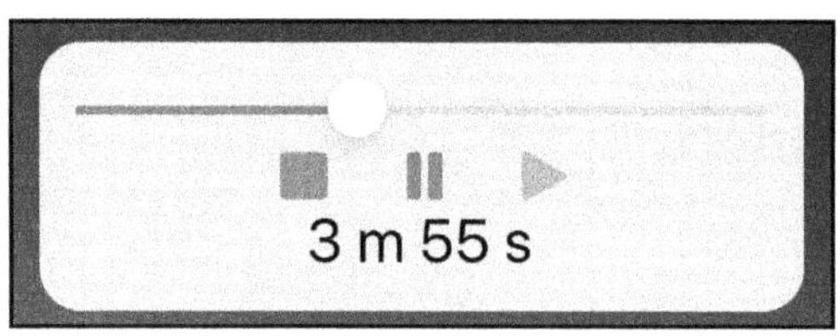

Steeping Timer with New Timer View

Open **TimerView.swift** and notice how much less code you need now that SwiftUI updates the views based on time. In addition, you no longer need the TimerManager class. As you can see, TimelineView greatly simplifies updating a time-based app. In the next section, you'll see how to draw graphics using a Canvas view.

Drawing With a Canvas

All animations are consecutive images that change over time to provide the illusion of movement. Most of the examples in this book change a view's state and then allow SwiftUI to manage the process of translating that state change into animation.

Since a `TimelineView` doesn't include a state change, you're responsible for creating the changing views yourself. In this section, you'll start developing an analog timer by combining the `TimelineView` with another SwiftUI view — `Canvas`.

Using a `Canvas` makes it much easier to produce two-dimensional graphics inside a SwiftUI view. Since drawing code is quite lengthy, you'll split the different parts of the timer into separate methods.

In **AnalogTimerView.swift**, add the following new method to it:

```
func drawBorder(context: GraphicsContext, size: Int) {
  // 1
  let timerSize = CGSize(width: size, height: size)
  // 2
  let outerPath = Path(
    ellipseIn: CGRect(origin: .zero, size: timerSize)
  )
  // 3
  context.stroke(
    outerPath,
    with: .color(.black),
    lineWidth: 3
  )
}
```

Separating the code keeps it manageable and makes your final view neater. Here's what this method does:

1. The method's `size` parameter provides the desired size for the timer. You create a `CGSize` with this value as the width and height.

2. You'll often use SwiftUI `Paths` when working with the canvas. In this case, you use the `Path` initializer that creates an ellipse using the `timerSize` from step one. Since the width and height are equal, the path defines a circle.

3. You have a path and now want to stroke the path onto the canvas. So, you call `stroke(_:with:lineWidth:)` on the canvas. It strokes the ellipse in black as a line three points wide.

Delete the current `TimelineView` and replace it with:

```
// 1
ZStack {
  // 2
  Canvas { gContext, size in
    // 3
    let timerSize = Int(min(size.width, size.height))
    drawBorder(context: gContext, size: timerSize)
  }
}
.padding()
```

Here's how your first canvas-based code works:

1. A `ZStack` lets you stack several views that SwiftUI aligns for you. Using the `ZStack` lets you separate the animated and non-animated portions of the view, so the result aligns as though created in a single canvas.
2. Then you declare a `Canvas`. SwiftUI passes two arguments into the closure. The first argument is a `GraphicsContext` you use for drawing. The second contains information about the view size you use to scale the view to match the container.
3. You determine which dimension is smaller, the width or height of the `Canvas`, and convert it to an integer. You pass this value to the `drawBorder(context:size:)` you created along with the graphics context.

Build and run the app. Tap any tea type, and you'll see the border for the new timer.

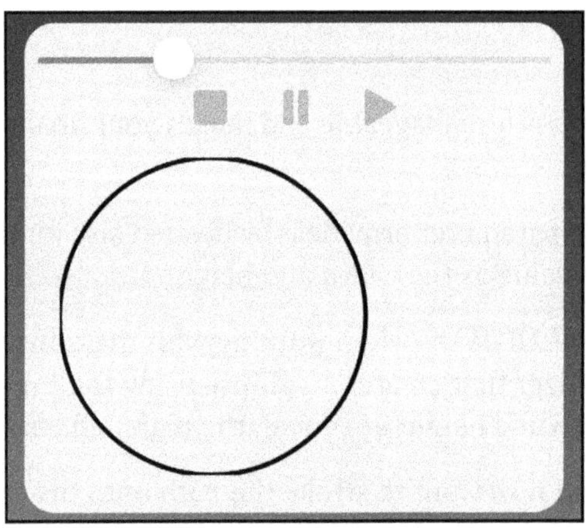

Timer with border.

You'll also see a problem with the border: the circle's edges are clipped on three sides, creating flat spots. The view shows there because you set the edge of the `CGRect` at the origin. Some of the extra thickness of the line gets lost outside the view. The circle also lies along the left side of the view and would look nicer centered.

First, you'll add a small border around the timer to fix these two issues. Change the definition of `timerSize` to:

```
let timerSize = Int(min(size.width, size.height) * 0.95)
```

You reduce the size of the timer to 0.95 of the canvas's smallest dimension. This reduced space allows the timer's thicker border to show within the view.

Now you'll calculate an offset to center the timer. Add the following code between defining `timerSize` and calling `drawBorder(context:size:)`.

```
// 4
let xOffset = (size.width - Double(timerSize)) / 2.0
// 5
let yOffset = (size.height - Double(timerSize)) / 2.0
// 6
gContext.translateBy(x: xOffset, y: yOffset)
```

Here's how this code centers the view:

1. You calculate the offset needed to center the view by subtracting the width of the timer in `timerSize` from the total width of the canvas after converting the latter to a `Double`. You divide this value by two to evenly split the space on both sides of the timer.

2. Then, you perform the same calculation in the vertical axis with the canvas height and the size of the timer. Again, you divide this by two to evenly split the space on both sides of the timer.

3. Finally, you call `translateBy(x:y:)` on the `GraphicsContext` to move future drawing operations by the amount calculated in the previous two steps. This method shifts the origin for future drawing operations by the amount specified. Note that when you change the `GraphicsContext`, *all* future drawing operations reflect this change.

Run the app and tap any tea. The timer now centers on the view and no longer clips the circle.

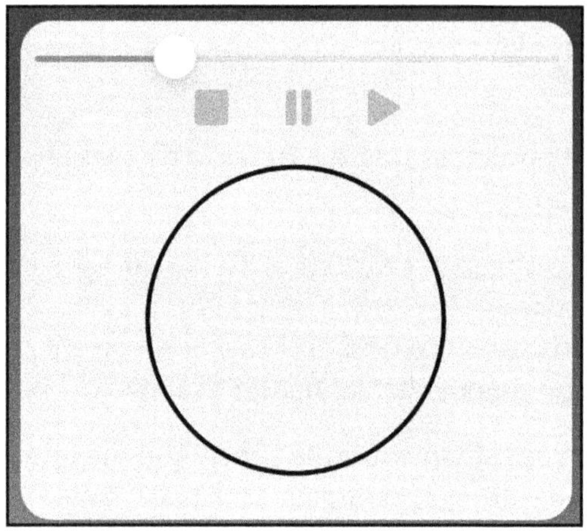

Timer centered in the containing view.

Now that you've explored the basics of `Canvas`, you'll add more features to the timer.

Drawing Tick Marks

Tick marks help the user interpret the position of the timer's hands. In this section, you'll add tick marks to the timer.

Add this new method in front of the `AnalogTimerView`'s body:

```
func drawMinutes(context: GraphicsContext, size: Int) {
  // 1
  let center = Double(size / 2)

  // 2
  for minute in 0..<10 {
    // 3
    let minuteAngle = Double(minute) / 10 * 360.0
    // 4
    let minuteTickPath = Path { path in
      path.move(to: .init(x: center, y: 0))
      path.addLine(to: .init(x: center * 0.9, y: 0))
    }
  }
}
```

Like before, drawing code tends to be long. So this code is split into two parts. Here's how it works step-by-step:

1. The `size` parameter provides the size of the full timer. You divide it by two to get the number of points from the center of the timer to the edge. You'll use this to position the different parts of the timer.

2. This loop counts through all integers between zero and nine. Since the maximum timer length is ten minutes, this provides minute marks and indicators for all possible numbers.

3. Then, you calculate the ratio of the current minute value to the total number of minutes. You then multiply that ratio by the 360 degrees that make a full rotation to get the fraction of a full rotation for the current position.

4. You create a `Path` and use `move(to:)` to move the current position to the edge of the timer at the right. You then add a line to the point one-tenth of the way back toward the center. Using a ratio instead of hard-coded points allows the timer to scale to different sized views.

Now add the following code to the end of the `for` loop:

```
// 4
var tickContext = context
// 6
tickContext.rotate(by: .degrees(-minuteAngle))
// 7
tickContext.stroke(
  minuteTickPath,
  with: .color(.black)
)
```

This code uses a technique that you'll use with a `Canvas`:

5. The `GraphicsContext` passed into the method is immutable, so you can't use methods that modify its state, like a rotation or translation. You create a mutable copy and change it instead. This step works because the `GraphicsContext` is a value type. With a value type, changes to the copy don't affect the original context.

6. You rotate the context by the negative number of degrees calculated in step three. Using a negative degree produces a counter-clockwise rotation.

7. `stroke(_:with:lineWidth:)` draws the path in black on the context using the default width of one point.

Go back to the view body and add the following code to the body after the call to `drawBorder(context:size:)`:

```
gContext.translateBy(
  x: Double(timerSize / 2),
  y: Double(timerSize / 2)
)
gContext.rotate(by: .degrees(-90))
drawMinutes(context: gContext, size: timerSize)
```

The `drawMinutes(context:size:)` method's implicit assumption is that the origin lies at the center of the timer. To make this accurate, you use `translateBy(x:y:)` to shift the origin to the center of the canvas. Recall that you already offset the origin by a small amount to draw the border. Since `timerSize` contains the size of the timer, then half of it will move its origin to the center.

You then rotate the canvas by -90 degrees. By default, a zero-degree rotation lies to the right of the origin. For this view, you want it to be above the origin, and this rotation accomplishes that. Now no rotation will appear above the center of the timer. You then call the new method to draw the tick marks.

Now run the app and tap any tea. You'll see your new tick marks added to the timer.

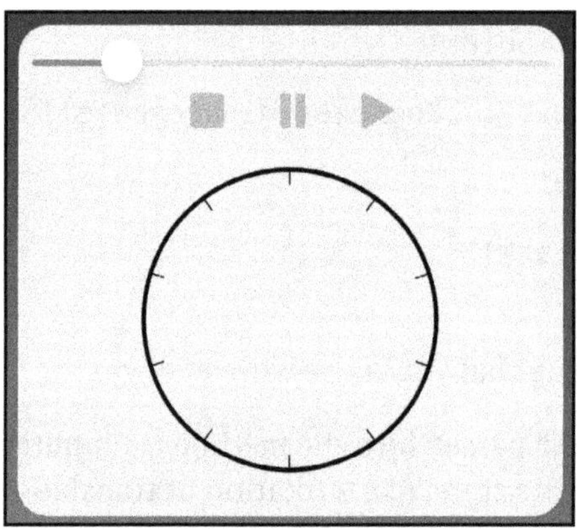

Timer with tick marks.

Adding Text to a Canvas

While the tick marks help the user interpret the timer's position, adding numbers increases understanding by clarifying the time for a given tick mark. Fortunately, adding text to a canvas isn't much more complex than adding other elements.

Still in **AnalogTimerView.swift**, find the `drawMinutes(context:size:)` you created in the previous section. Now add the following code to the end of the `for-in` loop after the call to `stroke(_:with:lineWidth:)`:

```
// 1
let minuteString = "\(minute)"
let textSize = minuteString.calculateTextSizeFor(
  font: UIFont.preferredFont(forTextStyle: .title2)
)
// 2
let textRect = CGRect(
  origin: .init(
    x: -textSize.width / 2.0,
    y: -textSize.height / 2.0
  ),
  size: .zero
)
// 3
let minuteAngleRadians = Angle(degrees: minuteAngle -
90).radians
// 4
let xShift = sin(-minuteAngleRadians) * center * 0.8
let yShift = cos(-minuteAngleRadians) * center * 0.8
```

Drawing text requires some additional setup. Here's how you prepare for it:

1. You create a string from `minute`. Then you use `calculateTextSizeFor(font:)`, an extension method found in **StringExtensions.swift** that calculates the size of the rectangle needed to contain this text for a `UIFont`. There's no way to easily convert between a SwiftUI `Font` and a `UIFont`, so you pass in the `UIFont` equivalent for the `.title2` font you'll use for the number.

2. You create a `CGRect` that centers an object with the size you calculated in step one. You'll use this later when drawing the text onto the canvas.

3. Up to this point, you used `rotate(by:)` to rotate objects to the proper location. That won't work for this case because it also rotates the text. However, you can use trigonometric functions to calculate the location of a desired angle and distance. Since you're calculating the location, the rotation you applied to the entire canvas no longer applies. You must subtract 90 degrees from the angle to set the zero angle vertically above the center instead of to the right. Finally, you convert the angle from degrees to the radians unit type expected by Swift trigonometric functions.

4. To calculate the position of a point along an angle, you use the trigonometric sine function to get the horizontal position and the cosine function to get the vertical position. Passing the negative of the angle to these functions causes the numbers to increase clockwise instead of in the default counter-clockwise direction. You multiply the distance to the edge of the timer by 0.8 to position the text inside the tick marks drawn in the previous section.

Add the following code to put these calculations to use:

```
// 5
var stringContext = context
stringContext.translateBy(x: xShift, y: yShift)
stringContext.rotate(by: .degrees(90))
// 6
let resolvedText = stringContext.resolve(
  Text(minuteString).font(.title2)
)
// 7
stringContext.draw(resolvedText, in: textRect)
```

Again, this looks complicated. Here's how each step works:

5. You create a second copy of the original graphics context. This copy won't contain the changes you made to `tickContext`. Then you translate the origin by the amount calculated in step four. While the initial -90 degree rotation doesn't apply to your calculation in step four, it will apply to drawing the text. You use the opposite rotation to undo it. Otherwise, the text would be rotated a quarter turn counter-clockwise.

6. You can draw a string, but using `resolve(_:)` on the `GraphicsContext` provides more flexibility. Here you use the method to apply `font(_:)` to format the text. Note the specified font matches the `UIFont` you used in step one.

7. The `draw(_:in:)` on the `GraphicsContext` draws the text onto the canvas. Using `ResolvedText` from step six produces formatted text matching the SwiftUI view. You use the `CGRect` calculated in step two to center the text around the current origin point you set in step five.

Run the app, select any tea and you'll see the new numbers on the timer.

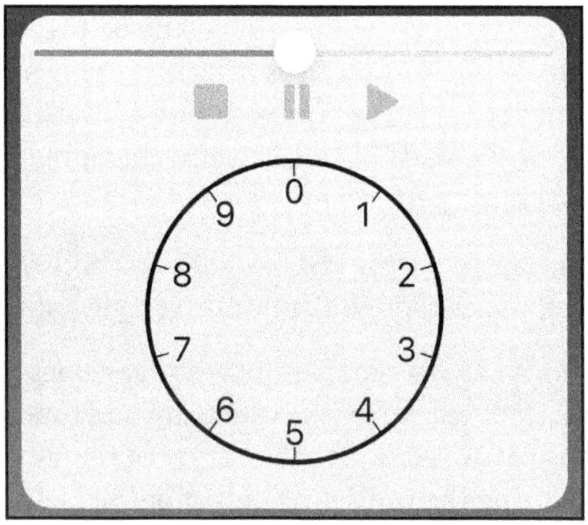

Timer with numbers added.

With the static parts of the timer in place, you can add the timer's hands and animate them.

Letting the Timer... Time

You want to animate the hands of the timer, so once you draw them, you'll also wrap them inside a `TimelineView` to control the timing of their movement.

In `AnalogTimerView`'s boy, add the following code after the current `Canvas` and inside the `ZStack`:

```
// 1
TimelineView(.animation) { timeContext in
  // 2
  Canvas { gContext, size in
    // 3
    let timerSize = Int(min(size.width, size.height))
    gContext.translateBy(
      x: size.width / 2,
      y: size.height / 2
    )
    gContext.rotate(by: .degrees(-90))
  }
}
```

Here's what the new code does:

1. You create a `TimelineView`, but pass in a schedule of `animation`. This value asks SwiftUI to reevaluate the view as often as possible. Doing so produces the smoothest animation at the cost of higher resource usage due to the frequency of redrawn views. Moving the parts of the view not changing outside the `TimelineView` reduces this performance cost.
2. You create a new `Canvas`. Since the `ZStack` contains both views, it aligns them, letting you draw on them as though they were a single `Canvas`.
3. While changes within a `Canvas` persist, a new `Canvas` doesn't inherit any settings of the other `Canvas`. Here you apply the centering and rotation you did to the first `Canvas`. You only draw relative to the center of the timer, so you can simplify the calculation and divide the width and height of the `Canvas` by two.

Now add the code for the following new method just before the body of the view:

```
func createHandPath(
  length: Double,
  crossDistance: Double,
  middleDistance: Double,
  endDistance: Double,
  width: Double
) -> Path {
  // 1
  Path {
    path.move(to: .zero)

    // 2
    let halfWidth = width / 2.0
    let crossLength = length * crossDistance
    let middleLength = length * middleDistance
    let halfWidthLength = length * halfWidth

    // 3
    path.addCurve(
      to: .init(x: crossLength, y: 0),
      control1: .init(x: crossLength, y: -halfWidthLength),
      control2: .init(x: crossLength, y: -halfWidthLength)
    )
    path.addCurve(
      to: .init(x: length * endDistance, y: 0),
      control1: .init(x: middleDistance, y: halfWidthLength),
      control2: .init(x: middleDistance, y: halfWidthLength)
    )
    path.addCurve(
      to: .init(x: crossLength, y: 0),
      control1: .init(x: middleDistance, y: -halfWidthLength),
      control2: .init(x: middleDistance, y: -halfWidthLength)
```

```
    )
    path.addCurve(
      to: .zero,
      control1: .init(x: crossLength, y: halfWidthLength),
      control2: .init(x: crossLength, y: halfWidthLength)
    )
  }
}
```

Both of the timer's hands have a similar design that only varies in width and length. This method creates the path based on the values you pass to it. Here's how it builds the path:

1. You create an empty path and move the current position to the origin. Recall that you already shifted the origin to the center of the `Canvas` in the view.

2. You take the desired width and divide it by two to get a half width that you'll use to mirror the shape, and also calculate a few values you'll need for the control points in the next step.

3. You then add four cubic Bézier curves to the path. A cubic Bézier curve uses two control points to define the shape of the curve. The combined curves trace out the hands as two parts, the first a more rounded curve with a longer, smoother curve at the end. You define the shape and width of the curves with the parameters passed to the method.

Now, add a method to draw the timer's hands. Add the following new method after `createHandPath(...)`:

```
func drawHands(
  context: GraphicsContext,
  size: Int,
  remainingTime: Double
) {
  // 1
  let length = Double(size / 2)
  // 2
  let secondsLeft =
remainingTime.truncatingRemainder(dividingBy: 60)
  // 3
  let secondAngle = secondsLeft / 60 * 360

  // 4
  let minuteColor = Color("DarkOliveGreen")
  let secondColor = Color("BlackRussian")

  let secondHandPath = createHandPath(
    length: length,
```

```
      crossDistance: 0.4,
      middleDistance: 0.6,
      endDistance: 0.7,
      width: 0.07
    )
  }
```

This method begins by drawing the timer's second hand:

1. You calculate the maximum length of the hands by dividing the size of the timer by two, as you've done before.
2. `truncatingRemainder(dividingBy:)` functions with a double as the remainder operator (`%`) acts on integers. Here it gives you only the seconds component of the remaining time.
3. You determine the ratio of the current number of seconds to the 60 seconds of a full rotation. You multiply this amount by 360 to convert this ratio to degrees of a full circle. Note that the `remainingTime` passed to this method includes fractional seconds, which allows you to calculate a more granular position and produce a smoother animation.
4. Then, you define constants for the colors you'll use for the hands and call `createHandPath(...)` to produce a path for the second hand.

With a path for the second hand, you can now draw it. Add the following code to the end of `drawHands(context:size:remainingTime:)`:

```
var secondContext = context
secondContext.rotate(by: .degrees(secondAngle))
secondContext.fill(
  secondHandPath,
  with: .color(secondColor)
)
secondContext.stroke(
  secondHandPath,
  with: .color(secondColor),
  lineWidth: 3
)
```

First, you create a copy of the graphics context and rotate it by the angle calculated in step three above. You then fill and stroke the path in the color you defined in step four. Doing both operations on the path produces a shape with more weight.

Now you'll add the calls to draw your clock's hand. Find the `Canvas` inside the `TimelineView` in your view. Add the following code to the end of the `Canvas`:

```
let remainingSeconds = decimalTimeLeftAt(timeContext.date)
drawHands(
  context: gContext,
  size: timerSize,
  remainingTime: remainingSeconds
)
```

First, you get the number of remaining seconds and store it in `remainingSeconds`. You then call `drawHands(context:size:remainingTime:)` passing the remaining seconds.

Run your app and start the timer. Watch it smoothly sweep through the seconds as the timer runs.

Timer with sweeping second hand.

With the second hand complete, you'll see that adding the minute hand to the timer in the next section works similarly.

Adding the Minute Hand

Add the following code to the end of `drawHands(context:size:remainingTime:)`:

```
// 1
let minutesLeft = remainingTime / 60
// 2
let minuteAngle = minutesLeft / 10 * 360
// 3
```

```
let minuteHandPath = createHandPath(
  length: length,
  crossDistance: 0.3,
  middleDistance: 0.5,
  endDistance: 0.6,
  width: 0.1
)
// 4
var minuteContext = context
minuteContext.rotate(by: .degrees(minuteAngle))
minuteContext.fill(
  minuteHandPath,
  with: .color(minuteColor)
)
minuteContext.stroke(
  minuteHandPath,
  with: .color(minuteColor),
  lineWidth: 5
)
```

This code matches the one you used to create the second hand with a few changes:

1. You divide the remaining time by 60 to get the number of minutes remaining. Note that the value includes the fraction of a minute. Dividing this value by the maximum timer length of ten minutes gives the ratio of the maximum timer.
2. You multiply this ratio by 360 to convert the minutes to a rotation in degrees.
3. Then, you create a path with different parameters, resulting in a broader and shorter hand than you used for the second hand.
4. Again, you create a copy of the context and rotate it by the value calculated in step one. You then fill and stroke the path as you did with the second hand, but use a wider width when stroking the path to add more weight to the broader minute hand.

Rerun your app, select any tea and watch the timer hands move as it counts down. The minute hand will move very slowly, and you may need to wait several seconds for it to move enough to notice.

Timer with second and minute hands.

You have a working animated analog timer. In the last section, you'll look at improving the performance.

Improving TimelineView Performance

A SwiftUI view should never update more often than it needs to. Right now, your `TimelineView` updates as often as SwiftUI can manage. In most cases, that's more often than necessary for the desired user experience and wastes resources.

While still in **AnalogTimerView.swift**, find the `TimelineView` in the body. Change the line to:

```
TimelineView(.periodic(
  from: .now,
  by: 1)
) { timeContext in
```

This change tells SwiftUI to update the view once per second, beginning immediately. Run the app now and start it for any tea. You'll see the second hand now "ticks". Instead of the previous smooth motion, it jumps to the next position every second.

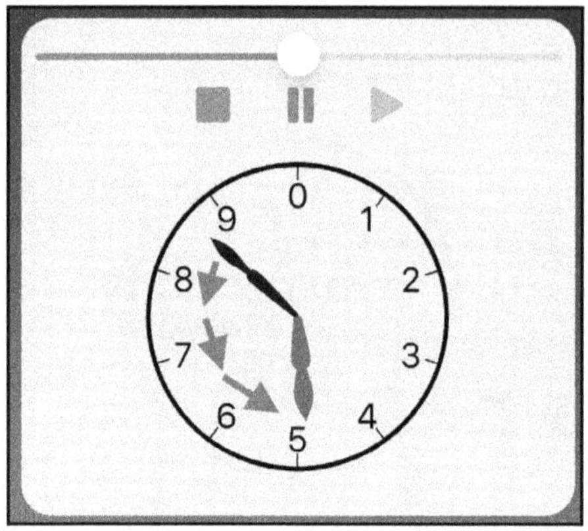

Timer with ticking second hand.

A view updating once per second produces better performance than one updating as fast as possible. The difference between a ticking timer and one with smooth motion is an aesthetic choice.

To keep the smooth motion while improving performance, you must find a balance where the second hand has smooth movement while updating as seldom as possible. You could do some complex math to calculate the minimum interval based on the view size, but it's just as effective to find a value that works for your app by trial and error. Change the `TimelineView` to:

```
TimelineView(
  .animation(minimumInterval: 0.1)
) { timeContext in
```

Run the app, and you'll see that the second hand appears to move smoothly, but updates will never occur more than ten times per second.

That solves the primary performance issue, but you must address one more point. Right now, the views inside the `TimelineView` update whenever the view is displayed. When the timer stops or pauses, the views update despite having no changes. SwiftUI provides a way to let it know when a `TimelineView` doesn't need updating.

Update the call to:

```
TimelineView(
  .animation(
    minimumInterval: 0.1,
    paused: status != .running
  )
) { timeContext in
```

You set the new `paused` parameter to true to let SwiftUI know there's no need to update the views in the closure. This app only needs to update the hands when the timer is running. You pause updates when the app isn't in the `.running` state.

Run the app and start a timer for any tea again. You'll notice no change when running since the timer no longer updates when not running.

Timer after performance improvements.

Challenge

Using what you learned in this chapter, add tick marks and numbers for the second hand to the timer. See one solution in the challenge project for this chapter.

Key Points

- A `TimelineView` redraws its content at scheduled points in time. You can specify this schedule in several ways or create a custom implementation for complex scenarios.
- `Canvas` lets you produce two-dimensional graphics inside a view. It resembles the pre-SwiftUI Core Graphics framework, though it still works with SwiftUI elements. You can call Core Graphics for complex methods or legacy code if needed.
- A `Canvas` also supplies a `GraphicsContext` within its closure. Methods that modify the `GraphicsContext` such as `translateBy(x:y:)` and `rotate(by:)` persist those changes to future drawing operations.
- You can create a mutable copy of a `GraphicsContext`. Since it's a value type, any changes you make to the copy won't affect the original `GraphicsContext`. You can use this to change a `GraphicsContext` without affecting its initial state.
- The `resolve(_:)` method on `GraphicsContext` helps you produce a text view that's fixed with the current values of the graphics context's environment. You can use this to change a SwiftUI Text view, including modifiers, to a format compatible with a `GraphicsContext`.

Where to Go From Here?

- The 2021 WWDC video Add rich graphics to your SwiftUI app (https://developer.apple.com/videos/play/wwdc2021/10021/) provides an introduction to the then new `Canvas` and `TimelineView` views.
- You can find another example using the Canvas and TimelineView in our Using TimelineView and Canvas in SwiftUI (https://www.kodeco.com/27594491-using-timelineview-and-canvas-in-swiftui) tutorial. This tutorial also shows how you can use **Core Graphics** and SwiftUI views with a `Canvas`.
- The Beginning Core Graphics (https://www.kodeco.com/3402-beginning-core-graphics) video course is an excellent resource for lower-level graphics operations.

Chapter 9: Combining Animations

By Bill Morefield

Most of this book's animations deal with user interaction. In earlier chapters, you used animation to draw the user's attention to the desired area in your app. These animations help guide the user while at the same time adding polish and improving the app's visual appearance.

In this chapter, you'll build an animation to act as a reward for the user when the steeping timer ends. This animation will show liquid pouring into the view's background and filling it up.

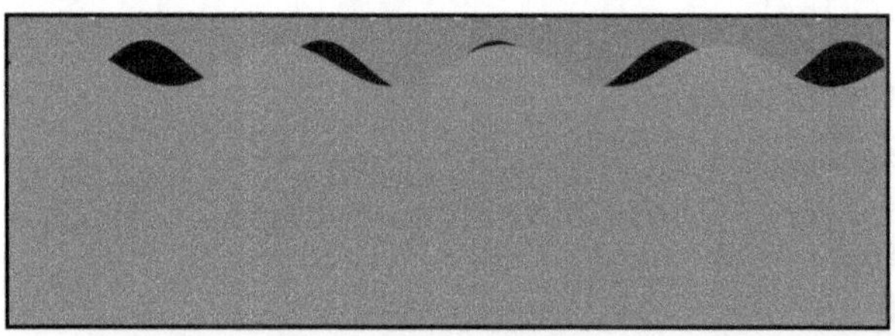

Since this is a more complex animation, you'll build it in two parts. First, you'll add the animation that resembles a rising liquid within a container. You'll then use **SpriteKit**'s particle system to add the pouring liquid that appears to fill the container.

Building a Background Animation

Open the starter project for this chapter. You'll see the familiar Tea Brewing from previous chapters.

The start project contains a new group called **PourAnimation**, which includes the `TimerComplete` view shown when a steeping timer finishes. To start the new animation, create a SwiftUI view file named **PourAnimationView.swift** in the **PourAnimation** folder`.

You'll use this view to contain the new animation's views. As with other animations, starting with a simple version and then expanding upon it to create the final animation is the easiest. At the top of the generated `struct`, add the following new properties:

```
@State var shapeTop = 900.0
let fillColor = Color(red: 0.180, green: 0.533, blue: 0.78)
```

This code adds a state property you'll use to control the animation. You also define a blue color you'll use as the liquid's color. Update the body of the view to:

```
// 1
Rectangle()
  // 2
  .fill(fillColor)
  // 3
  .offset(y: shapeTop)
  // 4
  .onAppear {
    withAnimation(.linear(duration: 6.0)) {
      shapeTop = 0.0
    }
  }
```

Here's what the code does:

1. You define a `Rectangle` shape that you'll replace with a more complex `Shape` later.

2. You fill the `Rectangle` with the blue color you defined earlier.

3. This offsets the rectangle by the amount of `shapeTop`. By changing `shapeTop`, you can change the position of the top of the rectangle on the view.

4. When the view appears, you use an explicit linear animation that takes six seconds to complete. SwiftUI will apply the animation when you change `shapeTop` to zero. The animation will then animate the movement of the `Rectangle` from the initial position to the top of the view.

You need to add this new view to the view that shows when the timer finishes. Open **TimerComplete.swift**. This view consists of a `ZStack`, which starts with a `backgroundGradient`. After the gradient and before the `VStack`, add the following code:

```
PourAnimationView()
```

Run the app and select any tea. Start the timer and wait for it to complete. Once the timer finishes, you'll see the animation as the blue rectangle fills the view over six seconds, like a cup filling with liquid. Remember, you can adjust the timer length.

Simple filled view clipped at the bottom.

The clipped area at the bottom seems out of place. By default, SwiftUI keeps a view from entering the device's safe area. To eliminate the bar at the bottom, you need to tell SwiftUI to allow the view to extend into that area.

In **TimerComplete.swift**, change the call to the view to:

```
PourAnimationView()
  .ignoresSafeArea(edges: [.bottom])
```

`ignoresSafeArea(_:edges:)` tells SwiftUI to allow the view to extend into part of that bottom part of the safe area.

Run the app, start a timer and let it complete. The `Rectangle`'s fill color now extends to the bottom of the screen.

Fill animation no longer clipped

Now that you've built the basics of the pouring animation, you'll make the top of the rising liquid more realistic in the next section.

Making a Wave Animation

If you watch a liquid pouting into a cup, you'll see the top of the liquid is anything but a smooth, flat surface. It makes a much more chaotic and complex flow.

While implementing actual fluid dynamics would be overkill, you can simulate a more complex shape to the pour using a sine wave. In this section, you'll implement a custom `Shape` and change the top of the animation to a sine wave.

In the **PourAnimation** folder, create a new SwiftUI view file named **WaveShape.swift**. You'll create a custom shape instead of a view, so replace the existing generated `struct` with:

```
struct WaveShape: Shape {
  func path(in rect: CGRect) -> Path {
    Path()
  }
}
```

A `Shape` returns a `Path` that defines the shape instead of a `View`. SwiftUI passes a `CGRect` struct as a parameter to the method. It contains the size of the container for the shape. This initial implementation only returns an empty path, but not for long.

To see your shape in the preview as you develop it, change the preview to:

```
WaveShape()
  .stroke(.black)
  .offset(y: 200)
```

This change strokes the path in black in the preview. It also uses a vertical offset, so the full path shows on the preview. Otherwise, you'd cut off the top portion when SwiftUI draws it on the view.

In previous chapters, you used sine and other trigonometric functions in animations when drawing lines at an angle. Here, you'll use it since the top of your shape will be a sine wave.

The plot of the sine function from zero through 360 degrees looks like this:

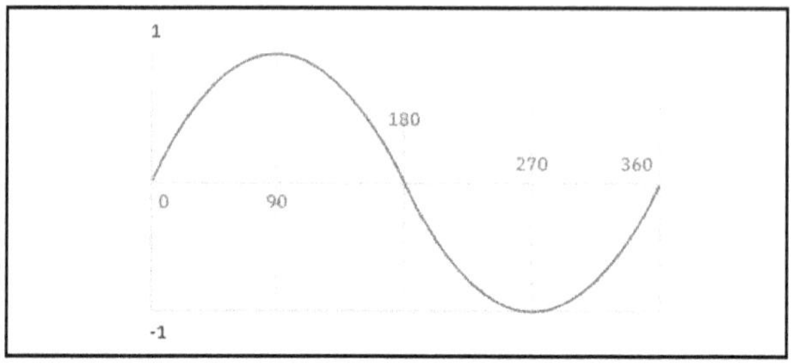

A sine graph

It produces a perfect wave shape with the vertical axis ranging between negative one and one over the distance. Due to the definition of a sine function, the wave varies regularly over the 360 degrees that make up a single revolution of a circle. After 360 degrees, the values repeat with y taking on the same value it did at the same angle minus 360 degrees.

To implement this shape in SwiftUI, replace the closure of `path(in:)` with:

```
// 1
Path { path in
  // 2
  for x in 0 ..< Int(rect.width) {
    // 3
    let angle = Double(x) / rect.width * 360
    // 4
    let y = sin(Angle(degrees: angle).radians) * 100
    // 5
    if x == 0 {
      path.move(to: .init(x: Double(x), y: -y))
    } else {
      path.addLine(to: .init(x: Double(x), y: -y))
    }
  }
}
```

Here's how this code draws the sine wave as a shape:

1. You create an an empty Path and accept a `path` to manipulate in the trailing closure's body.
2. You iterate all `x` positions in the rectangle using a `for-in` loop. This loop ensures you perform only the necessary calculations for the shape's size.

3. For each x position, you calculate the angle it should reflect by dividing it by the total width of the rectangle. This result gives you the position as a fraction of the full width. You then multiply this fraction by 360, giving you the position as a degree of a full 360-degree circle.
4. You get the sine of the angle from step three using the `sin` method. You convert from degrees to radians inside the function, as with other Swift trigonometric functions. Since this will provide a value between negative one and one, you multiply it by 100, increasing the wave's size.
5. The first time through the loop, you move the path location to the current horizontal position and the vertical position calculated in the last step. After that, you draw a line from the current position to the following path position. Since increasing values of `y` on a `Path` are downward on the view, you take the negative of `y` to flip positive values upward.

The preview for the shape shows you a simple sine wave:

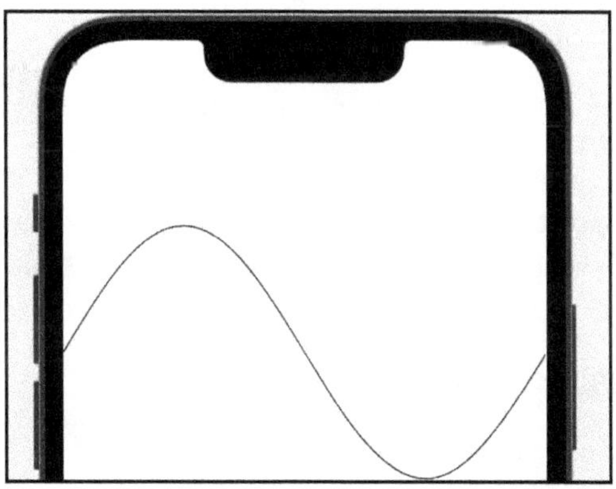

Initial sine graph drawn in a view

To make this work in your animation, it must produce a completely closed shape like the `Rectangle`. You also need to let the calling view specify a position for the top of the shape. You'll do that in the next section.

Animating the Sine Wave

Add the following new property to the top of the `Shape` before `path(in:)`:

```
var waveTop: Double = 0.0
```

This property lets the calling view control the location of the sine wave. Update the code under comment five to:

```
// 5
if x == 0 {
  path.move(to: .init(
    x: Double(x),
    y: waveTop - y
  ))
} else {
  path.addLine(to: .init(
    x: Double(x),
    y: waveTop - y
  ))
}
```

This change adds the value of `waveTop` to the vertical position of the view. A positive value shifts the wave's position down the shape.

To close the shape, add the following code after the `for-in` loop:

```
path.addLine(to: .init(x: rect.width, y: rect.height))
path.addLine(to: .init(x: 0, y: rect.height))
path.closeSubpath()
```

`for-in` ends with the position on the right edge of the view. So you add a line to the bottom-right of the view before adding a line to the left-bottom side of the view. You then call `closeSubpath()` on the path to ensure it forms a closed shape.

To better see the difference, change the preview to:

```
WaveShape(waveTop: 200.0)
  .fill(.black)
```

The shape fills in from the view's bottom up to a point specified by `waveTop`. You no longer need `offset(x:y:)` on the shape because you can control the location with `waveTop`.

Go to **PourAnimationView.swift** and change the body to use the new shape you just implemented:

```
WaveShape(waveTop: shapeTop)
  .fill(fillColor)
  .onAppear {
    withAnimation(.linear(duration: 6.0)) {
      shapeTop = 0.0
    }
  }
```

You'll see your new shape in the preview, but it immediately jumps to the new position without the animation. To confirm this, run the app and let a timer finish.

Wave movement not animating.

The `Shape` protocol supports animation but requires you to conform to the `Animatable` protocol. `Shape` already conforms to `Animatable`, so all you have to do is implement its requirements.

Go back to **WaveShape.swift** and add the following computed property after `waveTop`:

```
var animatableData: Double {
  get { waveTop }
  set { waveTop = newValue }
}
```

`Animatable` has one requirement, the `animatableData` property. This property provides a bridge SwiftUI understands when implementing custom animation for a shape or view.

Run the app and let a timer complete to see that the wave moves smoothly. See **Chapter 6: Introduction to Custom Animations** for more about the protocol.

Wave now animating the rise.

This wave shape works, but it's limited. It only produces a single shape that always looks the same. The current wave height also looks too big for the view. In the next section, you'll let the calling view modify the wave's shape.

Modifying the Filling View

You can change the shape of a sine wave by changing three properties: **amplitude**, **wave length** and **phase**.

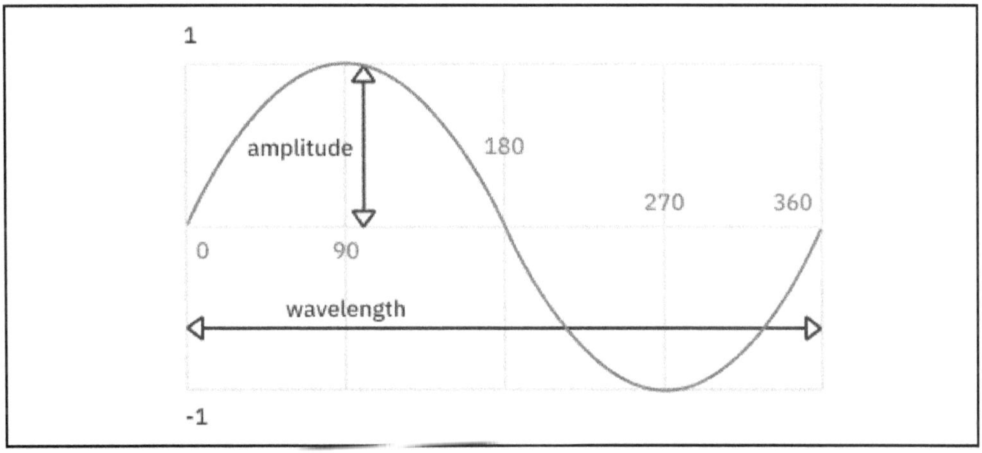

Elements of a wave.

Add the following new properties to `WaveShape` after `waveTop`:

```
var amplitude = 100.0
var wavelength = 1.0
var phase = 0.0
```

The `amplitude` determines the height of the wave. By default, the sine function's values vary between negative one and one. You can multiply that value by another number to change the shape's height. You already modified this in the initial shape using a fixed value of `100.00`.

To implement the amplitude, change the code under comment four to:

```
// 4
let y = sin(Angle(degrees: angle).radians) * amplitude
```

This change replaces the constant `100.0` value with the new property allowing any height wave.

Right now, the shape creates a single wave filling the entire space. The `wavelength` property lets you compress or stretch the wave.

To implement the wavelength, change the code under comment three to:

```
// 3
let angle = Double(x) / rect.width * wavelength * 360.0
```

The calculation adds a multiplication by the new `wavelength` parameter to the previous calculation. If this parameter is greater than one, it'll increase the number of waves appearing on the screen since the angle will rise more quickly. Think of the parameter as defining how many complete waves will show across the view.

To shift the wave horizontally, change the starting degree. Right now, you begin the wave at zero degrees, which produces a `y` of zero. The `phase` parameter lets you shift this beginning point so the wave can start at an arbitrary point.

You must adjust the angle calculated in step three to implement the phase parameter. Change the code to:

```
// 3
let angle = Double(x) / rect.width * wavelength * 360.0 + phase
```

You calculate an angle in step three and can change this angle by adding the desired change in degrees. The `phase` property provides the angle where the drawn wave should begin.

These new properties help you control the parameters of the wave. Open **PourAnimationView.swift** and change the call to `WaveShape()` to:

```
WaveShape(
  waveTop: shapeTop,
  amplitude: 15,
  wavelength: 4,
  phase: 90
)
```

Run the app and let a tea timer complete. You'll see your new animation. The wave shows more peaks and troughs with a smaller height and shifted to the right compared to before.

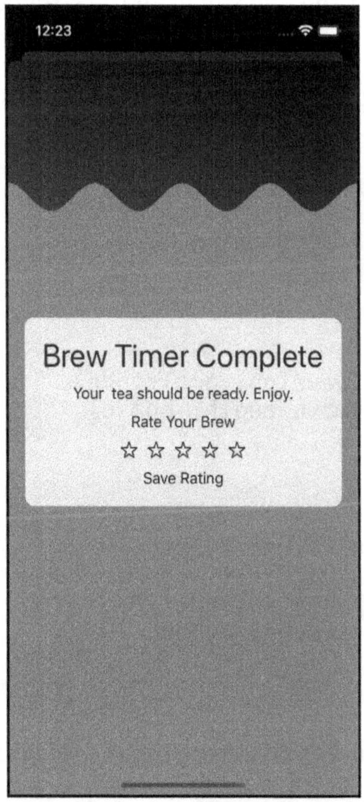

Wave shape after using new parameters.

This new wave produces a more realistic fill than a flat surface, but it's still too static. In the next section, you'll add some motion to the wave itself.

Animating Multiple Parts of the Wave

When you added `waveTop` to `WaveShape`, you needed to implement `animatableData` so SwiftUI could animate it. Therefore, you might expect to do the same for the three additional properties before you can animate them.

However, you have four properties to animate and only one property in the AnimatableData protocol. To handle these situations, SwiftUI provides the AnimatablePair struct. It lets you specify a pair of values for the animatableData property. In addition, each of the two values in the struct can be animatable, meaning you can nest values to support the number of properties you need.

Open **WaveShape.swift** and replace the animatableData property with:

```
// 1
var animatableData: AnimatablePair<
  AnimatablePair<Double, Double>,
  AnimatablePair<Double, Double>
  > {
  get {
    // 2
    AnimatablePair(
      AnimatablePair(waveTop, amplitude),
      AnimatablePair(wavelength, phase)
    )
  }
  set {
    // 3
    waveTop = newValue.first.first
    amplitude = newValue.first.second
    wavelength = newValue.second.first
    phase = newValue.second.second
  }
}
```

Here's how this code implements AnimatableData for your shape:

1. You define the animatableData property to have a type of AnimatablePair<AnimatablePair<Double, Double>,AnimatablePair<Double, Double>>. To animate four Doubles, you need four values. To get those, you need two AnimatablePair structs that you wrap inside an external AnimatablePair. This struct produces an AnimatablePair whose first and second values are AnimatablePair structs whose values are both a Double.

2. When SwiftUI requests the value for the property, you build an AnimatablePair struct. The first value of the struct is an AnimatablePair containing the waveLength and amplitude properties in the Shape. The second AnimatablePair struct consists of the wavelength and phase properties from the Shape.

3. When SwiftUI provides new values, you set the properties in the same order as you send them in step two. Notice the use of `newValue.first` to access the elements wrapped in the first `AnimatablePair` and `newValue.second` to access the second pair.

This diagram shows how the properties map through the `AnimatablePair` type of `animatableData`.

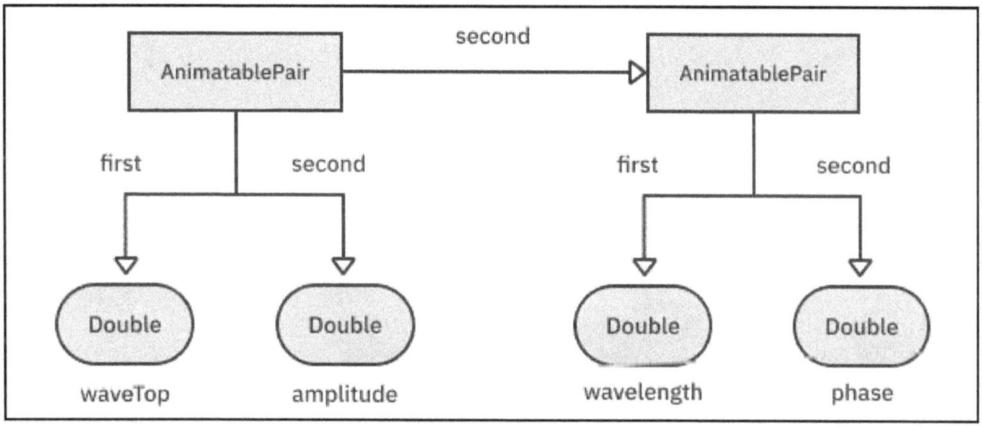

Diagram showing relation of AnimatablePair struct to properties.

For more on `AnimatablePair`, see **Chapter 7: Complex Custom Animations**.

With this change, you can animate all properties of the `WaveShape`. To put this to use, open **PourAnimationView.swift** and add a new computed property to the top of the view:

```
var waveHeight: Double {
  min(shapeTop / 10.0, 20.0)
}
```

This property calculates a wave height equal to the top of the shape divided by ten. The value of `waveHeight` starts at 20 and decreases as `shapeTop` decreases. `min` caps the value at 20, so the height isn't too large at the beginning of the animation.

Update `amplitude` in `WaveShape` to:

```
amplitude: waveHeight,
```

Using the new computed property for the shape's `amplitude` produces a larger wave that decreases as the animation nears the end. Run the app and let a timer complete to see the wave's height decrease.

Wave height shrinking as it nears the top of the view.

Since pouring a liquid produces a chaotic movement, you can make the animation more realistic by adding more movement to the wave. Shifting the `phase` for the `WaveShape` will do just that.

Open **PourAnimationView.swift** and add the following new property after `shapeTop`:

```
@State var wavePhase = 90.0
```

Change `phase` to the `WaveShape` view to read:

```
phase: wavePhase
```

This parameter has the shape use the new state property. Add the following code at the start of onAppear(perform:):

```
withAnimation(
  .easeInOut(duration: 0.5)
  .repeatForever()
) {
  wavePhase = -90.0
}
```

You do the same for the phase as you did when you changed shapeTop to animate a rising shape. Changing the phase adds a back-and-forth movement to the water in the view as it rises. You create an ease-in-out animation lasting one-half second. repeatForever(autoreverses:) tells SwiftUI to repeat the animation forever. Since autoreverses defaults to true, the animation will reverse before repeating.

Run the app and let a tea timer complete. You'll see the new motion in the animation.

Wave animation shifting horizontally.

Now that your animation resembles water rising in a cup, you'll add another wave in the next section to give the animation more complexity.

Adding Multiple Waves

While your wave resembles rising water, you can enhance the effect by adding more waves offset from the current wave.

Open **PourAnimationView.swift** and add the following new property after `wavePhase`:

```
@State var wavePhase2 = 0.0
```

Also, add a new color definition after `fillColor`:

```
let waveColor2 = Color(red: 0.129, green: 0.345, blue: 0.659)
```

Wrap the current `WaveShape` inside a `ZStack` by **Command**-clicking `WaveShape` and selecting **Embed in ZStack** from the menu. Keep `.fill(fillColor)` with `WaveShape` and move `onAppear(perform:)` to the `ZStack`. Add the following code inside the new `ZStack` and before the existing `WaveShape`:

```
WaveShape(
  waveTop: shapeTop,
  amplitude: waveHeight * 1.2,
  wavelength: 5,
  phase: wavePhase2
)
.fill(waveColor2)
```

This code produces a wave shape based on the existing one. It's 1.2 times higher and shows five complete waves across the view. You also use the newly added `wavePhase2` as the phase.

To animate this property of the new shape, add the following code to the `onAppear(perform:)` after the `withAnimation(_:_:)` that changes `wavePhase`:

```
withAnimation(
  .easeInOut(duration: 0.3)
  .repeatForever()
) {
  wavePhase2 = 270.0
}
```

Run the app, and you'll see a second, darker blue wave behind the existing one. It appears behind the first since you placed it first in the `ZStack`.

Second moving wave added to the view

Now that you have a nice animation of the view filling, the only thing missing is what's filling it. You'll start adding the pour in the next section.

Animation With Particles

The most efficient way to create a pour animation, the animation of a liquid acting under gravity, is to use a **particle system**. A particle system is a group of points that change under rules that affect their behavior and appearance. They work well to create effects such as smoke, rain, confetti and fireworks.

It's possible to write one natively in SwiftUI, but there's no need in this case since Apple provides particle systems in several libraries. In this section, you'll begin implementing a particle system in **SceneKit** and **SpriteKit** to add to your animation. SwiftUI supports SceneKit through the `SceneView` view, displaying SceneKit content.

To create the pour animation, you must build up several elements and combine them into a SceneKit scene. You'll start with the particle emitter.

Creating a Particle Emitter

Under the **PourAnimation** folder, create a new **SpriteKit Particle File**. For **Particle template**, select **Rain** and click **Next**. Name it **PourParticle**. The preview will show the new particle file, which resembles a light rain:

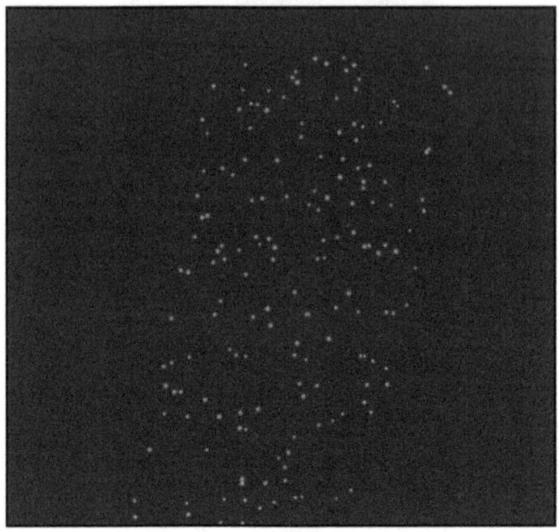

Default rain particle emitter

Select the **Attributes Inspector** for the particle file and change the following values:

- Change **Texture** to `dropshape` to select a drop shaped image for the particle.
- Change **Emitter ▸ Birthrate** to `600` to increase the number of particles.
- Change **Position Range ▸ X** to 55 as a lower number reduces the size of the space where the emitter creates particles.
- Change **Angle ▸ Start** to `270` to produce particles with a veritcal downward motion.
- Change **Speed ▸ Start** to `600` to speed up the particle motion.

Your final particle will look like this:

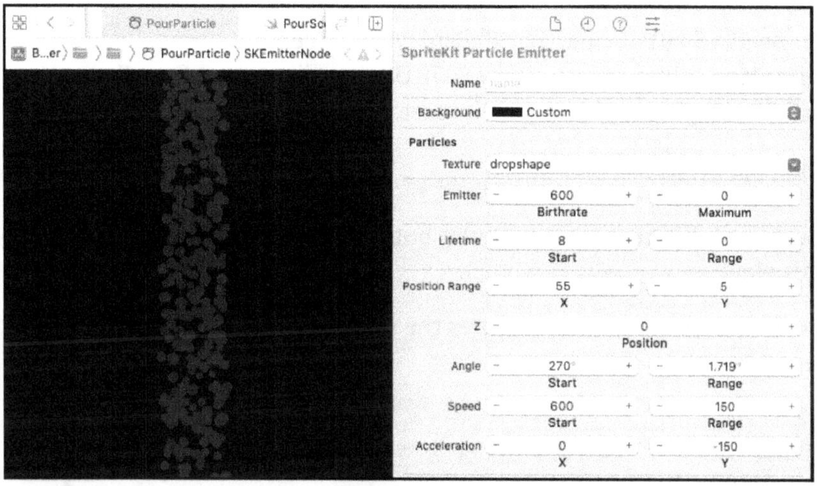

Final particle system

Click the circle next to **Color Ramp**. This selection will bring up a color picker. Select the second tab, which shows a slider option. Change the slider to **RGB Sliders** and change the **Hex Value** field in the bottom right to #1898FF.

The particles take on a blue color that may be hard to see on the default black background. You can change the **Custom** color to white to help them stand out.

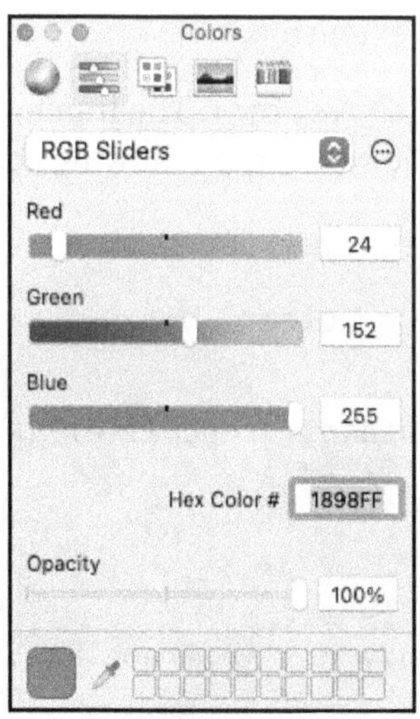

Color picker showing particle color.

With your completed particle emitter, you can create a SceneKit scene to hold the emitter. You'll begin that in the next section.

Building a SceneKit Scene

First, you need a SwiftUI view that'll display your SceneKit scene. Inside the **PourAnimation** folder, create a new SwiftUI view file named **PourSceneView**. At the top of the new file, add a second import:

```
import SpriteKit
```

You import SpriteKit because it includes both **SpriteKit** and **SceneKit**, which you'll use in this view.

First, you create a `SKScene` that defines the scene. At the top of the file before `PourSceneView`, add:

```
class PouringLiquidScene: SKScene {
  static let shared = PouringLiquidScene()
}
```

This bare-bones implementation contains only a single static property that creates an instance of itself. You'll use this class to define the view-independent properties for the scene. Add the following property to the class after the static property:

```
let dropEmitter = SKEmitterNode(fileNamed: "PourParticle")
```

`SKEmitterNode` loads the particle emitter you created in the last section. Notice you don't need to specify the file's extension,

You set up a `SKScene` inside `didMove(to:)`. The framework calls the method when the scene is presented to the view. Add the following code to your class:

```
override func didMove(to view: SKView) {
  // 1
  self.backgroundColor = .clear
  // 2
  if let dropEmitter,
     !self.children.contains(dropEmitter){
    self.addChild(dropEmitter)
  }

  // 3
  dropEmitter?.position.x = 100
  dropEmitter?.position.y = self.frame.maxY
}
```

Here's the setup for `SKScene`:

1. You set the scene's background color to `clear`. This change lets anything behind the scene, like other views, show through.
2. You attempt to unwrap `dropEmitter`. If successful, you then ensure the emitter isn't already present in the scene before adding it as a child of the current scene. Unwrapping `dropEmitter` can only fail if **PourParticle.sks** (the particle file you created) is missing or corrupt.
3. Particles from a `SKEmitterNode` appear at the location you provide to the `position` property. You set the horizontal position 100 points from the left edge. Unlike most SwiftUI-related coordinates, in a `SKScene`, the `y` value increases going upward in the view. Therefore, you set the `y` position to `self.frame.maxY`, placing it at the top of the view.

With that class in place, you can now use it in your SwiftUI view. Add the following computed property to `PourSceneView`:

```
var pouringScene: SKScene {
  // 1
  let scene = PouringLiquidScene.shared
  // 2
  scene.size = UIScreen.main.bounds.size
  scene.scaleMode = .fill
  // 3
  return scene
}
```

This property produces the `SKScene` you'll use inside your SwiftUI view by:

1. This gets the shared instance of the class through the `shared` property.
2. You set the size to match the size of the main screen, so the `SKScene` takes up the full view. You also set the scale mode to `.fill` to fill the entire view.
3. You return this modified view.

Finally, change the body of the view to:

```
SpriteView(
  scene: pouringScene,
  options: [.allowsTransparency]
)
```

You call `SpriteView`, passing in the scene's name from your `pouringScene` computed property. You pass `.allowsTransparency` to the options argument. Otherwise, the views below this in the stack wouldn't show through `SpriteView` and your `self.backgroundColor = .clear` setting in `didMove(to:)` would be ignored.

Check out the preview, where you can see the pouring liquid you created:

Preview of particle emitter in SwiftUI view.

With the SceneKit view added to a SwiftUI view, you can quickly finish the animation in the next section by combining the two.

Finishing the Animation

Open **PourAnimationView.swift** and add the following state property after `wavePhase2`:

```
@State var showPour = true
```

This property controls showing the pouring animation. Add the following code before the first `WaveShape()` inside the `ZStack`:

```
if showPour {
  PourSceneView()
}
```

Run the app, select any tea and let the timer complete. You'll see the new particle animation added to the view.

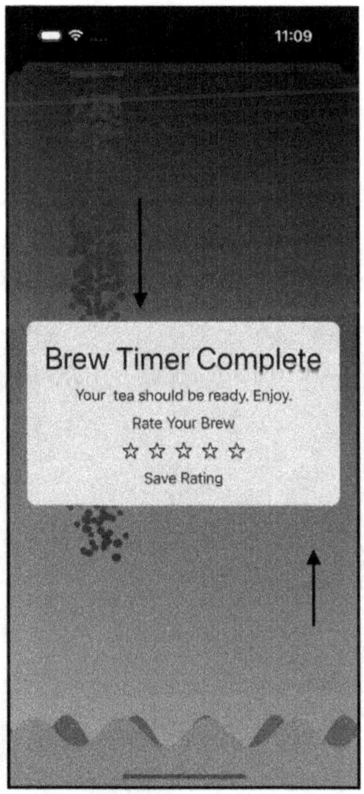

Timer complete with particle animation with timings wrong.

Since you added it before the `WaveShape` views, the pouring particle appears behind the rising liquid. However, the rising animation begins before the particles reach the bottom of the view, which spoils the illusion that the pouring causes the liquid to rise. To fix this, you can add a short delay before the liquid begins to rise. Inside `onAppear(perform:)`, find the last `withAnimation(_:_:)`, which changes `shapeTop`, and change it to:

```
withAnimation(
  .linear(duration: 6.0)
  .delay(1)
) {
  shapeTop = 0.0
}
```

You use the `delay(_:)` modifier on the linear animation with a value of 1 which delays for one second before changing `shapeTop` to zero and beginning the rising liquid animation.

For performance reasons, you don't want the particle emitter to keep running once the animation completes, which occurs when `shapeTop` reaches zero. If you directly compared `shapeTop` to zero, the explicit animation on `shapeTop` would cause SwiftUI to apply a transition to the view removal, fading it away. Instead, add the following code to the end of `onAppear(perform:)`:

```
DispatchQueue.main.asyncAfter(deadline: .now() + 7.0) {
  showPour = false
}
```

This code sets `showPour` to false after seven seconds, hiding the view. You get seven seconds from the one-second delay above plus the six seconds length of the animation. Run the app and let a tea timer complete to see your finished animation.

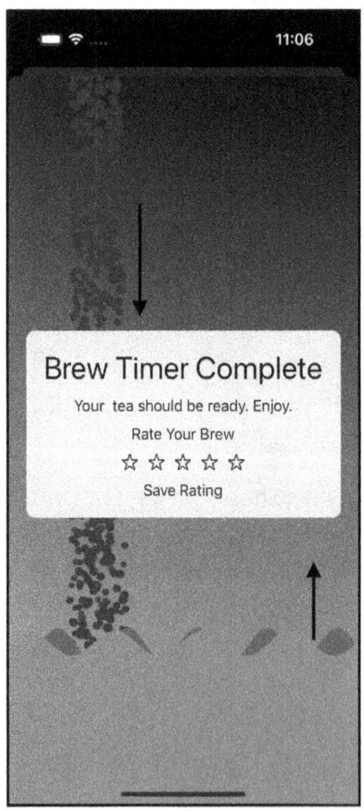

Final Timer completed animation

Key Points

- You can use animations to draw the user's attention to an element and add a nice visual to reinforce the user's action.
- You can combine multiple animations to produce a finished visual effect for complex animations.
- The SwiftUI animation system is robust and capable, but you can leverage other Apple frameworks when creating animations. SwiftUI lets you efficiently use them in your SwiftUI project.
- **SceneKit** includes a particle system that works well to produce smoke, rain, confetti and fire.

Where to Go From Here?

Chapter 6: Introduction to Custom Animations and **Chapter 7: Complex Custom Animations** of this book go into more detail on using the `AnimatableData` and `AnimatablePair` protocols.

For more about SceneKit, see SceneKit 3D Programming for iOS: Getting Started (https://www.kodeco.com/23483920-scenekit-3d-programming-for-ios-getting-started).

You can read more about the SceneKit particle system in SceneKit Tutorial with Swift Part 5: Particle Systems (https://www.kodeco.com/901-scenekit-tutorial-with-swift-part-5-particle-systems).

Chapter 10: Recreating a Real-World Animation

By Irina Galata

Building a component based on an existing UI solution differs from implementing something from scratch following your idea or a designer's prototype. The only thing you have at hand is an hours-long-polished, brought-to-perfection version of somebody's vision of functionality. You can't exactly see the steps they've taken or the iterations they've needed to get the result.

For example, take a look at Apple's Honeycomb grid, the app launcher component on the Apple Watch:

The view offers an engaging and fun way of navigation while efficiently utilizing limited screen space on wearable devices. The concept can be helpful in various apps where a user is offered several options.

In this chapter, you'll recreate it to help users pick their topics of interest when registering on an online social platform:

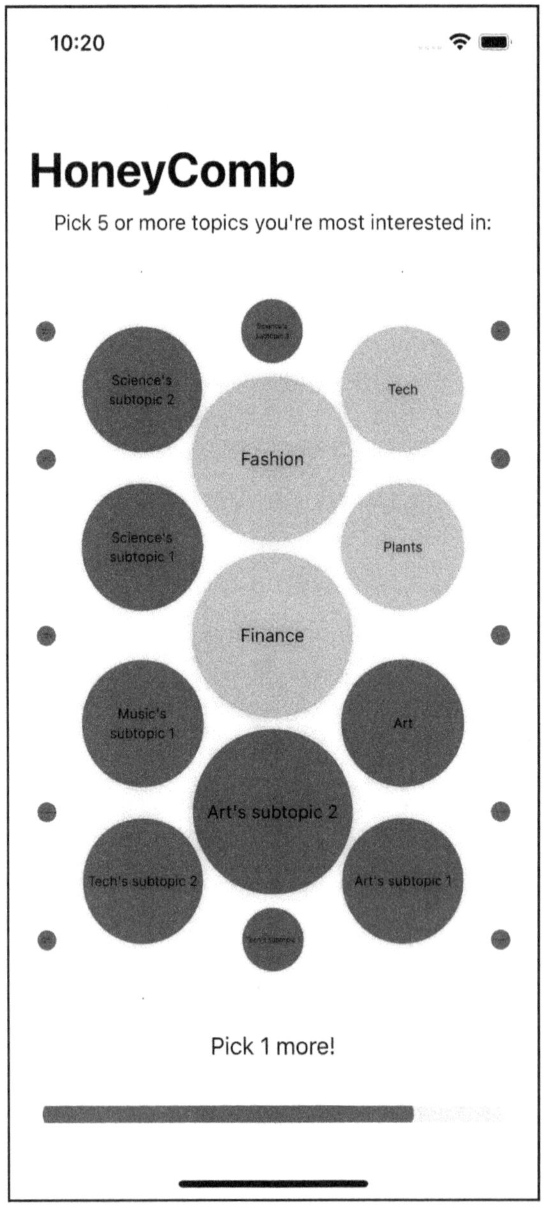

> **Note**: The calculations for drawing the grid would not be possible without Amit Patel's excellent work in his guide on hexagonal grids (https://www.redblobgames.com/grids/hexagons/).

This time, you'll start entirely from scratch, so don't hesitate to create a new SwiftUI-based project yourself or grab an empty one from the resources for this chapter.

Back to the grid. The essential piece of the implementation is the container's structure. In this case, it's a hexagonal grid: each element has six edges and vertices and can have up to six neighbors.

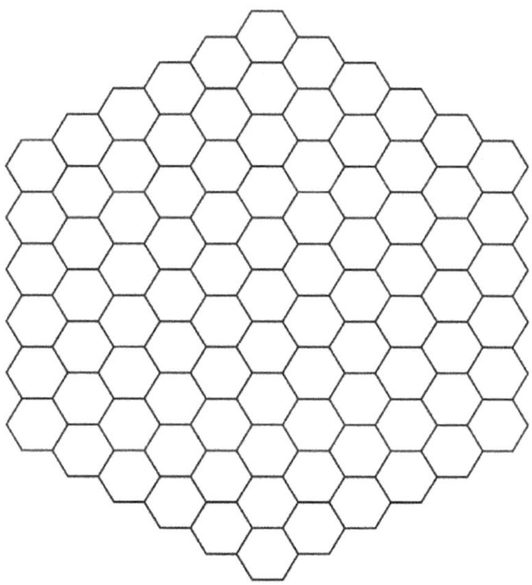

First, you need to know the fundamentals of the grid, such as its coordinate system and the implementation of some basic operations on its elements.

Applying Cube Coordinates to Building a Hexagonal Grid

While multiple coordinate systems can be applied for building a hexagonal grid, some are better known and easier to research. In contrast, others can be significantly more complex, obscure and rarer to find on the internet. Your choice will depend on your use case and the requirements for the structure.

Cube coordinates are the optimal approach for the component you'll replicate.

For a better understanding, picture a 3-dimensional stack of cubes:

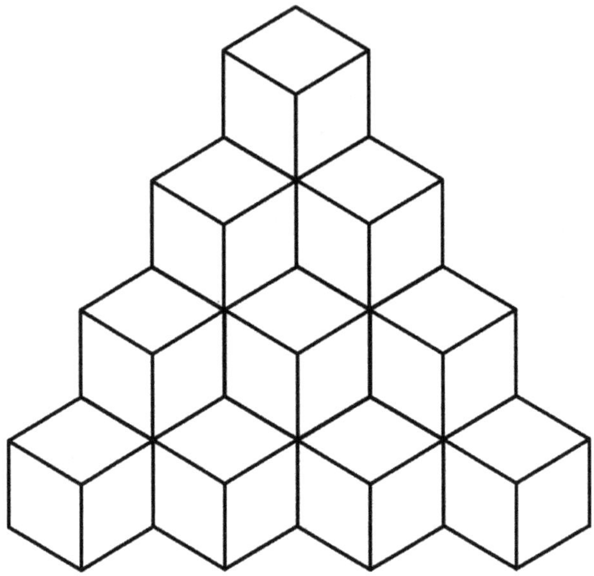

If you place this pile of cubes inside the standard coordinate system and then diagonally slice it by a `x + y + z = 0` plane, the shape of the sliced area of each cube will form a hexagon:

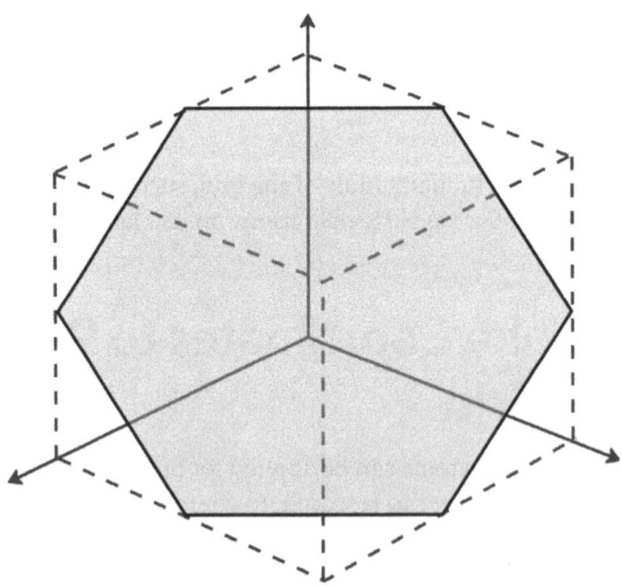

All the sliced cubes together build a hexagonal grid:

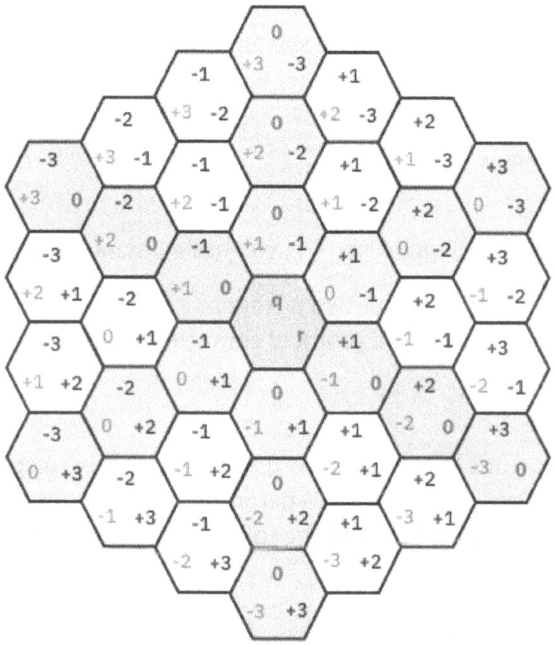

As you're only interested in the grid itself, namely the area created by the plane slicing the pile of cubes, and not in all the cubes' volume below or above the plane, from now on you will work with coordinates belonging to the `x + y + z = 0` area. That means, if x is 5, and y is -3, z can only be -2, to satisfy the equation, otherwise the said point doesn't belong to the plane, or to the hexagonal grid.

There are a few advantages to the cubes coordinate system approach:

1. It allows most operations, like adding, subtracting or multiplying the hexagons, by manipulating their coordinates.

2. The produced grid can have a non-rectangular shape.

3. In terms of hexagonal grids, the cube coordinates are easily translatable to the **axial** coordinate system because the cube coordinates of each hexagon must follow the `x + y + z = 0` rule. Since you can always calculate the value of the third parameter from the first two, you can omit the z and operate with a pair of values - x and y. To avoid confusion between the coordinate system you're working with in SwiftUI and the axial one, you'll refer to them as `q`, `r` and `s` in this chapter. You may often see this same approach in many other resources on hexagonal grids' math, but in the end the names are arbitrary and are up to you.

Now it's time to turn the concept into code.

Create a new file named **Hex.swift**. Inside the file, declare `Hex` and add a property of type `Int` for each axis of the coordinate system:

```
struct Hex {
  let q, r: Int
  var s: Int { q - r }
}
```

Since the value of `s` always equals `-q - r`, you use a computed property for its value.

Often, you'll need to verify whether two hexagons are equal. Making `Hex` conform to `Equatable` is as easy as adding the protocol conformance to the type:

```
struct Hex: Equatable
```

You can add two hexagons by adding their `q` and `r` properties, respectively. Swift includes another protocol you can use to naturally add and subtract two types together — `AdditiveArithmetic`. Add the following conformance to the bottom of the file:

```
extension Hex: AdditiveArithmetic {
  static func - (lhs: Hex, rhs: Hex) -> Hex {
    Hex(
      q: lhs.q - rhs.q,
      r: lhs.r - rhs.r
    )
  }

  static func + (lhs: Hex, rhs: Hex) -> Hex {
    Hex(
      q: lhs.q + rhs.q,
      r: lhs.r + rhs.r
    )
  }

  static var zero: Hex {
    .init(q: 0, r: 0)
  }
}
```

You have to provide three pieces to conform to `AdditiveArithmetic`: How to add hexagons, how to subtract hexagons, and what is considered the zero-value of a hexagon.

By incrementing or decrementing one of the two coordinates, you indicate a direction toward one of the neighbors of the current hexagon:

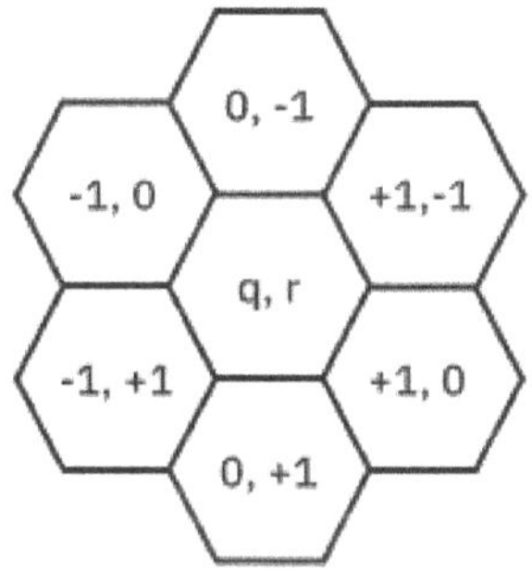

Since each of the directions from a hexagon piece has its own relative `q` and `r` coordinate, you can use `Hex` to represent them according to the chart above. Add the following code as an extension to Hex:

```
extension Hex {
  enum Direction: CaseIterable {
    case bottomRight
    case bottom
    case bottomLeft
    case topLeft
    case top
    case topRight

    var hex: Hex {
      switch self {
      case .top:
        return Hex(q: 0, r: -1)
      case .topRight:
        return Hex(q: 1, r: -1)
      case .bottomRight:
        return Hex(q: 1, r: 0)
      case .bottom:
        return Hex(q: 0, r: 1)
      case .bottomLeft:
        return Hex(q: -1, r: 1)
      case .topLeft:
        return Hex(q: -1, r: 0)
      }
    }
  }
}
```

Now fetching one of the current hex's neighbors is as easy as adding two `Hex` instances. Add the following method to your `Hex` struct:

```
func neighbor(at direction: Direction) -> Hex { // 1
  return self + direction.hex // 2
}
```

Here's a code breakdown:

1. Using the `direction` enum, you indicate which neighbor you want to get.
2. Then, you get the direction's coordinate and add it to the current coordinate.

Since obtaining a neighboring hexagon is now possible, you can also add a function to verify whether two hexagons are, in fact, neighbors:

```
func isNeighbor(of hex: Hex) -> Bool {
  Direction.allCases.contains { neighbor(at: $0) == hex }
}
```

To check whether two hexagons stand side-to-side, you iterate over all six directions and check if a hexagon in the current direction equals the argument. Using `contains(where:)` will return `true` as soon as it finds a matching neighbor, or return `false` if `hex` isn't a neighbor of the current coordinate.

Finally, you must obtain its center's (x, y) coordinates to render each element.

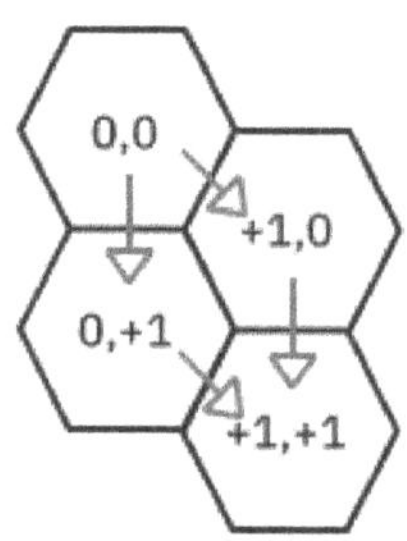

To calculate the center's position of a hexagon with the coordinates of (`q`, `r`) relative to the root hexagon in (`0`, `0`), you need to apply the **green** (pointing sideways) vector - `(3/2, sqrt(3)/2)` - `q` times and the **blue** (pointing down) vector - `(0, sqrt(3))` - `r` times.To allow for the scaling of a hexagon, you need to multiply the resulting values by the size of the hexagon.

First, in **ContentView.swift**, add the following constant above to the top of the file so you can change it later if you need to:

```
let diameter = 125.0
```

Here, you add the value for the diameter of the circle you'll draw in place of each hexagon on the grid. Where the *size* of a hexagon usually refers to the distance from its center to any of its corners:

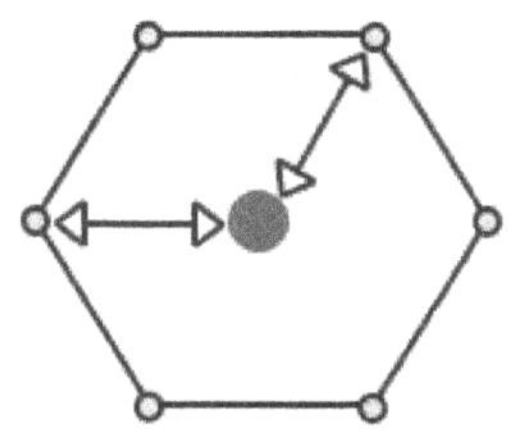

Therefore, a regular hexagon's width equals `2 * size`, and the height is `sqrt(3) * size`.

Add the following method calculate the `Hex`'s center, inside the `struct`:

```
func center() -> CGPoint {
  let qVector = CGVector(dx: 3.0 / 2.0, dy: sqrt(3.0) / 2.0) //
1
  let rVector = CGVector(dx: 0.0, dy: sqrt(3.0))
  let size = diameter / sqrt(3.0) // 2
  let x = qVector.dx * Double(q) * size // 3
  let y = (qVector.dy * Double(q) +
           rVector.dy * Double(r)) * size

  return CGPoint(x: x, y: y)
}
```

Here's a code breakdown:

1. First, you construct the green and blue vectors from the diagram above.
2. Then, you calculate the **size** of the hexagon based on the formula for the height.
3. You calculate the total horizontal and vertical shifts by multiplying a vector's coordinates by the hexagon's coordinates and size. Because a regular hexagon has uneven height and width, you use the same value for both height and width to fit it into a "square" shape because you're going to draw circles in place of hexagons, which would leave blank spaces on the sides otherwise.

Constructing a Hexagonal Grid

To represent an element of a hexagonal grid, make a new file named **HexData.swift** and define a struct inside it named `HexData`:

```
struct HexData {
  var hex: Hex
  var center: CGPoint
  var topic: String
}
```

Besides the grid's coordinates, `HexData` contains the coordinates of its center to render it and a topic, which the hexagon will display.

Make `HexData` conform to `Hashable` so you can iterate over a collection of it later:

```
struct HexData: Hashable
```

The compiler will prompt you to add `hash(into:)`:

```
func hash(into hasher: inout Hasher) {
  hasher.combine(topic)
}
```

In the current case, the represented topic can't be reused multiple times and, in a way, is a unique identifier of a `HexData` instance, sufficient for hash generation.

Iterating Over the Grid

You need to develop a method to generate an array of `Hex` instances to build a honeycomb grid.

Add the following declaration in the `HexData` struct:

```
static func hexes(for topics: [String]) -> [Self] {
  return []
}
```

You'll iterate over the elements moving along a spiral from the center of the grid toward the last ring. To keep track of the current coordinates and a ring's index, add the following variables to the top of the newly created method:

```
var ringIndex = 0
var currentHex = Hex(q: 0, r: 0)
```

Then, add a variable to append the hexes you're about to create, and initialize it with the root hexagon:

```
var hexes = [Hex(q: 0, r: 0)]
```

Now, the `Direction` enum you added earlier comes in handy since you need to move from one hexagon to another along a spiral. Add a variable to keep the directions along with their indices:

```
let directions = Hex.Direction.allCases.enumerated()
```

To start the iterations, first, create an outer `while`-loop until you reach the necessary amount of elements:

```
repeat {

} while hexes.count < topics.count
```

Inside the loop, add the following lines:

```
directions.forEach { index, direction in // 1
  let smallerSegment = index == 1 // 2
  let segmentSize = smallerSegment ? ringIndex : ringIndex +
1 // 3
  for _ in 0..<segmentSize {
    // TODO
  }
}

ringIndex += 1 // 4
```

Here's a code breakdown:

1. First, you iterate over the directions to reach the hexagons along the whole spiral.
2. As you progress along the spiral, the amount of hexagons grows with each consecutive ring. One of the six segments of each ring always has one less element than the five others though: the first spiral's ring contains only five elements. Likewise, the second one has `6 (amount of directions) * 2 (ring index + 1) - 1 = 11` elements, the third - `6 * 3 - 1 = 17`, and so on:

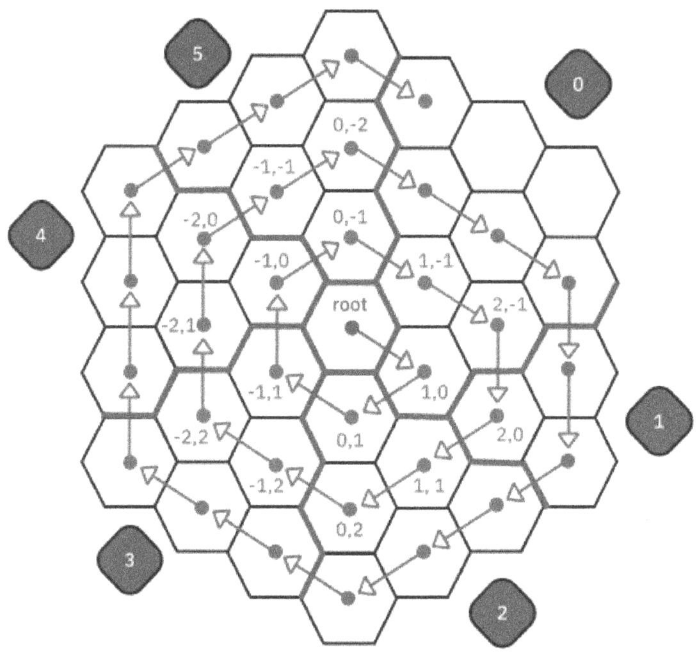

3. For a smaller segment you use `ringIndex` as the amount of hexagons in it, and `ringIndex + 1` otherwise.
4. After iterating over all the directions, you always increment the index of the spiral's ring.

Then, inside the inner loop, replace `// TODO` with:

```
guard hexes.count != topics.count else { break } // 1
currentHex = currentHex + direction.hex // 2
hexes.append(currentHex)
```

Here's a breakdown:

1. As a precaution, you verify if any new hexagons are still needed. Otherwise, you break out of the inner loop.
2. You update the `currentHex` by adding the current `direction`'s `hex` to it, namely adding their respective parameters - `q`, `r` and `s`, and append the result to the `hexes` array.

Finally, update the `return`-statement to map the array you've just computed to an array of `HexData`:

```
return hexes.enumerated().map { index, hex in
  HexData(
    hex: hex,
    center: hex.center(),
    topic: topics[index]
  )
}
```

Above, you calculate the center for each hexagon and fetch the respective topic from the array of strings.

Rendering the Hexagons

You're almost ready to display the first version of your grid view on the screen.

Create a new **SwiftUI View** file named **HexView.swift**, and add a property of type `HexData` inside the generated `struct`:

```
let hex: HexData
```

Inside `HexView`'s `body`, add a `ZStack` containing a `Circle` and a label to represent the grid's hexagon:

```
ZStack {
  Circle()
    .fill(Color(uiColor: UIColor.purple))

  Text(hex.topic)
    .multilineTextAlignment(.center)
    .font(.footnote)
    .padding(4)
}
.shadow(radius: 4)
.padding(4)
.frame(width: diameter, height: diameter)
```

To enable the preview, update HexView's preview like so:

```
HexView(
  hex: HexData(
    hex: .zero,
    center: .zero,
    topic: "Tech"
  )
)
```

Run the preview, and you should see a circle representing the current hex piece, with a topic in it:

Now, go to ContentView and replace its body content with a VStack:

```
VStack {
  Text("Pick 5 or more topics you're most interested in:")
    .font(.subheadline)

// TODO
}
```

Then, add these properties to the `ContentView` to keep the `HexData` array and a collection of topics:

```
@State var hexes: [HexData] = []
private let topics = [
  "Politics", "Science", "Animals",
  "Plants", "Tech", "Music",
  "Sports", "Books", "Cooking",
  "Traveling", "TV-series", "Art",
  "Finance", "Fashion"
]
```

The only thing missing is a container for the `HexViews`.

Building a Custom Layout

At WWDC22, Apple introduced a new convenient way of composing more complex containers, the `Layout` protocol, which is available on iOS 16.

There are two methods you must implement to conform to this new protocol:

1. `sizeThatFits(proposal:subviews:cache:)`, where you define the size your component requires to place its subviews.
2. `placeSubviews(in:proposal:subviews:cache:)`, responsible for placing each subview in the container.

Both methods receive a `ProposedViewSize` argument containing measurements suggested by SwiftUI. Additionally, the `Layout` offers caching functionality to improve your app's performance when a container needs to recalculate its size and the positions of its subviews often.

Create a new Swift file named **HoneycombGrid.swift** and add the following struct to it:

```
import SwiftUI

struct HoneycombGrid: Layout {
  let hexes: [HexData]

}
```

You'll use the `hexes` property to fetch each hexagon's center and position it inside its container.

Now, the compiler will prompt you to implement the methods mentioned above so the struct conforms to the `Layout` protocol:

```
func sizeThatFits(
  proposal: ProposedViewSize,
  subviews: Subviews,
  cache: inout ()
) -> CGSize {
  // TODO
}

func placeSubviews(
  in bounds: CGRect,
  proposal: ProposedViewSize,
  subviews: Subviews,
  cache: inout ()
) {
  // TODO
}
```

Start with `sizeThatFits(proposal:subviews:cache:)`. You want the container to take all the space available to it:

```
CGSize(
  width: proposal.width ?? .infinity,
  height: proposal.height ?? .infinity
)
```

If the measurement proposed by SwiftUI isn't available, you return `.infinity` as both width and height.

Inside `placeSubviews(in:proposal:subviews:cache:)`, you iterate over the subviews and fetch the corresponding hexagon from the `hexes` array:

```
subviews.enumerated().forEach { i, subview in
  let hexagon = hexes[i]

  // TODO
}
```

Then, add the following code snippet inside the loop:

```
let position = CGPoint( // 1
  x: bounds.origin.x + hexagon.center.x + bounds.width / 2,
  y: bounds.origin.y + hexagon.center.y + bounds.height / 2
)

// 2
subview.place(
  at: position,
  anchor: .center,
  proposal: proposal
)
```

Here's a code breakdown:

1. To calculate the position for each subview, you sum the coordinates of the container's origin, hexagon's center and half of the corresponding container's measurement. The origin is important to consider because a view's bounds often don't correspond to the whole screen's bounds, and its origin can differ from the `(0, 0)` point. Since you use the `(0, 0)` coordinates for the root hexagon, you add `bounds.width / 2` and `bounds.height / 2` to center the subviews around the `HoneycombGrid`'s center instead of its origin.
2. Then, you use `place(at:anchor:proposal:)` to position the subview at the point you just calculated using `.center` as an anchor.

Back in `ContentView`, below `Text`, add a `HoneycombGrid` containing all the hexagons to display in place of the `// TODO` comment:

```
HoneycombGrid(hexes: hexes) {
  ForEach(hexes, id: \.self) { hex in
    HexView(hex: hex)
  }
}
```

Finally, attach an `.onAppear` modifier to `HoneycombGrid` to compute the hexagons' positions right before `ContentView` displays:

```
.onAppear {
  hexes = HexData.hexes(for: topics)
}
```

Run your app to see the outcome:

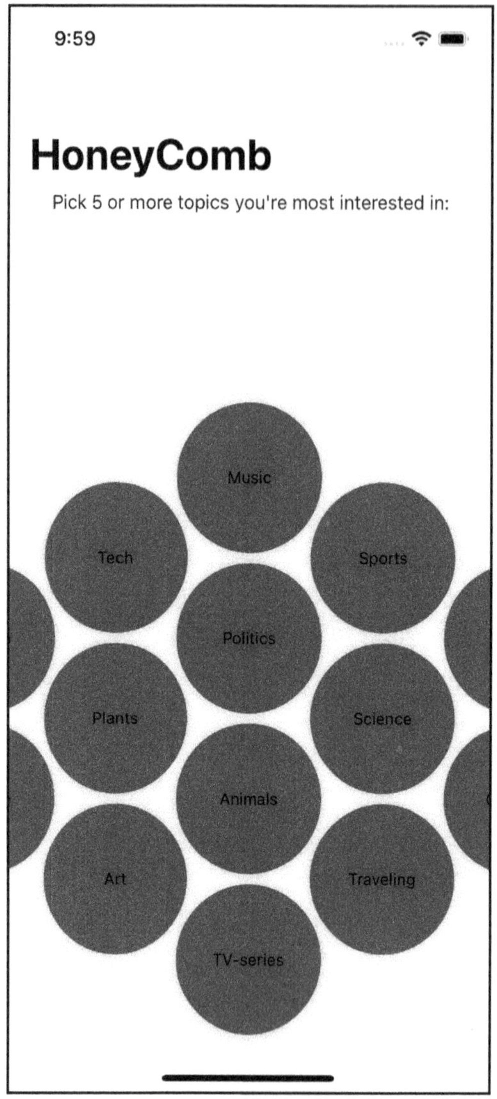

How cool is that? :]

Next, you'll enable dragging gesture handling to let users pan the component to access the corner cells. Additionally, users must be able to pick topics, so you'll also implement tap gesture handling.

Gesture Handling

Start with dragging gestures. Add a new `@GestureState` and `@State` properties to the `ContentView` to keep track of the offset:

```
@GestureState var drag: CGSize = .zero
@State var dragOffset: CGSize = .zero
```

Add a method to `ContentView` to invoke once a user completes a drag gesture:

```
private func onDragEnded(with state: DragGesture.Value) {

}
```

First, update `dragOffset` when the gesture is over to prevent the grid from jumping back to its initial position by appending the latest translation state to the values of `dragOffset`:

```
dragOffset = CGSize(
  width: dragOffset.width + state.translation.width,
  height: dragOffset.height + state.translation.height
)
```

If you take a closer look at the original Apple Watch honeycomb grid component, you'll notice that once you stop dragging the view, it moves slightly further, as if inertia was affecting it.

That may sound complicated to implement. But SwiftUI comes to the rescue and offers the `predictedEndTranslation` property of the `DragGesture.Value`, which produces a similar result if you apply it to the offset over time.

When a user drags a view, SwiftUI calculates the velocity and direction of the gesture and computes the approximate end translation. The actual end translation is often slightly shorter than the predicted one. Therefore the difference between those values comes in handy to recreate the effect from the original component.

To apply the difference between two offsets, first, create a variable *right at the beginning* of `onDragEnded(with:)` to keep the initial value of the offset:

```
let initialOffset = dragOffset
```

Then, *at the bottom* of `onDragEnded(with:)`, apply the predicted translation as follows:

```
var endX = initialOffset.width +
```

```
            state.predictedEndTranslation.width * 1.25
var endY = initialOffset.height +
            state.predictedEndTranslation.height * 1.25
```

You add the width and height of the predicted translation to `initialOffset` and the `1.25` multiplier to exaggerate the effect slightly.

Then, you must ensure the user can't accidentally drag the grid out of the screen's bounds. To do so, you'll verify that the offset distance value is always smaller than the distance from the center to the last hexagon. Add the following code below the variables you just added:

```
let lastHex = hexes.last?.center ?? .zero
let maxDistance = sqrt(
  pow((lastHex.x), 2) +
  pow((lastHex.y), 2)
) * 0.7
if abs(endX) > maxDistance {
  endX = endX > 0 ? maxDistance : -maxDistance
}
if abs(endY) > maxDistance {
  endY = endY > 0 ? maxDistance : -maxDistance
}
```

If the offset value is larger, you replace it with the maximum value allowed. The `0.7` multiplier ensures a few more circles are always visible to prevent the screen from going almost completely blank when the dragging value reaches its maximum.

After enforcing the dragging bounds, apply the calculated translation by adding the following code:

```
withAnimation(.spring()) {
  dragOffset = CGSize(
    width: endX,
    height: endY
  )
}
```

Now, similar to the way you did for the seating chart in earlier chapters, add a `DragGesture` to `HoneycombGrid` and invoke the newly created `onDragEnded(with:)` in its `onEnded` callback:

```
.simultaneousGesture(DragGesture()
  .updating($drag) { value, state, _ in
    state = value.translation
  }
  .onEnded { state in
    onDragEnded(with: state)
```

```
  }
)
```

You use .simultaneousGesture because you'll add a couple of gesture handlers later, and SwiftUI must recognize them simultaneously.

The last step is to apply the offset to the HoneycombGrid. Add .offset above .onAppear:

```
.offset(
  CGSize(
    width: drag.width + dragOffset.width,
    height: drag.height + dragOffset.height
  )
)
```

Run the app to try the gesture handling out:

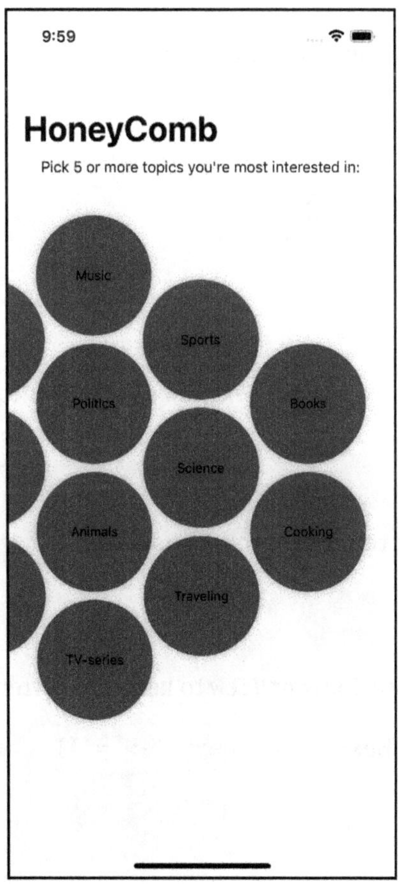

Selecting a Grid's Hexagon

To highlight the selected cells, add these properties in `HexView` below the `hex` property:

```
let isSelected: Bool
let onTap: () -> Void
```

Update `.fill` to alternate colors depending on the state of the hexagon:

```
.fill(isSelected ? .green : Color(uiColor: .purple))
```

Then, add a tap gesture handler to `Circle` below `.fill`:

```
.onTapGesture {
  onTap()
}
```

Update `HexView_Previews` once again to display `HexView`'s preview:

```
HexView(
  hex: HexData(
    hex: .zero,
    center: .zero,
    topic: "Tech"
  ),
  isSelected: false,
  onTap: {}
)
```

Go back to `ContentView`, and update `HexView`'s initializer to include `isSelected` and `onTap`:

```
HexView(
  hex: hex,
  isSelected: selectedHexes.contains(hex)
) {
  select(hex: hex)
}
```

Then, add a new property to `ContentView` to keep the currently selected cells:

```
@State var selectedHexes: Set<HexData> = []
```

Below `ContentView`'s `body`, add a new method to handle a cell's selection:

```
private func select(hex: HexData) {
}
```

Place the following code inside `select(hex:)`:

```
if !selectedHexes.insert(hex).inserted { // 1
  selectedHexes.remove(hex)
}

withAnimation(.spring()) { // 2
  dragOffset = CGSize(width: -hex.center.x, height:
-hex.center.y)
}
```

Here's what you did:

1. You attempt to insert the selected `hex` into the set and check if it was successfully `inserted`. Since `Set`s only include unique values, adding the same value more than once will return `false` for `inserted`, in which case you will remove it from the set instead.
2. Then, you update `dragOffset` to the opposite value of the center of `hex`. This way, the grid moves to center the selected hexagon on the screen.

To give the user a hint of how many more topics they need to choose, add a text and a progress indicator at the bottom of the root `VStack` of `ContentView`'s `body`:

```
Text(
  selectedHexes.count < 5
    ? "Pick \(5 - selectedHexes.count) more!"
    : "You're all set!"
)

ProgressView(
  value: Double(min(5, selectedHexes.count)),
  total: 5
)
.scaleEffect(y: 3)
.tint(selectedHexes.count < 5 ?
Color(uiColor: .purple) : .green)
.padding(24)
```

To make `ProgressView` update its state smoothly, attach the `animation` view modifier to it as follows:

```
.animation(.easeInOut, value: selectedHexes.count)
```

Run the app to see the outcome:

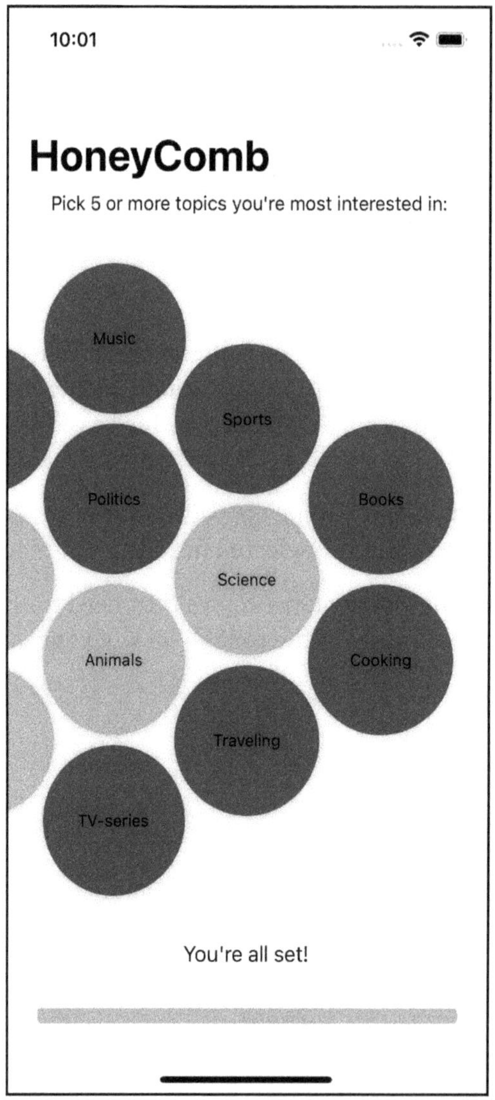

If you have an Apple Watch nearby, look closely at its launcher component again. When you drag the view around, the closest bubble to your finger and those surrounding it are slightly dimmed and shrunk.

You can implement this effect by adding one more gesture handler.

Go back to `HexView`, and add a new `@Binding` above `onTap`:

```
@Binding var touchedHexagon: HexData?
```

Then, add an `.overlay` to the `Circle` right below `.fill` to dim it if the user is touching it:

```
.overlay(
  Circle()
    .fill(touchedHexagon == hex ? .black.opacity(0.25) : .clear)
)
```

Below `.onTapGesture`, add `.simultaneousGesture` to handle one more gesture:

```
.simultaneousGesture(
  DragGesture(minimumDistance: 0)
    .onChanged { _ in // 1
      withAnimation(.easeInOut(duration: 0.5)) {
        touchedHexagon = hex
      }
    }
    .onEnded { _ in // 2
      withAnimation(.easeInOut(duration: 0.5)) {
        touchedHexagon = nil
      }
    }
)
```

Here's what you did:

1. When the gesture is ongoing, you update `touchedHexagon` with the current `HexData`.
2. Once the gesture ends, you set it to `nil`.

Pass the following as the `touchedHexagon` parameter of `HexView`'s initializer in `HexView_Previews`:

```
HexView(
  hex: HexData(hex: .zero, center: .zero, topic: "Tech"),
  isSelected: false,
  touchedHexagon: .constant(nil),
  onTap: {}
)
```

Go back to `ContentView`, and append the following property:

```
@State var touchedHexagon: HexData? = nil
```

Then add a new variable inside `ForEach` above `HexView`'s initializer to determine whether the current cell should dim:

```
let hexOrNeighbor = touchedHexagon == hex ||
    touchedHexagon?.hex.isNeighbor(of: hex.hex) == true
```

Pass `touchedHexagon` to the initializer of `HexView`:

```
HexView(
  hex: hex,
  isSelected: selectedHexes.contains(hex),
  touchedHexagon: $touchedHexagon
) {
  select(hex: hex)
}
```

Finally, add `.scaleEffect` to `HexView`:

```
.scaleEffect(hexOrNeighbor ? 0.9 : 1)
```

Run the app:

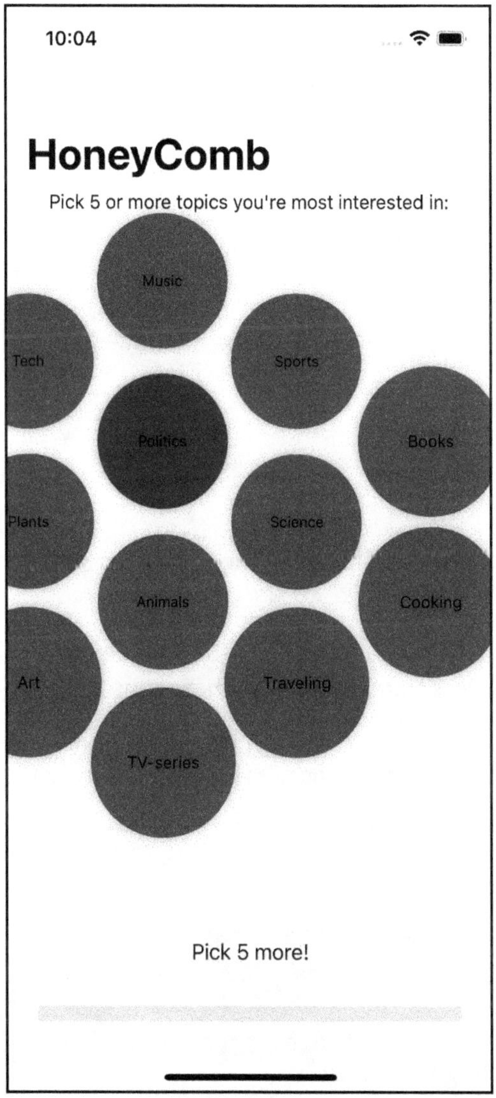
10:04
HoneyComb
Pick 5 or more topics you're most interested in:
Music
Tech
Sports
Politics
Books
Plants
Science
Animals
Cooking
Art
Traveling
TV-series
Pick 5 more!

Expanding the Grid

The currently presented topics are rather generic. Once a user picks a topic, you could offer subtopics to them to be more specific in defining their interests.

Add a new method to calculate the positions of additional hexagons below the `hexes(for:)` static function you added earlier inside **HexData.swift**:

```
static func hexes(
  from source: Hex,
  _ array: [HexData],
  topics: [String]
) -> [HexData] {
  var newHexData: [HexData] = []

  //TODO

  return newHexData
}
```

The method receives the source hexagon, the one a user selected, the current array of `HexData` and new subtopics.

First, iterate over the potential neighbors of the `source` hexagon to see whether there are any empty spaces to insert the new hexagons into:

```
for direction in Hex.Direction.allCases {
  let newHex = source.neighbor(at: direction) // 1

  if !array.contains(where: { $0.hex == newHex }) { // 2
    newHexData.append(HexData(
      hex: newHex,
      center: newHex.center(),
      topic: topics[newHexData.count]
    ))
  }

  if newHexData.count == topics.count { // 3
    return newHexData
  }
}
```

Here's a code breakdown:

1. You fetch a neighboring hexagon in the current direction.
2. If the array doesn't contain a hexagon at that position, you append a new hexagon to `newHexData`.
3. At the end of each iteration, you check if you've already added all the needed hexagons and return `newHexData` in such a case.

In a scenario when the `source` hexagon doesn't have enough space around it to insert all the needed cells, you need to append them further away. Add the following condition below the loop:

```
newHexData.append(contentsOf: hexes(
  from: source.neighbor(at:
Hex.Direction.allCases.randomElement()!),
  array + newHexData,
  topics: Array(topics.dropFirst(newHexData.count))
))
```

Here, you pick a random neighboring hexagon and try to insert the needed hexagons near it recursively.

There can be multiple ways to approach this problem. You could always pick the last hexagon of the array as the new `source` or the first neighbor of the `source` or even come up with an algorithm to search for the nearest corner hexagon with enough spare space. In the end, the grid shouldn't contain that many elements for the approach to make a difference: a user must be able to navigate through the whole grid without easily getting lost.

Create a new method to append subtopics in `ContentView`:

```
private func appendHexesIfNeeded(for hex: HexData) {
  let shouldAppend = !hex.topic.contains("subtopic") &&
    !hexes.contains(where: { $0.topic.contains("\(hex.topic)'s
subtopic") })

  if shouldAppend {
    hexes.append(contentsOf: HexData.hexes(from: hex.hex, hexes,
topics: [
      "\(hex.topic)'s subtopic 1",
      "\(hex.topic)'s subtopic 2",
      "\(hex.topic)'s subtopic 3"
    ]))
  }
}
```

You add the subtopics based on whether the current hexagon represents a subtopic or if it already contains subtopics somewhere else in the grid.

Find the condition `if !selectedHexes.insert(hex).inserted {` in `select(hex: HexData)` and replace that block with:

```
if selectedHexes.insert(hex).inserted {
  appendHexesIfNeeded(for: hex)
} else {
  selectedHexes.remove(hex)
}
```

Then, still in `select(hex:)`, wrap `dragOffset` into the `DispatchQueue.main.async` to prevent two animations, new hexagons appearing and shifting toward the selected cell, from glitching:

```
DispatchQueue.main.async {
  withAnimation(.spring()) {
    dragOffset = CGSize(width: -hex.center.x, height:
-hex.center.y)
  }
}
```

Add `.transition` to `HexView`:

```
.transition(.scale)
```

Finally, to animate the transitions, add the following modifier to `HoneycombGrid`:

```
.animation(.spring(), value: hexes)
```

Rerun the app and try to select a topic:

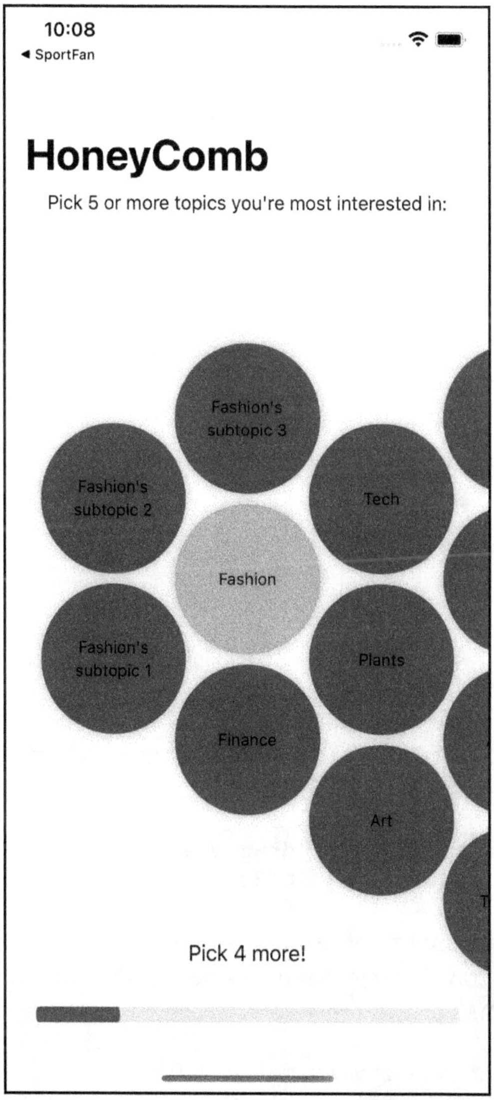

Recreating the Fish Eye Effect

What makes Apple's honeycomb grid so special and recognizable besides the grid structure is its "fish eye" effect. The cells closer to the center of the screen appear larger, while those at the corner shrink until they disappear entirely when reaching the screen's borders.

`GeometryReader` is handy for determining the borders of the parent view. Wrap `HoneycombGrid` into a `GeometryReader`:

```
GeometryReader { proxy in
  HoneycombGrid { ... }
}
```

Create a new method in `ContentView` to compute the size for each hexagon depending on its position relative to the borders of the parent view:

```
private func size(
  for hex: HexData,
  _ proxy: GeometryProxy
) -> CGFloat {
  return 0
}
```

First, you need to calculate the total offset of a hexagon from the origin point `(0, 0)`, counting in the position of its center and the drag gesture's offset. Add these two variables in the beginning of the method:

```
let offsetX = hex.center.x + drag.width + dragOffset.width
let offsetY = hex.center.y + drag.height + dragOffset.height
```

Then, you calculate the amount of "excess" along the x-axis and y-axis, namely what distance the hexagon traveled behind the borders of the container along each axis starting from the `(0, 0)`:

```
let frame: CGRect = proxy.frame(in: .global)
let excessX = abs(offsetX) + diameter - frame.width / 2
let excessY = abs(offsetY) + diameter - frame.height / 2
```

You add the total value of the diameter instead of a half because once the center of the circle is precisely at the border and only half of its diameter is technically behind the borders, you want it to shrink to 0, thus deducting its full diameter.

Finally, calculate the size based on the "excess":

```
let excess = max(0, max(excessX, excessY)) // 1
let size = max(0, diameter - excess) // 2
return size
```

Here's a code breakdown:

1. You pick the largest excess measurement out of the two. To preserve the 1:1 ratio of the cell's width and height, you need to decrease both by the same amount. Moreover, you only consider the values bigger than 0; a negative value would mean that the hexagon is still not close enough to a border.
2. Then, you deduct the `excess` from the size of a hexagon and return the result.

To apply the computations you just implemented, add these two variables below `hexOrNeighbor` inside `ForEach`:

```
let size = size(for: hex, proxy)
let scale = (hexOrNeighbor ? size * 0.9 : size) / diameter
```

Then, update `.scaleEffect` as follows:

```
.scaleEffect(max(0.001, scale))
```

Using `0.0` as a scale multiplier may produce unexpected values in the projection matrix SwiftUI applies under the hood, which you could observe from the console logs. Until this issue gets fixed, use a small value barely above 0, like `0.001`, to achieve the needed effect.

Run the app and drag the grid around to see how the cells constantly change their size to fit into the container:

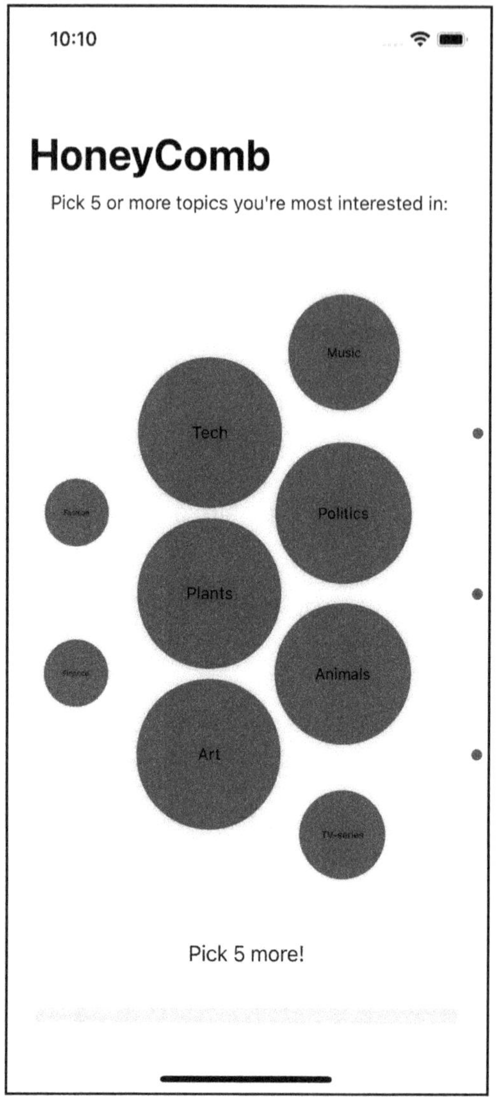

Only one small detail is missing to recreate the fish eye effect precisely. In Apple's component, when the corner cells shrink, the distance between the centers of those cells decreases as well.

They move slightly closer:

Since you'll move the corner hexagons slightly further away from the borders and decrease them simultaneously, you need to "split" the excess value you calculated above between the resizing and repositioning.

Update the signature of `size(for:_:)` to return a pair of values, and rename it `measurement(for:_:)` to keep the code base readable and clear in its intention:

```
private func measurement(
  for hex: HexData,
  _ proxy: GeometryProxy
) -> (size: CGFloat, shift: CGPoint) {
```

Then, add the position calculations above `return` and update the return value:

```
let shift = CGPoint(
  x: offsetX > 0
    ? -max(0, excessX) / 3.0
    : max(0, excessX) / 3.0,
  y: offsetY > 0
    ? -max(0, excessY) / 3.0
    : max(0, excessY) / 3.0
)
return (size, shift)
```

This way, you apply a third of the excess on both axes. Depending on whether the value of the offset is positive or negative, you set a negative or positive shift, respectively.

Now update the `size` variable declaration inside `measurement(for::)` to decrease only by three-quarters of the excess measurement:

```
let size = max(0, diameter - 3.0 * abs(excess) / 4)
```

In total, you are negating `1.0/3.0 * excess + 3.0 * excess / 4.0`, which is slightly above the `excess` value. You do it as a precaution against the cells not having sufficient spacings or "colliding".

Go back to `ContentView`'s `body` and replace the `size` and `scale` variables inside `ForEach`, since now you receive a pair of values instead of a single one from the calculations:

```
let measurement = measurement(for: hex, proxy)
let scale = (hexOrNeighbor
  ? measurement.size * 0.9
  : measurement.size) / diameter
```

Finally, add the `.offset` modifier to the `HexView` below `.scaleEffect`:

```
.offset(CGSize(
  width: measurement.shift.x,
  height: measurement.shift.y
))
```

Build and run the app one final time to see the outcome:

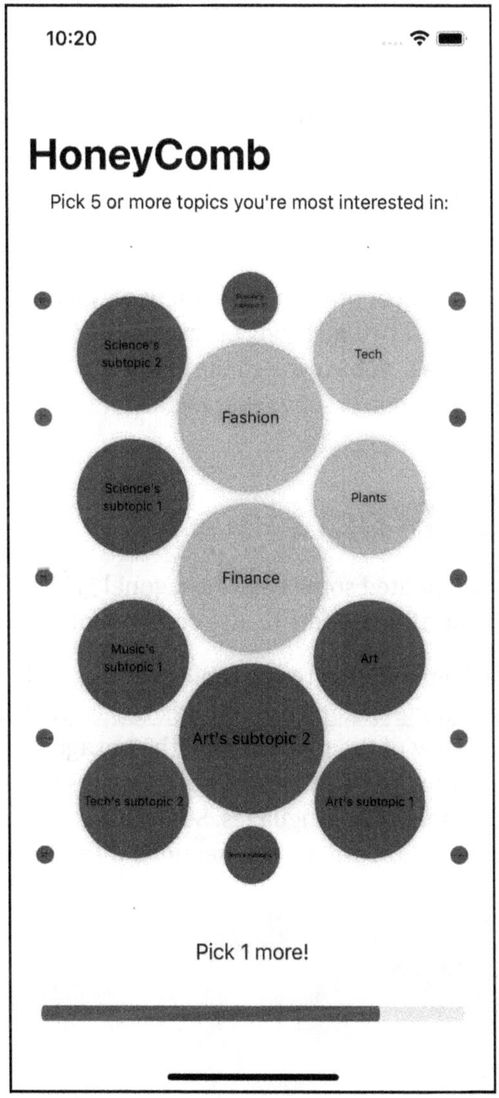

Key Points

1. When recreating an existing UI component, it's often helpful to break larger concepts into smaller ones. For instance, find a way to build the outer parts of the component, the parent container, recreate its layout and proceed with the smaller views or child controls.
2. One optimal way to build a hexagonal grid is *cube* or *axial* coordinates, with the third, `s`, parameter computed as `-q - r`.
3. Apple's new `Layout` protocol offers a convenient way to build more complex containers. You only need two methods to implement it: `sizeThatFits(proposal:subviews:cache:)` and `placeSubviews(in:proposal:subviews:cache:)`.

Where to Go From Here?

In this chapter, you implemented some basic hexagonal grid operations, which helped you recreate a beautiful and fun-to-use component.

However, if you want a deeper dive into the topic of hexagonal grids, go to Red Blob Games blog (https://www.redblobgames.com/grids/hexagons/). You'll find the best and most extensive overview of the math behind the hexagonal grids, the implementation peculiarities, different coordinate systems and the existing solutions for various programming languages. Some of the functionality of the grid container in this chapter and the theoretical sections were implemented relying on this resource.

11 Conclusion

The journey has come to an end, and what a delightful journey it has been. You started by learning some simple animations and how to apply them to your app, blazed through using both built-in and custom transitions and finished up with an entirely custom component from a real-world product!

The technical, creative and conceptual concepts you've learned in this book will aid you in adding much more liveliness and richness to your apps. From small, yet experience-enhancing animations, all through bold and impactful transitions.

We hope your learning journey has been pleasurable and you're motivated to explore the many options SwiftUI provides for creating your very own animations. We're looking forward to seeing what you make! ;]

In a swift *transition*, if you want to dive deeper into SwiftUI itself, you might enjoy some of our other books, such as *SwiftUI Fundamentals* and *SwiftUI by Tutorials*.

If you have any questions or comments as you work through this book, please stop by our forums at https://forums.kodeco.com and look for this book's forum category.

Thank you again for purchasing this book. Your continued support is what makes the books, tutorials, videos and other things we do at kodeco.com possible. We truly appreciate it!

– The *SwiftUI Animations by Tutorials* team

www.ingramcontent.com/pod-product-compliance
Lightning Source LLC
Chambersburg PA
CBHW061201240926
51846CB00006B/1081